The following is a partial list of horse and cattle brands in use in the Columbia Basin and surrounding area, around the turn of the century, as quoted by no other than the "Sage of Frenchman Hill", Martin Burke.

"Old" Ben Hutchinson—3 brands
The Hanging H
Quarter Circle W
and LX Brand
Crab Creek

Sam Hutchinson
Hanging H on left stiffle
Crab Creek

Henry Gable
Flying H horse brand
Scootney Springs

Tony Richardson
Dipper Brand
Upper Crab Creek

Harvey Hite
Bar A Brand
Ephrata

Billy St. Clair
Double X Quarter Circle
Lower Crab Creek

Bill Switzler
Horse Brand Twenty-Two
Horse Heaven country

Sailing Bros.
Horse Brand, Circle S
Horse Heaven country

Chas. Peterson
Quarter Circle K
Marlin

Earl Savage
Horse Brand, Oar Lock
Pasco

John Peters
Horse Brand
Warden

Sam Blake
Ear Brand
Warden

Drumhellers
Railroad Cattle Brand
Moses Lake

Drumhellers
Bar Seven Horse Brand
Moses Lake

Ed Latimer
Flying Satellite Cattle Brand
Yakima

L. Coffin
House Cattle Brand
Ellensburg

Press Connors
Horse Brand
Ephrata

G. Seeburger
Cattle Brand, Lazy S
Frenchman Hill

Sagebrush Homesteads

LAURA TICE LAGE

WSU
PRESS

Washington State University Press
Pullman, Washington

In collaboration with the
Othello Community Museum, Othello, WA

Washington State University Press
PO Box 645910
Pullman, WA 99164-5910
Phone 800-354-7360; FAX 509-335-8568
©1999 by the Board of Regents of Washington State University
All rights reserved
First printing 1999

Library of Congress Cataloging-in-Publication Data

Lage, Laura Tice.
    Sagebrush homesteads / by Laura Tice Lage.
        p.   cm.
    Originally published: Yakima, Wash. : Franklin Press, 1967.
    Includes index.
    ISBN 0-87422-174-9 (alk. paper)
    1. Frontier and pioneer life   Columbia River Valley. 2. Columbia River Valley—Social life and customs. 3. Columbia River Valley—Biography. 4. Lage, Laura Tice—Childhood and youth. 5. Pioneers   Columbia River Valley—Biography. 6. Othello Region (Wash.)—Biography. I. Title.
    F897.C7L34   1999
    979.7'34—dc21
    [b]
                                                                    98-33104
                                                                         CIP

WSU Press Reprint Edition

Dedication

The Othello Community Museum is pleased to bring together, in this reprint publication, the intentions of two of Othello's original families.

This edition of *Sagebrush Homesteads* is dedicated to the memory of Ralph Hedrick Barton, only child of homesteaders Ralph and Blanche Barton and a former Museum member. His gift of an assigned legacy has greatly assisted making Laura Tice Lage's story available again. Her original 1967 book, self-published, has been long out of print.

Born Feb. 14, 1896 in Troy, Missouri, the author lived many of her retirement years in College Place near Walla Walla, WA. Her death in Coos Bay, OR, was announced in the *Walla Walla Union Bulletin*, August 29, 1985. Her children, Jerry Lage and Genevieve Lage Tanczos, have been helpful with the work of seeing this new edition into print.

Dedicated Spring, 1999
Bill L. Morris, President,
Othello Community Museum
Othello, WA 99344

Ralph Hedrick Barton

Introduction

The author's original, self-published 1967 edition of *Sagebrush Home-steads* was printed only little more than half a century after Othello's incorporation as a city in the state of Washington. Now, after a few more decades have passed, driven by the community's present irrigated agribusiness economy, Laura Tice Lage's story of the hard reality of local Columbia Basin beginnings seems at once both safely behind us, yet very near and familiar.

Laura arrived as a child, age 10, in 1906 with her parents to the bleak "panhandle" region of Adams County, Washington, where its shallow, sandy acres offered settlers one last chance to become wheat farmers.

Childhood in the large and caring Tice family was a happy one, full of the small comforts Laura learned to treasure, earned by working together under unpromising conditions. But the scuffed shoes she wore that first spring were never replaced by a new pair, all her own, until she could grow old enough to buy them with her own earnings.

She grew up fast when her mother died. Suddenly, life became very simple. Life meant doing without: without her mother; without water or food enough; and always without clothing that was new. Ultimately the family was also without enough cash for Laura to complete a high school education: no horse could be spared for waiting all day in the Othello school yard. Equally impossible it was, to divert the cash from her own labor to support her lodging in Ritzville as a working student. Laura watched her neighbors' crops fail for too many years for them to catch up and her friends look for work instead with the newly established Milwaukee Railroad. Selling out to stay alive seemed the best decision for most. While attending the 10th grade in Othello High School and working in town at the same time, Laura concluded that she, too, must leave, and set about to accomplish her education alone. Her life's effort toward this goal included attending adult writing courses at Skagit Valley College, Mt. Vernon, WA. Following the death of her husband, William Lage, and her successfully raising of their five children, this book has resulted from that experience.

Othello Community Museum members, many of whom have known Laura Tice Lage, and her sister Mary May's Othello family, are pleased to bring Laura's book back into print. She brings energy and life to those local years, not so long ago, that we no longer can know without stories like hers.

Gladys C. Para,
Othello Community Museum
1999

1st Edition, 1967

The Author

Laura Tice was born near Troy, Missouri and came to Washington with her parents, brothers and sisters in 1903. After three years on a section of wheat land near Cunningham, it was sold and the family moved to a homestead north of Othello Post Office.

She experienced the hardships, the happy times and slow developments of the area, and attended high school in Cheney and Othello. In 1914 she left Othello to take a secretarial course in Spokane. She also attended Skagit Valley College.

Following her marriage to William Lage, five children were born to them, Gerald, Patricia, Richard, Zelpha and Genevieve. In 1929 they moved to California and her husband's death occurred in 1940, leaving her with the children to raise alone.

Returning to Washington in 1943, she found great changes taking place in the Columbia Basin, and on a visit to Othello about 1950 she saw the Potholes Canal which crosses the old homestead about two hundred yards from where the home stood. It was the sight of water flowing in the canal that brought vividly to her mind the early struggles, and she conceived the idea of relating the early history as a memorial to the pioneers. She remembered hearing them say, "If we just had water, this soil would grow anything." Six years were spent in research and writing her book.

Dedication

To the memory of my father and mother, Joseph W. and Susie A. Tice and Otis; and to James, Mary, Dona, Headley, Nellie and J. W. May who shared with me those homestead days, I lovingly dedicate this record.

Acknowledgments

In attempting to recall the events recorded here, I gratefully acknowledge the encouragement and assistance given me by others;

To my brothers and sisters who have supplied some early data; to J. W. May for information regarding his first homestead experiences; to Mrs. Mary Pierce, the Adams County Superintendent of schools for her assistance in obtaining information from early school records; to Roxie Gillis for incidents in the Corfu-Smyrna area; to many old school friends and neighbors, all of whom bear their part in the story, and to many others who have given their encouragement and suggestions that have helped to make this record more readable and of greater historical value. Among the latter are Mrs. John Para, former President of the Adams County Historical Society, Archie Binns, author of several books of the northwest, Dr. Norwood M. Cole, Dean and Historian at Skagit Valley College at Mount Vernon, Washington, and to A. G. Smith who suggested the title.

To each and every one of these, I offer my sincere thanks.

Front Row: Laura, J. W. Tice, Susan Tice, Otis.
Second Row: Nellie, Dona, Headley.

Prologue

THAT SECTION of eastern Washington lying near the heart of the Columbia Basin Irrigation System, has seen such vast changes since those early days it is difficult for the present generation to visualize how it once looked, or picture the conditions met by the pioneers.

Only a few of those who first took up homestead claims and lived on them long enough to get a patent of ownership, have stayed by during the long years of battling dust and drought to see the wish that was almost prophetic, have its fulfillment. Many times have I heard it expressed in this way, "If we only had water, this soil would grow anything."

Many of the old-timers moved to places where life did not seem so grim, or living such a fight when the battle seemed over-rugged and there was little to soften its stern outlines. Others remained until their tired bodies gave up the fight, and their dust found quiet rest beneath the arid soil. Above their graves the dry dust they hopefully tilled shifted back and forth with every whim of the wind; never quite at rest.

Rugged though the conditions may have been, the men and women of pioneer stock were not accustomed to soft living. They were establishing homes and providing for the future of their children. Traveling twenty or more miles to the nearest grocery, or to a railroad for shipping the wheat they expected to raise, were some of the conditions they understood and accepted from the beginning.

While neighbors were not usually more than a mile apart, the lack of roads, the work involved in clearing the land of sagebrush and getting it ready for cultivation, and the lack of social centers such as churches and granges made for few social contacts except those directly connected with the schools or the yearly Fourth of July picnics on Crab Creek.

A return visit brings such developments and changes to view, that recognition comes slowly. Only by looking at the familiar outline of Saddle Mountain lying to the southwest, the Royal Slope once familiarly known as Frenchman Hill to the northwest, or still farther to the west where the Cascade Mountains and Mount Rainier are etched against the warm colors of sunset, can one be sure this is the same place. Where once sagebrush, bunch grass, coyotes, jackrabbits and rattlesnakes had undisputed possession, now stands a modern city. Othello, with other Basin cities, has come far since those days.

As the eyes are raised to take in the once-familiar countryside, the change is apparent. Where once was a dun-colored slightly rolling stretch of land, there are leveled sweeps of green fields. No longer do tumbleweeds roll across the bare fields until they come to rest against a barbed wire fence. Dust devils of whirling wind funneling dust and debris, whose courses could be marked by the boiling dust they raised, have, to a large extent, vanished. So rich and luxuriant are the growing crops that one is reminded of the early vision, "If only we had water, this soil would grow anything." That statement has proved to be true.

The little cemetary, once a part of the Adams homestead, set aside by the family when the wife and mother died, has undergone the same change. It has been taken over as a community burial place under the care of the American Legion. The barren alkali soil which would scarcely support a weed has lost its grim look, and now wears the smooth green of a well-kept lawn. Nothing more graphically portrays to the returning visitor the tremendous changes everywhere apparent.

A few of the first pioneers have remained to see their faith justified through the years. They, with their children, have had a vital part in this accomplishment.

When a former resident, who had spent the years of her childhood there, returned after years of absence and was asked what she wanted to see first, the answer was, "The big ditch with water in it." That ditch, a main canal, now runs across the old homestead not more than two hundred yards from where the house once stood.

Such were the dreams, and such the fulfillment that sixty years have seen come to pass. Now let us take a closer look at some of the incidents and struggles that made up a part of the daily life of those who lived those pioneer days.

Hedrick Merc. Co. in Cunningham, Wash. Thompson and Snead, co-owners. About 1901. L to R: Fred Damon, unknown, unknown. Seated, Delbert; Standing, Jim Snead, Elmer Thompson, Roland Hedrick, Harry S. Snead.

Chapter I

Homestead Bound

"GID'UP! PETE! FRANK!" Jim snapped the long lines across the backs of the team of horses and the loaded wagon began slowly to move as the farm team leaned into the traces for the long pull to the new homestead. Papa had recently filed on a quarter section of homestead land farther west in the Columbia Basin, and we were moving from Cunningham to our new home.

Cows, chickens, pigs and a major portion of the household things had been moved out the week before. Mamma had gone along to get things settled for the family, and to cook for Papa and Jim. Jim was the eldest brother who was helping Papa, and Frank Barton, a homestead neighbor, with the building now under construction. We younger children who were in school, were left to the supervision of Dona, an older sister, for the final week of school. Now Jim had come for the rest of the family which included Headley, Nellie, Otis and me.

Two more stops were to be made in the small town we were leaving. One stop was at the post office where A. O. Lee was the postmaster, to have the mailing address changed to the farmhouse post office which had been given the name of Othello. Another stop was at the Hedrick Mercantile Store run by Harry Snead, where anything from axle grease, nails and farm tools to calico and gingham for the family wardrobe might be purchased, along with crackers, cheese and other groceries. These stops would give us an opportunity to wave good-bye to some of our schoolmates who lived in town.

It was about noon when we pulled up beside the false-fronted frame building that housed the store. Since it was twenty miles from our new home to town and the grocery store, and the all-day trips by wagon were taken only when the supply of

1

staples was getting low, Mamma had sent in a list of groceries to be purchased.

"Here is the list of things Mamma wanted," and Jim gave the slip to Dona after handing the lines over to Headley while he went across the street to Henry Myers' hardware store to see about getting more nails for the building.

"Dona, we are getting hungry. Can we have some cheese and crackers to eat on the way?" came from Otis and me. Our breakfast seemed a long way in the past, and it would be night before we reached the homestead. But Dona was already entering the store to arrange with Harry for the groceries.

Mamma had sent in for a five gallon can of coal oil for the lamps, five pounds of dried prunes and dried apples, three fifty-pound sacks of flour, ten pounds each of red and navy beans, five pounds of coffee beans which would be ground in a small hand coffee grinder as needed, a can of K. C. baking powder, a box of soda, (Papa liked his hot biscuits for breakfast), two packages of Magic yeast, (though Mamma usually kept potato water starter from one bread baking to another,) a three gallon can of molasses and a case of tomatoes. A half dozen spools of thread, sizes forty and fifty in black and white, filled out the list.

Jim soon had these stowed away on the loaded wagon, and on his last trip into the store he emerged with packages we found to contain cheese and crackers, and a bag of candy Harry had put in for us children as a parting gift. He then climbed to the driver's seat.

Meanwhile, Mary and Tat Logan, (Tat's real name was Frances) had come from their father's hotel, and Marie Tulles, Nellie's chum, had appeared from the Tulles Drug Store to stand around the wagon for some last visiting. Now with a chorus of "Good-byes" and much waving of hands we were finally on our way.

The warm May sun shone from a clear blue sky, and meadow larks flitting from post to post, sang with a lilt that ignored the sand dunes that had drifted along the road in the two recent severe dust storms, half burying the fences. These had almost made a dust bowl of the wheat farms around the town we were leaving.

Most fortunately for us, our section of land had been sold and the sale consummated a few days before the first three-day storm had struck and begun its destruction of whole sections of promising wheat. Then only a few days after wives and daughters had finished cleaning out the fine dust that had sifted through and into everything, another equally severe storm followed. This one completed the devastation, and left the light volcanic soil blown into drifts that buried the uprooted wheat along with the hopes of those who planted.

One incident in particular during that second storm stands out in memory. It was the second morning and breakfast time. By the light of a kerosene lamp, Mamma had gotten breakfast and called the family to the table. There was a layer of fine dust over everything; and though the table had just been set, already a film of dust was settling on the dishes. We quickly assembled to take our places. Just at that moment a wide strip of paper tore loose from the ceiling, letting all the dust from previous storms cover the table and food. Breakfast was delayed while the mess was cleaned away and a new meal prepared. Mamma was glad to be moving to fresh country.

Now we were on the road to that new country. It would take at least five hours for the steadily plodding team to cover the distance from the old home to the new, and children soon tire of inactivity. Sometimes we sat at the rear end of the wagon where a little space had been left. It was easy to drop off now and then to walk, holding on to the rear of the wagon, enjoying the soft dirt as it squeezed up between our bare toes.

At the top of the hill just west of Cunningham, we passed the Logan homestead. The Logans had moved into town to run the hotel.

"Are Fred and Julia living here now?" Dona asked as we passed the place. Fred Damon had married Julia Kelly, a daughter of Mrs. Logan, after we moved to Cunningham.

"No, I think they are living on his father's homestead about three miles north of here," Jim said.

After the new brick schoolhouse had been built in Cunningham, John and Arilla Damon bought the old white frame school building and remodeled it for their home, leaving the homestead to Fred and Julia. Fred's little brother, Harry, was a schoolmate of ours.

Here and there, dotted across the country-side were small homes on land which had developed from homestead to farm status. Around some were tall poplar trees and a few fruit trees. These were where a windmill stood near, merrily spinning to bring up the life-giving water from below. Here too, small gardens provided welcome additions to the table, or a bush of bright yellow roses bloomed in a yard. While fragrant, those rose bushes had so many thorns the toughest-tongued cow would never have tried them a second time. But in the main, most houses were little more than shacks, and water was supplied by being hauled in water tanks from some distant well.

As we rode along, Jim pointed out the homes of others whose names we had heard.

"The Shinings live up in that direction," he said, pointing toward the north. "Do you know Mina Shining, Dona?" he asked.

"Not very well, but I have seen her. I don't know much about their family," she answered.

"Whose is the big white house over there with all the trees around it?" Dona wanted to know. The house stood about a half mile off to the left several miles out of Cunningham. It had a windmill.

"That is the Lucy place. Dennis Lucy lives there." Headley had already been out to the homestead, and didn't mind showing off his knowledge of the country. Patty Lucy had taught the first term of school we attended at Cunningham. This was her home.

Miss Patty, (we never called her Miss Lucy) and I had had a few brushes that school year when she discovered me sur-

4

reptitiously transferring a piece of candy from my desk to my mouth during school hours, or turning to whisper a question to the one seated just behind me. On these occasions she seemed to think a ruler applied vigorously to the palm of my hand might act as a successful deterrent to such breaches of school room decorum.

Miss Patty, whom we had heard called an "old maid", was a firm believer in schoolroom discipline, as her firm jaw indicated. One time she had become impatient with the children bringing their words and problems across the room to her desk, and she had issued a directive that this would no longer be permitted. When such a problem in our studies arose, we were to raise the hand and wait until her attention was gained; she would then either come to the individual, or grant permission to bring it to her. No snapping of fingers to get her notice was permitted either.

On this day, two or three students in the seventh and eighth grades had been granted permission to bring their problems to her desk for solution. I had been holding my hand aloft for some time to get a word in my second reader pronounced, but without getting any notice. Another second grader, Lena Hedrick, having failed to gain the teacher's attention by waving her hand, took her word to the teacher's desk, had it pronounced and returned safely.

"Aha!" I thought, "If she can do that, why can't I?" Leaving my seat with my finger accurately placed on the word I was needing pronounced, I approached Miss Patty's desk. She seemed to have been waiting for just such an opportunity, or at least it seemed so to me; perhaps she had suddenly remembered her directive.

In the corner of the room on a small shelf barely large enough to hold it was a large Webster's dictionary. It was about three feet off the floor and a curtain hung from the shelf to the floor.

Grasping my arm, she propelled me swiftly across the room to this little shelf, drew the curtain aside, and told me to remain down under there out of sight until she gave me permission to emerge. Then she dropped the curtain and went on with class recitations.

Squatting there in that little fourteen by sixteen inch space with no chance to change position soon became torture. Class recitations and other schoolroom activities in the eight-grade school room went on, and to the shy little seven-year-old girl in that cramped corner, they seemed endless.

Finally came the order to put away books for recess, and a quick flurry of noise. Then I heard, "One!" That was the signal to sit up straight in their seats. "Two!" That was the signal to turn with the feet in the aisle. "Three!" sent them marching in orderly column to the door. Passing the place of my incarceration, a few thought it amusing to tweek the curtain in passing, or shove it aside for a momentary glimpse of the object lesson in school discipline. It was only after the schoolroom had been emptied that I was permitted release.

So this big house had been Miss Patty's home. I remembered that first year at the Cunningham school and was glad to have had a new school and another teacher the next year.

"Mandy Maguire lives out this way, doesn't she, Jim?" asked Nellie. Mandy had worked for us the first summer we were in Cunningham when Dona was sick with typhoid fever. We would never forget Mandy's Irish brogue, nor how she placed the big dishpan of bread dough on the floor and got down on her knees to give it the vigorous working it needed to make the beautiful loaves of bread she turned out.

"Yes, she lives off in that direction," he said, pointing to the south. "You can't see her house from here." He pointed out other places as we drove along; Jim Hanrehan's place, Jabe Couch's farm. "That is where Reddin Couch lives now," he told us. "Shinrock's is farther on."

Gradually the drifted sand disappeared and more sagebrush and bunch grass appeared. Interspersed were sections of school land where the plow had never touched. New grass showed green, and patches of tiny pink flowers added touches of beauty.

6

At a distance these were just blobs of pink, but they became more numerous as we drove farther west until we came to a field of about twenty acres. At some time this had been cleared off; now the whole field was carpeted in delicate pink. The wind had evidently broadcast the seed. What child could resist a quick dash for samples and a closer look? They were a specie of low growing phlox.

"How much farther is it?" we began to ask before we had gone much more than half way. Jim would reply with a good-natured grin, "Oh, we've got a long way to go yet. Are you gettin' tired of ridin'?" We were; not only of riding, but of the dust that fogged from those wagon wheels. Occasionally, we met a buggy and team that generously turned out of the road to pass us, and the occupants and we would exchange greetings as we passed. Already, we were feeling the kinship of fellow homesteaders.

About sundown, dusty and weary, we pulled up beside the little black, tar-paper covered shack which was the home of our married sister and brother-in-law, Mary and Billie May, who had influenced our decision to homestead. Queen and Longtail, their hounds, bawled us a welcome from the shade of the barn.

"Well! Well! You finally got here," was Billie's greeting. He and Mary were trying to find some relief from the heat inside the cabin by bringing their chairs outside to the shade cast by the building. He continued; "You are going to like it out here on the homestead. You can run through the sagebrush and hunt jack rabbits, or pick wild flowers, and ride all over the country." He was always a booster for the area, and right away he wanted us to see it through his eyes.

"What time did you leave Cunningham?" Mary asked. "It was just about noon by the time we started from town," Dona informed her.

"Are you hungry?" was Mary's next question. We felt that "starved" would have been a better word for the way we felt. That cheese, crackers and candy had long since disappeared leaving us with a feeling of hollowness inside.

Jim was anxious to get on to the home place before dark, and it was still nearly two miles to go. The last part of the road was newly broken through sagebrush. The horses too, needed to rest and be fed. They had been on the road most of the day since four o'clock that morning with only some grain before noon.

"Dona, why don't you and Nellie and Laura stay here with us tonight?" Mary asked. "You can walk across in the morning. It is only about a mile by the path." It had been some time since she had seen us, and after several months in the cabin she felt the need of company. Dona and Mary, near the same age, had felt the separation. So it was arranged. Otis and Headley would go on home with Jim and the wagon.

While these things were being arranged, some sliced potatoes were frying in a skillet on the small four-holed stove in the cabin. After our long ride the smell of food was good, but when we looked into the small mirror hanging over the enamel wash basin and water pail on a bench beside the door, it showed our dust-covered faces and hands needed some soap and water. A roller towel of coarse crash material hung near on which we could dry our faces and hands.

"How are they coming along with our house, Mary?" Dona asked as she watched Mary setting the dishes on the oil-cloth covered table that had been pulled out to the center of the room. "Is it about finished?"

"I think Billie said everything was done except some of the window casings, the inside ceiling upstairs and the outside trim," she answered. "What is going on in Cunningham? Has Stella come home from Pullman yet?"

"No, school isn't quite out at the college, so I didn't get to see her before we left." Dona and Stella saw a good bit of each other until Stella went away to school.

Curiously, we had been looking at the arrangements of the cabin. Shelves were nailed to the wall to serve as a cupboard. These were covered with curtains made of bleached flour sacks to serve as doors. Below these stood a kitchen cabinet in which

8

were deep drawers for the flour and vegetables. Mary's tall organ in one corner of the room, and a bed in another corner completed the furnishings of the room. This was the small home to which they had come following their wedding some seven months earlier.

The May's homestead had originally been filed on by Billie in 1901. On it he built this small fourteen by sixteen foot one-room cabin of upright boards. The outside was covered with tar-paper, and the inside had once been papered with a heavy pink building paper which had long since lost most of its color. Small sliding windows on three sides gave a view of the sagebrush surrounding it. Cracks between the boards of the wall and floor assured plenty of ventilation. He furnished it with a bunk bed, a rough board table and a few dishes with which he could do the necessary batching on the rare occasions he was there. It was never locked when he was away, and one time when he returned after a year's absence, he learned that others had used the cabin while he was away. Tools, bedding and furnishings were just as he left them, and the passing visitors had registered their names on the wall paper to show who had used it.

Having failed to spend the required time living on it, and not having done the necessary cultivation, he learned someone was about to contest his claim; thus he would lose it. Knowing he and Mary were soon to be married, he decided on a quick move to forestall the loss. Together, they went to the land office in Hatton where he relinquished his claim to the homestead, and she immediately filed on it in her name. They were just in time. When the other interested party came to the land office the next day, it was to find the homestead had already changed hands. This opened the way for Billie to file on another claim sometime later.

I had also been seeing that there were five plates on the table, but only four chairs. "There ain't enough chairs for all of us at the table," was my worried comment. Having had to stand to eat a meal at some previous times when company out-numbered chairs, it looked like it might happen again this time.

"Billie can bring in an apple box for a seat," Mary reassured me as she pulled her loose Mother Hubbard dress away from the hot stove. I noticed she seemed to be getting heavier.

"Where will we all sleep?" Nellie asked, noting the one bed in the room.

"You and Laura can take a quilt out to the barn and crawl in with Longtail and Queen in the straw, can't you?" asked Billie to see what kind of reply she would make.

"You can go out there and sleep with them," she retorted, "We'll stay in here and sleep with Mary."

The problem was solved after the dishes had been washed and put away, by taking the straw-filled tick from under the feather bed, and placing it on the floor. Extra quilts placed on this made a firm, but not uncomfortable bed for healthy young people. Even with three in the bed, we slept soundly.

After breakfast, the trail was pointed out to us. There was no new house in sight, only a stretch of sagebrush, but Billie assured us, "It will take you right across to where your house stands. You will see it when you get over about half a mile."

"Just watch out for rattlesnakes," was the caution from Mary.

Chapter II

New Things

THE TRAIL we followed was made by the hundreds of range cattle and horses being pushed farther west into the area of cliffs and potholes by the barbed-wire fences of the homesteads. The trails were seen here and there throughout the whole area, and led in the general direction of small lakes and a creek lying some seven or eight miles farther west. The trail was fairly straight except now and then curving around some sagebrush. Much of the brush was from eighteen inches to two feet tall, but where moisture had stood it came above my shoulders.

Remembering the caution Mary gave us, we watched the ground on all sides. Nellie was in the lead, I followed and Dona brought up the rear. About a half mile from the May's cabin we caught our first sight of the new buildings on ahead of us about three quarters of a mile away. Its new lumber showed up clearly, and we could see two other buildings near by the house.

"Those must be the barn and chicken house," was Dona's conjecture. We were forgetting to watch the ground.

Suddenly, a rasping buzz sounded from a sagebrush beside the trail as we were nearing it. "There's a rattlesnake," yelled Nellie as she jumped back in fright.

"Where?" "Did you see it?" Dona and I fired the questions at her as we followed her example in getting away from prox-- imity of that bush.

"No, but it must be right there in that bush." With beating hearts we scanned the ground from a safe distance to find the snake we were sure was there. Then, a large, clumsy, dark-colored insect launched into the air from this same bush, still making the same rasping buzz. We relaxed guardedly as we recognized it for what it was, a locust. We had seen them in Missouri.

These were the cicadas, or seventeen year locusts which appeared that year in countless numbers. We had many a frightened jump, and found it disconcerting to be going along the trail and one of those cicadas would sound off within a few feet of the trail. We jumped involuntarily, and stopped with pounding hearts while we examined the adjacent ground for the source of the sound, or made a wide detour around the bush. At first, this happened any number of times between our house and the May's, but we gradually learned what to expect from the locusts so that, after the initial start their buzz always gave us, we walked with more confidence.

Mamma and Papa were waiting for us. It was the first new home they had owned in the twenty-five years of their marriage, and Mamma's delight in its newness was plainly evident as she showed us the rooms, closets and built-in cupboard. She and Papa had planned it together. Papa's face reflected Mamma's

Tice Homestead house. J. W. Tice and Dona.

pride in it. Slightly less than a full two-stories high, and approximately eighteen by thirty-four feet in size, it had two rooms on the ground floor.

"Some day we can put on the addition of another two rooms like the Lucys did," she explained. She and Papa had seen the Lucy house and liked their L shaped house.

The first room we entered was the kitchen which would also serve as the dining-room for all the family meals. At once, the doors to the new cupboard drew our interest.

"This is the dish cupboard," Mamma said as she opened the upper doors to reveal her dishes inside. "The lower part is where we shall keep the food supplies. It will make a good storage place."

The second room was the living-room which was usually referred to as the front room. The big double windows on the east end made the whole room bright, and with the other full-length window in the north wall gave a good view of the country in both of those directions. This room would serve as our parents' bedroom at night. A small hall connected the two rooms, and was the front entrance to the house.

"Oh Mamma, isn't that pretty!" was my excited comment as my eye caught the large square glass in frosted design in the front door. In it was pictured a forest of trees with a stream of water. With a smile of sympathetic understanding as I pointed to the deer among the trees, she replied, "Yes, it is pretty."

A stairway led from the front hall to the two bedrooms on the second floor. Mamma pointed with pride to the width of the stairway.

"See how wide it is? It is almost four feet wide. That leaves a good space for a closet underneath off the front room." It also gave space for another closet between the two upstairs bedrooms.

Stovepipes from the lower rooms, coming up through the thimble-lined holes that had been cut in the floor, to connect with the chimneys, would help to take the chill from these rooms on cold winter nights. Seeing the advantage, we girls

13

immediately laid claim to the one over the living room. Fire would be kept burning later in the front room heater than in the kitchen range. The house was sealed throughout with ship-lap which could afterward be papered. The outside was covered with a beveled siding, which had already received its prime coat of white paint. It would have green trim.

After seeing the inside, Nellie and I, with Otis as guide, went to explore the outside while Mamma and Dona set about plans for arranging things in the house.

A new barn with eight stalls for the horses was in process of erection, and the pigs were grunting happily in their new pens. The hen house was nearly ready for shingling. While referred to as a hen house, it is not to be supposed that only hens were admitted to the building. Three or four roosters of varying and nondescript breeds kept watch over the flock in their usually lordly manner, and shared the harem with a reasonable degree of harmony.

Another practical lesson on the need for being alert to the hazards that might be encountered in the new land, was very effectively impressed on our fourteen-year-old brother a few days later.

Papa was shingling the hen house and Headley climbed the ladder to the roof to watch. An unbroken bundle of shingles was lying there and looked like a good seat. As he sat down he felt a prick. Thinking it was a splinter, he raised up, moved slightly and sat down again. This time he felt a more decided stab and got up in time to see a scorpion run down over the side of the shingles. Now, we had always understood the sting of a scorpion was deadly poison. Headley's face turned pale, and he stammered to Papa as he started for the ladder; "I've been stung by a scorpion."

"Where are you going?" Papa asked as he saw Headley starting down the ladder.

"I'm going to Mamma," was the scared reply as he lost no time getting there.

It was twenty miles to the doctor, and no team available at

the time, so first aid in the form of Cuticura salve was applied. A little soreness similar to that of a yellow jacket which lasted a few days was all that resulted. A girl living in the neighborhood, Gertrude Lee, was stung on the arm by a scorpion. It gave her a painfully sore arm, but it soon healed.

"What have you got there?" I asked Otis that afternoon as I saw him curiously examining something he had in his hand. Otis was seven, and curious about anything new that came along.

"I don't know, I found it hanging on the sagebrush out by the chicken house," he replied, holding it out for me to take.

"Will it bite?" I wanted to know before accepting the queer looking object.

"No, but watch it. You'll see it do something funny." As we watched, it suddenly began to split right down the middle of the back. It was still clinging to a twig of sagebrush on which he had found it, and made no effort to crawl away. Its legs seemed to have become quite rigid. Slowly the split widened, and we could see it was a sort of outer skin or shell enclosing something that was trying to emerge. We could see it had a head with what appeared to be eyes on each side. It was the queerest looking object, and its actions were even more queer, and as the split widened it seemed to be trying to get its front legs pulled out of the outer shell. The head looked like one of the locusts heads, but it was a pale green color instead of the dark, almost black color of the locusts flying about. Finally, after about a half hour, it had freed itself from its outer shell and clung weakly to the twig. It had only slight nubbins of wings, otherwise, its body resembled the locusts so we concluded that was what it was.

Most children seem to have a natural bent toward biology; and watching those locusts, or cicadas from the time they left the ground in the pupa stage through to flight, was a never ending source of interest to us. We would find the cocoons, split down the back, clinging to a branch of sagebrush while the insect struggled to draw its body and legs out of the thin shell that encased it. After it was out it clung weakly to the

15

limb, its pale body trembling with the effort. The thin membrane of wing would gradually fill and spread to full size, and the body turn to the dark color of the adult insect. They were then ready for the mating song given by the male, and the short life above the ground. This ended the life cycle, but in the meantime they had their brief moment in the sun, and made possible future generations to carry on. We occasionally found little round holes about the size of a lead pencil from which they had emerged, in the dry soil under the bush. In turn, the next generation would hatch from the egg, drop to the ground as small larva, and disappear for the next seventeen years.

Another biological specimen we observed crawling along the dusty road or across the dry grass-less yard, was a hard-shelled black bug from three quarters to an inch long. It was indelicately called a "stink bug" from its habit of elevating its posterior in self-defense at any approach of danger.

Sometimes, Otis, with his boyish delight for teasing, would call his particular chum, Shadow, (a name suggested by Mamma because the little white dog was invariably at the heels of the boys whenever they appeared out of doors,) and pointing to the bug would say, "Sic 'um, Shad!" Shad was usually obliging, and promptly responded to the challenge, but one sniff of that elevated rear caused her to back off and refuse further investigation.

Whether the bug threw off a gas, or an invisible spray, we never discovered. The indescribable odor carried for ten or fifteen feet in all directions. I had always had the notion that a little salt sprinkled on that obnoxious odor might have improved it a bit, but doubtless this would not have served the purpose of the bug. At other times, Otis would flip it to a distance with a stick, then the bug would take off out of the danger zone in high dudgeon with its head tucked down and its posterior still high in the air.

Water for the household needs and for the stock was one of the most urgent problems. It was hauled from various sources; the North well some three or four miles due north

16

of us; Skootenai Springs[1] ten or twelve miles south, or Crab Creek to the west.

A wooden tank drawn by a four horse team, was used to haul water. At these sources the water was either dipped up or drawn up with a bucket on a rope, and poured into the tank. Since it took a long time to fill the ten-barreled tank in this way, it took the major portion of a day to make the trip to the more distant sources. If someone else had been to the well earlier, a wait was necessary while the water renewed itself in the well. When the horses were not being used they were turned out to graze on the open range where they could drink from a small lake or pond northwest of our place.

At first we did not have a cistern in which to store the water, and it was left in the tank until used. During the hotter part of the day it became unpleasantly warm to drink, so water for that purpose was best drawn during the early hours before the sun was high. Later, a cistern was dug and cemented, then covered with planking to exclude, as far as possible, dust, bugs and an occasional field mouse. We usually ignored mere bugs that dropped in, but a mouse called for a bit of dredging. The cistern also served as a cooler. In hot summer weather cream and butter, placed in pails, were suspended just over the water by a string fastened to the edge of the opening.

A caution we heard often repeated was, "Don't waste the water." In fact, so thoroughly was this impressed upon us, that much of the water served more than one purpose. Water from the family wash was used on the garden or around the fruit trees after they were planted. Water in which the dishes were washed went as slops to the pigs. The weekly baths were either in a wash basin, or a few inches of water in the galvanized tub in which more than one was expected to take his turn.

On one occasion, Otis and I paid a visit to the small lake that had formed from melting snow about a mile up the coulee.

---

[1]There is reason to believe the original spelling was either Skootenai or Skutenai Springs, which has since been corrupted to Scootney Springs. The early Indians called it Skookum Spring, meaning "good water."

17

It had remained long enough that frogs had increased to a sizeable population. While pursuing our biological interests, we had transferred a large supply to a tub in the back yard where we could observe the metamorphosis from tadpole to frog.

This day found me at the house alone while Otis was away with the family. It seemed a good time to take a solitary bath. After finishing with it, the idea occurred to me that here was a nice supply of water, and I could give the tadpoles a much better depth for swimming and development. I dumped it in with a glow of satisfaction, and thought how pleased Otis would be to find the tub half full of water.

Sometime later, I heard a howl of indignation from the back yard. "Who poured all this soapy water in here and killed all my polliwogs?" Only then did I realize the horrible mistake I had made. The sight of all those tadpoles floating belly up convinced me there were better uses for soapy bath water. Most abject apologies were in order.

There was the problem of fuel. Coal at six dollars a ton was expensive; and twenty miles was a long way to haul either coal or wood from town.

One feature that aroused our curiosity when driving past the John McCulloch homestead which adjoined ours, was a huge pile of sagebrush in the yard. We had noted the same thing beside the Frank Barton's and Adams' places. We knew the land must be cleared of the brush before it could be planted to wheat, but it seemed odd they would pile it near the house to burn.

One day we stopped at the neighbors to get acquainted. Mrs. McCulloch had a fire in the kitchen stove, and an odd odor hung in the air. When she replenished the fire, as she did every little while, we learned the source of the odor and why there was the big stack of brush in the front yard. It was a new lesson in homestead economy which we at once adopted. After using it for a short time the odd smell was no longer noticed. It made a quick hot fire, but needed to be replenished so frequently it

18

almost required one person to stoke the kitchen range. A thin piece of board shaped like a paddle was used to push the brush into the stove. The brush top was usually discarded and only the woody trunk used in the stove.

"There are two old hens that are wanting to set," Nellie told Mamma one evening after bringing in the eggs from the hen house. "I've thrown them off the nest for the last two days, but they are back again to-night."

Mamma already had three hens setting on their clutches of fifteen eggs, and two batches of chicks had been hatched.

"I'll put eggs under them tomorrow," Mamma told her, "We shall need a good-sized flock of chickens." The baby chicks that had been hatched out needed good care for a start in life, but the Plymouth Rock hens made good mothers.

A small plot of ground near the house was plowed, cleared of the brush and planted to potatoes. Beside it, Papa prepared a spot for the garden in which Mamma planted a variety of vegetable seeds, some of which were already coming up. Jim began clearing land where he could sow the winter wheat.

With a four-horse team hooked to the moldboard plow that turned two furrows, it was not difficult to uproot the sagebrush and turn it over onto the preceding furrows. But then came the tedious task of pulling the uprooted brush from the soft dirt, and stacking it to be hauled to the house. Headley and Otis were given this task. Day after day the monotonous pulling and piling went on, sometimes with a bit of help and encouragement from Papa.

One day the boys came in at noon and told us about what fun they were having out in the field pulling the brush from the soft dirt.

"We saw a meadow lark's nest," Headley told us. "There were five young ones. They scattered into the brush when the team came along."

"The plow turned out a field mouse's nest. Headley killed them," Otis added his bit. It sounded real interesting to hear them tell it.

19

"Nellie, you and Laura ought to get on some overalls and come out there with us," came next from Headley who somehow forgot to mention there was any work connected with it. "It's lots of fun playing in the soft dirt," he continued.

Nellie saw through their ruse to get some company and help in their work and would have none of it, but I was more gullible and learned the hard way. The family was adjusting to homestead life, but with a lot yet to learn.

Chapter III

Neighbors

"Mamma, may I go up to see Flossie?" was an oft repeated request that summer. Not always was the request given a favorable answer, for Mamma did not believe we should be always going to the neighbors. She had probably read what the proverb said about "withdrawing thy foot from thy neighbor's house, lest he get tired of thee," but sometimes she permitted me to go. At other times she would say, "Go ask your father." Off I would go to ask Papa and get his answer, feeling the request was almost granted.

"What does your mother say?" Papa was too cagey to give his permission until he knew what Mamma had said.

"Well, she said to ask you," was the answer I would pass on to him without any unfavorable remarks she may have made.

"How long has it been since you were up there?" would be his next question.

Even though it seemed ages since Flossie and I had been together, I would confess to the number of days, and after considering this for a moment he would either give his consent outright or return me to Mamma for her final assent.

This referral to Papa was noticeably true if it involved going on horseback or had something to do with things that came especially in his domain. They must have had some private understanding or code by which they granted or denied our requests for permission to carry out our plans. If a request was denied by one it did no good to go to the other to have the decision reversed.

The McCullochs were our nearest neighbors and lived on the homestead adjacent to ours in the same section. It was three quarters of a mile to their house.

John H. and Fannie McCulloch, with their family, had originally come from Wisconsin to North Dakota in a covered wagon, remaining there to farm and work for a year before coming on to Washington by train. From Lind they explored for land that could be homesteaded and settled on their present quarter section. Leaving the family in Lind until he could construct a place for them to live, he put up a small fourteen by sixteen foot, story and a half house. To this was added another room shortly before we moved to the homestead, and within two years another room was added.

John was a jovial friendly man. He had been badly injured when a horse he was riding stepped into a badger hole, stumbled and fell so heavily it broke the horse's neck and knocked John unconscious. When he regained consciousness some time later, it was to find his leg pinned under the dead horse. He was several miles from home, having gone to round up the farm horses which were allowed to run loose to graze in the open country when not in use. No one would know where to look for him. It was with difficulty that he worked himself loose from under the dead horse and removed the saddle.

Among the horses running loose was a gentle little white pony belonging to the girls, named Pearl. Mr. Mac, as he was usually called, coaxed Pearl to him, placed the saddle on her back and rode home. Not realizing he had broken his hip, it was about two weeks before he was able to drive to Lind to see the doctor. By that time the hip had already started to knit crookedly. It left him with a life-long limp, but it in no way slowed him down.

Fannie was a soft-voiced woman whose quiet mien concealed a strength of character that showed up more and more as you became better acquainted with her. She was an immaculate housekeeper despite the occasional dust storms that came along. The McCullochs were progressive farmers, hard working and laying strong plans for the future. Already, much of their land was under cultivation and sowed to wheat as they increased the number of cattle, horses and hogs. Fannie had a flock of some two hundred hens which were allowed to roam freely, and was making a start with turkeys and ducks.

There were three girls in the family. Alice, the eldest, was married to Homer J. Tipton who had a general store in Hatton, but Xerpha and Flossie were still at home, helping their mother in the chores about the house and chicken yard.

Flossie and I became chums after we got acquainted. It was part of her chores to gather the eggs, feed the little ducks and turkeys and throw grain to the flock of hens, a chore we sometimes shared.

Since the hens were allowed to roam freely, they sometimes chose their own nesting places. Hunting those nests in the hay mow, under the mangers or around the grainery, and occasionally finding a hidden nest, was exciting. Watching the baby ducks gobble down their food and run to wash it down at the shallow pan of water, was an amusing sight. We had no turkeys and ducks at our place yet.

McCullochs had a turkey gobbler which was very belligerent. He would come strutting after us ready to fight any time we were outside the yard, or in the barnyard which he seemed to think was his own domain. Flossie carried a stick to discourage any attacks from him, and we kept close watch for him whenever we were outside the yard fence.

One day the gobbler slipped up behind Mr. Mac, who was seated on the ground repairing some harness, and had failed to notice the gobbler's approach. When the gobbler without any warning, landed on his back in fighting fury, John reached around and got the gobbler by the neck, giving the bird several dizzying turns before releasing him. Mr. Gobbler never tried that again. One lesson was enough. He had learned who was boss of the barnyard.

Several of the Adams family took homesteads in the section that cornered on the McCulloch place. The elderly parents, Francis M. and Frances Adams, Ed, a bachelor son, and a widowed daughter, Cora Gorsuch, built their homes near the inner corner of their land so they formed a compact little group.

23

Charles Showalter who married Clara Adams, had the fourth quarter in the section. They built at the other side of their land beside the section line road. The community school was built on a corner of their homestead.

Frank Barton, who was helping to build our house, had a homestead two miles northeast of our place; but he walked the distance night and morning. Frank and Belva homesteaded in 1903, and their son Ralph filed on the claim next to theirs. There were five girls in the family, Mary, Bonnie, Nellie, Jennie and Ruth, but Mary was married and living in Oregon. The younger girls were near the age of Nellie and me.

Their mother was a motherly, pre-maturely white-haired woman, who always gave a hearty welcome to her children's friends though their house was small when we first knew them.

About the time Mr. Barton was finishing up his work on our house, the three younger girls came over to invite Nellie and me to stay all night at their house. They had come over on horseback.

"Mamma can we go?" we pled with Mamma. It would be an unusual treat for we had rarely had the privilege of overnight visits with our friends.

"Won't it be an inconvenience to your mother to have the girls stay over night?" Mamma asked them, knowing the Barton house was rather small. "How will you sleep so many?"

"Oh no, Mrs. Tice, Ma wants them to come. We five girls will sleep together, and it will be fun," the girls assured her. It did sound like fun. We would have to sleep cross-wise of the bed.

Riding double behind two of the girls, it did not take long to reach the Barton home. Several guinea fowls set up a noisy "Pu thrac! Pu thrac!" as we rode into the barn lot. They had several of the loud-voiced birds running around.

Lying cross-wise of the bed to the accompaniment of much giggling, and talking in one of the small upstairs bedrooms, we forgot that others might be wanting to go to sleep.

"You girls quiet down and go to sleep," Bonnie would chide

us from the other upstairs room, "You'll keep Pa and Ma awake."

Shortly before this, while Frank was still helping with the building at our place, he urged Nellie and me to go visit his girls. They had ridden over to see us one day, but we would have to walk the two miles across open sagebrush land to get there. The upper end of a deep coulee lay between the two places, and we were afraid there might be rattlesnakes on the way.

Yielding to his urging, and our desire for other children to play with, we put on fresh calico dresses, donned sunbonnets and started to make our call. We had gone not more than two hundred yards into the brush when a sinuous movement beside a bush stopped us.

"A rattlesnake!" we both yelled, and never stopping to verify whether it was a rattlesnake or a harmless squirrel snake, we headed for home on flying feet. Nothing could pursuade us to continue on for our visit that day.

The Willis Thorp claim lay just beyond the Barton's. He was a surveyor, and sometimes when he was away from home with a surveying crew, he left his wife and two girls, Grace and Edith, at the little cook shack he had converted into a homestead house.

One of their problems was getting groceries from one of the distant towns if they ran out of groceries while he was away. They could send for supplies by a neighbor who was going to town, but on one occasion there was a delay in receiving their order, and the girls' school lunches consisted of cold beans and nothing to go with them for three days. They, like other families used jack rabbits for meat part of the time until they were thoroughly tired of rabbit.

Grace liked to practice shooting ground squirrels and rabbits with her twenty-two rifle. One day she shot herself in the foot. It was late afternoon, and the nearest doctor was at Lind. Fortunately, her father was at home. Another neighbor, Clyde Powers, helped put Grace into the hack and started at once for

Lind. It took several hours over rough country roads to make the trip, and it was in the wee morning hours when they arrived at the doctor's. Grace was put to bed with a sedative that permitted both Grace and the doctor to sleep until morning.

At the doctor's office next morning, Grace had a new experience when he took an X-ray picture of her foot. Neither Grace nor her father had ever seen an X-ray machine or picture before. They were much interested in seeing how it showed up the little piece of lead and the bones of her foot. Incidentally, the doctor did not remove the bullet, and presumably she is still carrying that little memento of homestead life.

An exciting adventure came to Edith one morning on the way to school. She was alone, coming across a lonely section of sagebrush where there were no houses in sight when she was surrounded by coyotes. With no other place of refuge in sight, she climbed a fence post to get away from them. Curiously, they sat down to watch that crying little human on the fence post, and she did not dare to get down.

No one was ever heard to have been attacked by a coyote unless it was rabid, and plainly these were not sick coyotes, but she thought they might be hungry. Finally, they either tired of their fun, or may have heard a wagon coming; they slipped away like shadows into a coulee leaving a badly frightened child to continue on to school.

Another family we came to know very well was the John F. Lee family which lived two miles east of us. Gertrude married soon after we first knew them, but Roy, Ethel, Johnny and Marion attended the small country school we attended. Ethel was a pretty brown-eyed girl near Nellie's age. She and Roy completed the grades of the small country school, and Ethel went on to attend the State Normal School at Cheney, but Roy remained at home to help his father with the farm work.

Johnny would show up at our house with his twenty-two rifle over his shoulder, and he and Otis would spend the day ranging through the sagebrush. Often they came home with stories of coyotes they had seen, or a rabbit to feed to the dogs. One time they told of seeing a bobcat and her kittens while over in the Deadman Lake area.

Farther south was the Don P. Estep homestead, with the Jay Kellenbergers, Littles, Harry and Essie Gregg, B. W. Reynolds, and the three Rosevear families as near neighbors. The Mays became acquainted with some of these families right after their wedding and arrival at their homestead.

One social activity of the neighborhood young folk was a charivari, better known as a shivaree, given for any young couple who were newly married. Rarely were any allowed to escape the serenade. Gathering quietly after dark near the home of the couple to be honored, the serenaders broke forth with wild yells like a band of raiding Siwashes. Around and around the cabin they raced, firing guns, pounding on pans, tin buckets and cans; anything that would produce a lot of noise.

There would be no sleeping for the ones inside the cabin when a shivaree was going on. After some fifteen minutes of this, the leader would call a halt and the party pounded on the door for the appearance of the bridal couple. Since the shivaree took place well after night had fallen, a hasty robing was necessary. The crowd expected to be treated cakes, candy and drinks of some kind, and usually these were on hand. Congratulations and good wishes were given, and the crowd dispersed to their homes.

The usual shivaree had been planned for Mary and Billie by the young people of the surrounding area. The Bagwells, Chavises, Littles, Ed Lees and others living farther south were the conspirators. They planned to give them the works, knowing Mary would be their teacher for the coming school term. The Mays were expecting such an event, but had no way of knowing when it would occur.

It was late evening when Mary and Billie got to their cabin on their wedding day. By the time they had unloaded the buggy which had been piled high with the feather bed, bedding and other household things, besides Mary's luggage, and arranged things for the night, there was no time to go for water. They had brought along a five-gallon can of water to last until they could get more. The light of their kerosene light showed the Bagwells they were at home, and other young folks were alerted for the following night.

It was getting late in the afternoon the following day when Mary said, "We are about out of water." Only a small amount was left in the can.

"I'll hook up the team, and we can drive over to the Adams place," Billie said. "I'll take some five gallon cans and we'll go visit a while. They will let us have a supply to last until we can fill the cistern."

As they were nearing the cabin after visiting for a while, they heard the din of racket around their shack. The shivaree was on. When Billie saw what was taking place, he quietly turned the team around and went for a nice long drive in the opposite direction. Not until the noisy festivities had ended and the crowd dispersed did they return to the cabin.

The crowd had silently surrounded the darkened cabin supposing the recipients of their attentions were inside. The shivaree went on in the usual way, but when loud pounding failed to produce anyone, they realized they had been serenading the empty cabin. Not to be entirely unrewarded for their efforts, the crowd opened the unlocked door and entered. Only the crumbs of cake and other goodies from the wedding dinner in Cunningham were left to greet the newlyweds on their return.

"Billie, come here!" Mary called after lighting the coal oil lamp on the table while Billie was unloading the cans of water from the buggy.

"What is it, darlin'?" Then as he saw the table to which she pointed, he exploded! His language was sometimes a bit sulfurous. It was quite evident what the young folk had been doing while he and Mary were taking that nice quiet drive.

Several of the serenaders registered for school a few days later and Mary learned more about the evening's happenings.

Rory McDonald, a batchelor in his late forties, had the quarter section next to ours on the south. He had lived so much alone he

28

was more than a little shy when in the presence of women, hardly raising his eyes when answering a question put directly to him. Mamma had a good sense of humor, and his embarrassed responses to her attempts to draw him out when he was at our house, led her to further attempts to make him feel at home. It amused all of us. One incident in particular comes to mind.

We sometimes had an occasional visitor from Cunningham to stay with us for a few days. Jeanie Bristow, whose father had bought the section of land from Papa, was visiting us, and we went for an afternoon chat at the May's. Returning home, we decided to walk past McDonald's little cabin so Jeanie could have a visit with her cousin, Will West, who was drilling a well just south of McDonald's homestead. Will was taking his meals with the bachelor.

It was getting near the time to quit drilling for the day, so Will suggested we should go on to the cabin and wait for him there. Mamma was teasing the two twenty-year-old girls about calling on the bachelor, and the kind of reception they might expect. She suspected that Rory would find this visit an unexpected experience.

Rory was quite flustered to have five females stop at his small two-room shack, especially when he learned we were to stay until Will came, and it would be his duty to entertain us until relieved. For protection, he picked up the twice-a-week Spokesman Review, and opening the newspaper to full width, retired behind it. With his back to the wall, he stood with legs' braced far apart, only his hands on the edge of the newspaper and his legs visible.

With a twinkle in her eye, Mamma began asking questions on various topics to try and set him at ease.

"It looks like you are going to have a good stand of wheat," was her opening comment.

"Pretty fair," came from behind the newspaper.

"Are the jack rabbits doing any damage to your potatoes?" was her next try.

29

The paper was lowered slightly as Rory's face appeared momentarily to say, "Some."

"How is your garden doing?" Mamma was still trying to find a common interest that would take away his embarrassment. This time the paper came down barely long enough for his answer, "Fairly well," and again his defenses were raised. Questions about the railroads coming and how much of his land it would cross met with similar results. Beleaguered man! It must have been with quite a feeling of relief that he saw Will belatedly arrive to take over the social amenities. The girls took more teasing from Mamma on their failure to make a greater impact on the bachelor. However, he must have felt Mamma's friendliness, and enjoyed it, for later in the summer when his garden was producing under irrigation from the well, he sent quantities of vegetables to her.

Two miles west of us where there were more outcroppings of the lava, was the homestead of Charles Morgan. He was a brother of Simon Morgan who lived farther west. Charley brought his bride to the lonely little homestead shack he built, in December of 1906. With nothing but sagebrush and cliffs surrounding their place, it was indeed a lonely beginning of their life together, and tears of loneliness were sometimes shed when Charley was in the field or at work. The loneliness for her was somewhat mitigated when their first baby, Gilbert, was born. In the next few years more little brothers came to fill the home and make an addition to the house necessary.

Chapter IV

More Homesteaders

FURTHER DOWN CRAB CREEK after it turned west between Saddle Mountain and Frenchman Hill were two outstanding and colorful men who took up homestead land along the creek about 1884. Ben and Sam Hutchinson would attract attention anywhere for Ben was six feet eight inches tall, and Sam topped him at seven feet and four inches. Their sister Bessie was also six feet, and her son, Cash McLeod, who homesteaded farther west near the Columbia River, was the same height as his Uncle Ben.

The part of Sam's land lying along the creek bottom was rich hay land, yielding good hay crops for his herd of horses whenever the heavy snows covered the tall rich bunch grass in that area. His ranch house and corrals lay near a bluff about a mile from the east end of Frenchman Hill. For a time Sam served as sheriff of Yakima County, and his daughter Ruth, who was also well over six feet tall, was her father's deputy.

Ben never married. His bachelor cabin was a little one-room cabin of rough timbers that looked across Crab Creek toward a long row of cliffs at the foot of the Hill. Ben was a top rider noted for outstanding skill with his long rawhide lariat. Both he and Sam had been riders for Ben Snipes in the Yakima Valley when Snipes was the cattle king of the northwest.

One day some of the riders working for Ben stopped at his cabin for a noon-day meal. Ben was not at home, and the boys prepared to cook some sourdough biscuits to go with their meal. They closed the oven door to the small low stove, which had been standing opened, and built a sagebrush fire in the stove. Soon the fire was burning hotly, and by the time the biscuits were ready to place in the oven, an odor of roasting meat began to fill the room. Perhaps Ben had left a roast of some kind! Opening the

Ben Hutchinson cabin on Lower Crab Creek. Built in 1888.
Photo by Joseph H. Tice.

oven door to see what kind of meat was there to add to their meal, they discovered some nicely roasted rattlesnakes which had crawled into the oven from the nearby cliffs while the oven door was open.

Ben had been on his homestead only a short time when Indian trouble came to some of the homestead people on and around Saddle Mountain. The Columbia Basin Indians were apprehensive because the grazing lands were being taken by homesteads, and they decided on direct action. The Wanapums were battling the homesteaders on Saddle Mountain down toward Priest Rapids. Ben knew of the battle going on and realizing the danger to the families living farther up the creek, he set out to take the word to the Tom McManamon family above Deadman Lake. It became necessary for him to hide out under a deep overhanging rock for a good part of a day until he could escape the Indians.

Indian troubles had ended by the time the Harry Hays family, Charley Johnsons and Charles Toskeys came by wagon in September of 1906, to take up claims a few miles from Hutchinson Lake. At first they camped beside the lake while lumber and supplies were hauled from Cunningham with which to build their homestead houses.

One night while the women and children were alone, the dogs set up an excited barking and commotion. "What kind of a

32

Cowboys about 1900. L to R: Billy Walker, Sam Hutchinson,
Jack Borden.

varmint do you suppose that is sneaking around?'' wondered
Mrs. Hays. The children, too, peered into the darkness not
knowing if they might see some shadowy form ready to engage
the dogs in a fight. Taking the shotgun, Mrs. Hays fired it off
into the air to scare away any wild animal that might be around.

A moment afterward, they heard loud talking as several riders
went past. Ben and his cowboys were taking no chances of being
mistaken for wild animals by those women with a gun. Again, as
they returned later they let their presence be known.

Another family that came to take up homestead land in 1906
was Jennie Tiffany and her children. Her husband had died a
short time before in North Dakota, leaving her with six children,
the youngest, George, being only three months old. Jennie's
brother, Ed Miller, had a claim at the foot of Saddle Mountain
a few miles west of the Othello post office; and he sent for Jennie
to come west.

The mail came to the Othello post office only three times a

week, and Ed did not always go to the post office on mail days, so he failed to get her letter telling just when they would arrive.

"Hatton! Hatton!" the brakeman called as the train approached the small town which was their destination.

"Well, children, it looks like we are there," said Jennie as they gathered their things together. "Ina, you take George, and Effie you can help the boys with some of these things," she continued as the train slowed to its brief stop. After their long ride in the day coach in which she had bedded the children down on the seats to sleep, it would feel good to get away from the coal dust and occasional flying cinders of the train. It would be good to see Brother Ed, too. But the platform of the small depot failed to disclose any familiar face. Ed was not there, and the train pulled out leaving the family wondering what to do next. It looked like it was up to Jennie to find out.

Securing a team and wagon, and leading a cow which she had purchased knowing the children would need the milk, and getting directions for the long drive to Ed's homestead, they came in the late afternoon dusk to a cabin. They thought it might be Miller's. It set back some distance from the dim road, and in their rush to the cabin, they left the wagon and team in the road. The cabin was vacant. They had no way of knowing who the owner might be or when he would return, but the door was unlocked.

Finding a lamp containing some oil and a box of matches, Jennie decided it would be the wisest thing to remain there for the night. They got a fire started in the stove, and further investigation turned up some flour with which they could make pancakes. Then they remembered the team, wagon and cow that had been left standing in the road.

"Ina, you and the boys go bring the team and cow," Jennie directed. But it had gotten dark by this time, and in the unfamiliar surroundings they were at a loss to remember where the wagon had been left. All their hunting in the dark failed to produce the wagon and animals.

With only a supper of pancakes to satisfy their hunger, they bedded down on the floor until daylight, when they could find their way on to Ed's homestead. Jennie and the family shared the one-room cabin with her brother until a house could be built on the claim she took adjoining his.

As with so many others, Jennie had her problems of getting water. Sometimes when the team got lost in the open country, she walked and carried two pails of water from over a mile away.

One time when Jennie was working in the new little town that was just coming into existence, she left the small children in the care of Ina and Effie. Gaynell, the eldest daughter who had now come out from North Dakota, was also working away from home to help provide for the family. Effie went to bring in the cow from the open range toward evening, not realizing that little George was following her through the brush. When she returned with the cow George was nowhere to be found.

Effie and the boys were hunting frantically when Ina returned from an errand to town a few minutes later, and learning of the baby's disappearance she immediately returned on the long walk to town to carry word to her mother.

The alarm was sent out. Men from town and homestead neighbors joined in the search. All night the hunt went on among the rocks and sagebrush for the missing child. A terrible fear for the safety of the child where so many rattlesnakes were to be

Horse-powered ferry on Columbia River at White Bluffs, 1899-1904. L to R: First two unknown; on ferry, Matt Wiehl and George Borden. Horses: Pete and Ginger. Courtesy Harvey Yeager, Sr.

35

found was in the heart of the searchers. It was not until the next forenoon that little George was found unhurt.

The railroad had not yet been built when the August Lawrenz family moved to their homestead two miles north of where Corfu was afterward located on the railroad, in 1905. It was a long trip to Hatton for groceries and other supplies. Sometimes the two boys, Bill and Fred, walked or rode horseback over Saddle Mountain to the Columbia River where they could take a little ferry to White Bluffs. This ferry replaced an old horse-powered ferry that had been in use there, and the boys saw the old abandoned ferry on the bank of the river. Matt Wiehl operated the new ferry.

We had seen and ridden on the horse-motivated ferry when we camped on the east bank of the river in 1904, when George Borden was the operator with Matt as his helper.

This ferry had been built in 1899 by the Carter Brothers who were sheep people, probably for transporting their flocks of sheep from one grazing ground across the river to the other side. It had an enclosed pen in the middle of the boat in which wagons, buggies, riders or animals could be transported across the river. Around this enclosure was space wide enough for a horse to walk; two horses on opposite sides followed the passage around and around to supply the motive power. An upright beam in the center of the boat to which was attached a sweep served to steer the boat. In making the crossing, the ferry was first steered upstream for some distance before getting into the strong current of the river. Then, with the force of the current combined with the two-horse power, it was able to make a landing across from where it started. The two horses, Pete and Ginger became known to many of those using the ferry, but a few months later George Borden was drowned in the river and another ferry was secured and put into operation by Matt in 1905.

Realizing the need for a road across the mountain to White Bluffs for the homestead people living on the north side, Road Commissioner Joyce of South Grant County, was able to get a grant of $1,000.00 for a wagon road from where the town of

36

Corfu was located, over Saddle Mountain and terminating at the Wahluke ferry.

It was surveyed, and the crew of road builders from the surrounding homesteads went to work at twenty-five cents an hour. The pay for horses to pull the Fresno scrapers was fifty cents a day. Lloyd Nelson, a homesteader in the area, guided the first team while Joyce held the plow handles to make the first furrow along the surveyed route up and over the mountain. Faint traces of that old road can still be seen.

Other homestead men and boys who helped with the road building were Nate and Jim Lewis, Clyde and Fletcher Madison, Gus Seeburger, Bill and Fred Lawrenz, Roy and George Ellsworth, Mannie Simonson, John Mason and others. The income from the work helped out with homestead finances, along with the convenience of the new road.

Martin Burke, a cowboy and rider for Henry Gable and others, homesteaded on Frenchman Hill about twenty-five miles south of Ephrata. During the early years he saw eighteen thousand horses shipped from that point. He was acquainted with all the horse and cattle brands from all over that section of the state. Others who took up claims on the Hill, or just north of there were Tom Berry, Gus Seeburger, Bert and Dwight Cole. Quincy was their nearest town. Most of these families lived too far away from our homestead for us to get acquainted except at the yearly Fourth of July picnics on Crab Creek, or the Pioneer's picnic at Moses Lake.

Site of cowboy's fall, Deadman's Bluff.

Chapter V
Rocks, Rattlesnakes and a Railroad

WHILE LOOKING FOR HOMESTEAD LAND, Papa met another colorful and unusual personality in the person of Thomas S. Blythe. He was generally called Lord Blythe behind his back by those who knew him.

It was rumored that Lord Blythe was a remittance man from Scotland whose father was a duke in Scotland. It was said he had attended Oxford, but because of some trouble in which he became involved, he came to America, receiving from his titled father some ten to twenty thousand dollars a year.

Blythe became intrigued with the wide open spaces around Moses Lake and Ephrata, and decided to become a cattle baron. He bought a large tract of land along Crab Creek south of Moses Lake on which he built a large mansion. It even included a beautifully tiled bathroom, but without any bathroom fixtures. From time to time he bought up more land from homestead people who had proved up on their land and wanted to move on, until his holdings comprised more than six thousand acres. Another method he used in acquiring more range land was to have his cowboys file on a homestead, then buy them out when they got title to the land.

Blythe bought the cattle, horses, equipment and cattle brand of another man by the name of Fobina who had run stock in the area, and extended his holdings up into the Ephrata country where he built another large house. It was furnished with the finest in furniture, silver, china, books and a piano.

At first the only means of getting around was by horseback, but as roads were made, the buggy and buckboard came into more general use. However, Blythe wanted something more befitting what he considered his station, so he ordered a glassed-in coach. Its mohair upholstery, silver trimmings and beveled glass to separate the occupants from the driver outside, presented a vehicle never before seen in that dusty, sagebrush country. Wearing his tailored suits, his high stiff hat and monocle, Lord Blythe presented a picture of a gentleman cowboy entirely unfamiliar to the cowboys who rode for him. None of them would have been caught dead in the contraption except one of the men who was fond of getting "likkered up," and who sometimes gave his employer some wild rides from town to the ranch.

Blythe sold his entire outfit to George Drumheller in 1904, with the possible exception of the royal coach.

Henry Gable owned many of the range horses running in the open range around us and south to Skootenai Springs where he had his headquarters and corrals. From there the horses spread out to graze toward the south and to the north toward Deadman's Lake, Goose Lake and Crab Creek. Trails led across this rough country from different directions and converged on these sources of water.

Henry Gable's headquarters and horse corrals at Skootenai Springs, 1900-1906. Courtesy Mrs. Matt Wiehl.

On the week-long camping trip our family, in company with several friends had taken to the Columbia River in 1904, we camped overnight at Skootenai Springs. Next morning we were treated to an impromptu rodeo that was put on by Gable's buckaroos for our benefit, riding the wild horses filling the corral.

From the outside of the strongly built corral, constructed of strong poles, we watched as a rider entered the corral on foot holding his lariat in which was a large open loop. Swiftly the loop of the lasso shot out, catching the running horse by the front legs and throwing it to the ground. Before it could struggle to its feet it was blindfolded, a rope was put around its neck, and it was allowed to scramble up. A heavy cowboy's saddle was placed on its back and cinched tightly. The rider climbed into the saddle while we watched with breathless interest, and settling his spur-equipped boots firmly into the stirrups, reached over and removed the blinding bandana.

With an explosion of energy the horse went into action, using every stratagem its wild instincts could devise to unseat the rider. How that horse could buck! Rearing, pitching, sunfishing, springing into the air with its back bowed in an endeavor to snap the unwanted rider from its back, and coming down on stiffened legs, only to find none of these tricks worked. No bucking straps were needed to make those wild cayuses buck. As the horse began to tire, the buckaroo pulled his hat from his head and slapped the horse first on one side and then on the other to show the horse who was the master. It was part of our early experience with what we had heard called "The Wild and Woolly West."

The Springs were surrounded by the same lava cliffs that lay beyond our homestead. That this country had once undergone violent convulsions of natural forces was evident. Beds of rocks that had at one time been molten lava which cracked into almost hexigon shapes as it cooled, were everywhere. Higher outcroppings and long rows of cliffs of this same lava added to the wildness of the country. Traces of an ancient shoreline indicating a great inland sea or body of water had at some time existed there, could be seen part way up on Frenchman Hill. It could also be traced along the bench of land running north and south on which our homestead was located. Our house and the farm buildings lay on top of this bench with the land extending into the flat.

In digging a hole for the cistern we found beneath the top two feet of soil was a loose layer of smooth rounded stones similar to those found on the seashore. This layer seemed to be several feet in thickness and had little soil mixed with the stones to bind them together.

In the deep coulee lying a half mile north of our home were huge boulders of true granite, unlike any other rocks in the area. In a sharp bend of the coulee was a large pocket of sand that had been caught during some water action. It lay several feet above the floor of the coulee. Sometimes we children stopped to play there when something took us across the coulee; sand for plastering and cement work was sometimes obtained there. Diatomaceous earth was found there and in other places, though we children had no knowledge of such a long name, nor of what it consisted.

This rough country provided an ideal incubator for rattle-snakes. Nor were they content to remain in The Flat, as we came to call the area below the bench. They spilled over, or rather,

Deep Coulee one-half mile north of Tice Homestead.
Picture by Joseph H. Tice.

crawled up onto the bench where we frequently found them. This called for the necessary caution, "Look out for rattlesnakes!"

"I killed a rattlesnake in the yard today," Mamma told us one day soon after we moved there. We had just returned from a walk over to see Mary.

"Where is it?" we asked. We were curious to see what one looked like, never having seen one of those poisonous reptiles. We had seen copperhead snakes in Missouri.

"It was not a big one," Mamma said, "But I want you to see it so you will know what a rattlesnake looks like."

"What did you kill it with?" Dona asked as we looked at the snake which was about eighteen inches long.

"I did not have anything else handy, so I used that little baseball bat the boys made," was her reply. That bat was not over two feet long, and we thought how brave she was to get that close to a rattlesnake.

"Every rattler must be killed if possible, but you children must keep back if you see one, and call Papa or me," she cautioned.

We were sitting at the dinner table one day when Dona, having finished her meal, stepped out the front door. She immediately stepped back in to say in a frightened voice, "Papa, there is a big rattlesnake out here."

"Where?" Papa was already on his feet as he asked.

"Right outside the front door," she told him. Papa took the shotgun down from the wall where it hung, always kept loaded for possible coyotes looking for chickens, and stepped outside. The snake had disappeared.

"It crawled under the house," Dona told him getting down on the ground to look from a safe distance. Papa could see it only a couple of feet from the edge, but since the house was only about eight inches off the ground he was compelled to lay the gun on its side, and he could not sight along the barrel. Dona told him when he got the gun lined up with the snake. He killed it, then hauled it out with the garden rake to examine and cut off the rattles. We gradually added specimens of rattles to our collection.

There was a good-sized coyote population around there. Jack rabbits were plentiful to provide plenty of food for their pups in the spring. Occasionally, they varied the diet with chicken, or other poultry from some barnyard. We were often serenaded in the night or early dawn by what sounded like a dozen. Beginning with several short yips that extended to a long howl, it carried across the sagebrush in the still air. When two sang in duet, it became the very personification of that wild desolate country. It was a puzzle to us how two could sound like so many.

Papa kept some hounds, two of which he had brought from Missouri. (One of these Mamma had named Aggravation when Papa brought two skinny little fox hound pups home to raise. The other pup, which she named Starvation, glutted himself on freshened cow's milk and died; but Ag survived to come west.) The dogs frequently engaged in the sport of chasing coyotes for the mocking yell of the coyotes seemed to infuriate the hounds. Soon we would hear them coming down the flat, their deep voices rising on the morning or evening air.

One particular evening, at the close of a busy harvest day, we heard the chase heading down the flat. As the sound came nearer, some of the men headed on a run for the brow of the bench hoping to get sight of the chase. One of the men heard a warning rattle as his foot landed beside the snake and he gave a wild leap over, but not in time to escape the deadly strike of the ugly head. It was fortunate for him that the strike landed a half inch below his shoe top of tough muleskin leather where some of the venom was left to show how near it came to the flesh. He lost all interest in the chase, and returned to the house with a very pale face.

"Miz. Tice, if that rattler had a struck any higher last night, I woulda been up arguin' with Saint Peter at the gate this mornin'." Charley had gotten over his bad scare of the previous evening, and was in a jocular mood when he came to breakfast.

"Well, Charley, it is a good thing for you that snake didn't strike any higher," Mamma told him as she took a large pan of biscuits from the oven to place before the harvest hands who were coming to the table. "It would have been no joke for you then," she continued, smiling as some of the men were trying to decide just how she meant it. It would have been a serious matter when there was no doctor nearer than twenty miles, and she knew of no effective antidote to counteract the poison.

Even in the midst of the busy harvest season mail day was an important day to us on the homestead.

"Nellie, I think Papa has the horse saddled for you and Laura to go after the mail. Take this letter to mail, and be sure the sack is tied good and tight to the saddle horn so you won't lose any." We always enjoyed these trips after the mail on the three days each week the mail was brought to the country post office. The Othello post office was the gathering place for many of the younger folk from the surrounding homesteads.

Nellie and I rode double on a gentle old horse; Nellie did the steering and set the pace while I clung to the back of the saddle. "Please don't let him trot," I would beg. As there were no stirrups to the rear seat, a gallop was much to be preferred to a jog trot. It was three miles to the Ed Lee home where we first went for the mail. Shortly afterward the post office was moved to the Harry Gregg homestead where it remained for about a year until it was again moved, this time to the J. P. Price home. This brought it a mile nearer.

There are different stories as to how Othello came to get its name. Previous to the establishing of the post office at this place, the nearest post office for homestead folk as far away as Crab Creek was another farmhouse post office five miles farther east. It was known as Hamlet. Probably the name had nothing to do with Shakespeare, but it may have suggested another Shakespearean name. Some credit William Hodson, a school teacher, with selecting the name of Othello. Others give the credit to Mrs. A. O. Lee, another teacher who taught at the Billington school. However, her daughter, Helen, discounts this report. Perhaps the best authenticated credit should go to Mrs. Robert M. Chavis as the one who suggested the name that was adopted. Two of her sons, Will and Sam, vouch for the accuracy of this account.

Their mother was a lover of Shakespearean plays, and in reading some of them she liked the sound of Othello. "Why not give the name to the new post office?" she suggested, "It would be unique, and some day we might have a town here by that name."

Several other names were offered by others, but when A. O. Lee, the postmaster at Cunningham circulated the petition among the settlers who would be benefitted by the new post office, the vote was in favor of Othello.[1]

On our trips to the post office we usually could bring home some of the neighborhood news. Rumors were flying that a railroad might be built through the country. We had found stakes from a preliminary survey across our land, but had not known for what they were intended. Now these rumors were confirmed our first summer when further surveying was done with only minor shifts in the stakes.

One day a member of the surveying crew came to our house to see Mamma. "Mrs. Tice, our surveying crew will be working in this section for a few days. I wonder if we could arrange with you for our noon meals while we are here?" he asked.

"How many of you will there be?" she inquired. "There are usually five of us," he informed her. Arrangements were made, and we became acquainted with Orin Rook, "Nig" Pringle, Morris Brink and the two other members of the surveying crew. Through them we learned more about the railroad that was coming.

Interest was keen as the settlers discussed how the railroad would aid in the development of the country. The Chicago, Milwaukee and Saint Paul was extending its main line through from Chicago to the coast. That would bring towns, stores, shipping facilities and passenger service to homestead people.

Next followed negotiations between agents for the railroad and the land owners for a right-of-way across their lands. Papa

---

[1] Data on early postoffices at Othello and Hamlet from the National Archives and Records Service, Washington, D. C.

46

came home to discuss the sale of the right-of-way across our land with Mamma.

"It will take about five acres of our land," he told her. "They offer twenty-five dollars an acre."

"Is that what they are paying for other land?" she asked.

"I think that is the price most of the homesteads are getting. Chavis sold his entire homestead to them at that price; I hear it is to be the townsite," Papa assured her. "I heard a rumor that the railroad will put a division point with freight yards here and make a town."

"Then we shall have stores where we won't have to go twenty miles for groceries," she was pleased at the idea.

Meanwhile, homestead life went on. A barbed wire fence was built around the one hundred and sixty acres as part of the requirements the government imposed on homestead land. It was also necessary in order to keep out the wild range cattle that had free run throughout the unfenced land. At times the single strand of wire proved insufficient barrier, and they had to be driven out by someone on horseback. Those wild cattle would promptly take after anyone incautious enough to attempt it on foot.

As a pleasant interlude from the daily routine of chores, an all-day outing and picnic over on Crab Creek was enthusiastically welcomed by the younger members of the family.

Young cockerels who were reaching the crowing stage and needing to be reduced in numbers, formed a delectable piece de resistance. Home made bread fresh from the oven the day before, freshly churned butter and a gallon of buttermilk which still had tiny flecks of butter floating on top, potato salad made with a generous supply of eggs from the hen house; what more could be desired to make the day a joyous occasion?

Bathing suits consisted of an extra pair of bib overalls for the boys; an extra calico dress for the girls.

"Did you girls put in some extra panties and underwaists to wear under your dresses when you are in the water?" Mamma knew our dresses would stick tightly enough to be rather revealing when wet if we wore nothing underneath; but these garments made from bleached flour sacks helped to fulfill the requirements of modesty. Nellie had seen we were provided with the needed articles.

Papa hitched Pete and Frank to the wheat rack while Headley assembled fish hooks and twine for fishing gear, and we children climbed in to wait with what patience we could muster while the food baskets and necessary things were loaded into the wagon. Mamma saw that the chickens had enough water to last all day and Papa checked a few last items; then we were off across the sagebrush and rim rocks, making a new road that joined a more plainly marked one to the creek.

"There goes a jack rabbit!" exclaimed the boys excitedly as a long-eared rabbit sprang away from in front of the team and went bounding off a little way, then sat up to look around. Headley grabbed the twenty-two rifle and aimed it as the wagon continued on over the rough ground, but his aim was not good enough and only served to send the jack bounding away through the brush with occasional higher leaps and quick changes in direction to make good its escape.

We frequently saw the jack rabbits, but rarely was a coyote seen in the daytime, especially if there was a gun in the wagon.

Where Edward O'Roarke rode off the bluff while night herding cattle. April — 1880. Photo by Joseph H. Tice.

We wondered if they could detect the gun powder in the cartridges, or how they knew when to stay out of sight.

A little farther on we turned north toward a long row of cliffs. Papa pointed out a pile of rocks at the foot.

"There is where the boy and his horse went off the cliff," he told us. "He was herding cattle up on top."

"Is that why they call this Deadman's Bluff?" we asked.

"Yes, and the lake just beyond is called Deadman's Lake," he added.

These names were given as a result of some earlier cattle history. Deadman's Bluff was a long bluff with an approach to the top from one end. Ben Snipes, the cattle king, Blythe and Drumheller had all run cattle in the area. At times, when a cattle round-up or drive was under way, the herd would be held on top of this bluff under the care of one or two cowboys, ready to start the herd on the long drive the next day. If the herd became restless or alarmed during the night, the cowboys rode around the herd to quiet them. Often they sang as they rode.

This time a young lad of fifteen, by the name of Edward O'Roarke,[1] was on night herd duty. In riding around the milling cattle herd on his mule, he was somehow pushed off the cliff by the cattle, and fell to his death on the rocks at the foot of the cliff. His body was taken to the Columbia River near Priest Rapids, and sent by Indian canoe to Wallula, and from there to Walla Walla where his parents resided, for burial.

A five foot pillar of rocks at the bottom marked the place where his body was found, and the skull of his steed was still beside the pile of rocks as we passed in the early days. Two smaller piles of rocks stood on top of the cliff directly above where they found the last tracks leading to the edge of the cliff. The pile of rocks were a cowboy's tribute and memorial to a lad's courage.

The road we traveled by Deadman's Bluff was the same one

[1] The death of Edward O'Roarke, mentioned as Roark in the book *Kamiakin*, by A. J. Splawn, and whose tragic death at Deadman's Bluff happened in April, 1880, is recorded on page 69, of the Parish Register of Saint Patrick's Church in Walla Walla, Washington.

A portion of the White Bluffs road used by Ben Snipes in his cattle drives. The Author herded horses here in 1911.
Photo by Joseph H. Tice.

Ben Snipes used when he took some of his herd of cattle from the Yakima Valley to sell at the mining camps in British Columbia. On some of these drives they swam the herd across the Columbia River near White Bluffs with the help of the Priest Rapids (Wanapum) Indians. Other cattlemen sometimes followed the same route.

"Look over there and you can see the face at the end of the cliff," Papa told us. We didn't know just what to look for, but as we got to the north end of the bluff he pointed it out to us. From a certain point it did look like a face outlined on the rocks. Just beyond was Simon Morgan's place.

When we got to the creek the team was unhooked from the wagon and staked out to graze until needed again. We children found our swimming clothes and sought private dressing rooms among the willows and wild roses lining the creek. The creek was only about a foot deep with a few places up to three feet in depth.

Papa looked for a slender willow he could use for a fishing pole and fitted it with a strong twine, a rifle bullet for a sinker, and a bottle cork for a float. Grasshoppers, or crawfish from the creek supplied the bait.

50

Mamma was satisfied to enjoy the beauty of the wild roses blooming mingled with the willows along the stream, or to watch the cliff swallows darting to and from their nests along the face of the cliffs which lined the valley; satisfied that the members of the family were all happily occupied with their own activities and requiring no attention on her part until it was time to eat.

The odors of frying fish and coffee made in a blackened can over an open fire, sent out an invitation to our healthy appetites. The call "Dinner!" needed no repeating. We gathered around the cloth spread on the grass in the shade of a willow tree, and bowed our heads while Mamma gave thanks for the bounties given. Life was good and satisfying.

A little after mid-afternoon Papa began to hook the team to the wagon.

"Do we have to start home this early?" we children queried. It seemed awfully early to be starting home.

"We want to stop by Simon's place and visit a while," Mamma explained. We thought of the big patch of watermelons we had seen at his place and were quite reconciled to start.

Papa heard that Simon was using some kind of system to irrigate his truck garden and melon patch, and wanted to see how he did it.

While Mamma and the older girls visited with Simon's wife in the house, we younger children trailed Papa and Simon as he showed the improvised irrigation system he had devised with water from the lake. A sort of sweep had been set up to be powered by hand to pull the water from the lake into the series of flumes along the higher side of the garden. Minnie and the boys provided the hand power while Simon directed the water to where he wanted it to go.

Melons were ripening on the vines; large good-looking melons that made our eyes shine in anticipation. He cut several for us to sample. The samples were generous slices of juicy sweetness that left us wishing our capacity was greater.

"Come on, try this rattlesnake melon," he urged as he cut into a striped melon that snapped open with a crisp sound to reveal a beautiful deep pink interior. He had several varieties, round dark green ones, long, lighter splotched green and huge rattlesnake melons. We tried all kinds. In the shade beside the house was a large pile he had picked in readiness to haul to Lind next day for door-to-door delivery. It would take two full days for the trip.

Harvesting Scene—Showing header, 5 header boxes, cook house, and water wagon or tank, background center. Courtesy Nellie Tice Kluss.

Chapter VI

Resources

SOURCES OF REVENUE on a homestead are somewhat limited, especially before the land is cleared and a crop can be harvested. Advantages are taken of every avenue that will add a bit of cash to the budget for the purchase of staples and clothing. Butter and eggs could be sent to the store and traded for other commodities from time to time, but the distance made this practical only occasionally. Older sons and daughters took work where they could find it.

Before we moved from town Mamma sometimes did sewing for other families such as the doctor's or hotel keeper's who could afford the expense, but this source of revenue had been removed by distance.

After coming to Washington in 1903, Mamma hired a man to build a carpet loom for her so she could weave rag carpets for our home. This loom, a large, crude, but strongly built affair which took up considerable room, was installed in the boys' room upstairs. Now she decided to put it to use weaving for others. Some of the women in town who had seen carpets Mamma had woven, became ready customers.

Rag carpets require a lot of rags. Cotton dresses, shirts, sheets, pillow cases or any cotton material no longer suitable for its original use, were torn into strips, the ends tacked together and wound into balls ready for the weaving. A large willow clothes basket was kept filled with the torn rags, and when other work was out of the way, or in the evening, Mamma and the girls gathered around the basket to sew and chat. This was frequently high-lighted by Mamma's stories of when she was a little girl. She was a delightful story teller, making rag sewing a not unpleasant task.

"Mamma, tell us a story about when you were a little girl," and she would begin another story.

"It was the next year after the close of the Civil War. Our father, your grandpa, had been in the Northern Army and had been with his army unit when it was fighting down in the South. He got sick with the measles. There were no hospitals where he could be cared for, and because he got wet and cold while he was sick, he died. Word was sent to our mother of his death, but he was buried down South. This left Mother with four little children, your Uncle Minor, Aunt Harriet, Aunt Ellen and me, to take care of and support. I was the youngest, about three years old." Mamma broke off the story long enough to wind the sewed rangs onto the ball, thread another needle with a long thread, and reach for more of the rag strips. Then she continued.

"It was hard work on the little farm, so when Father's brother wanted to marry Mother and help her raise the family, she accepted him and they were married. We called him 'Pappy,' and he was a good father to us."

"One morning Pappy got up real early before it was light, and as he went outside to start the chores at the barn, he saw a beautiful sight in the sky. Stepping back to the door, he called Mother to come outside and see all the shooting stars. There seemed to be hundreds of them. She had never seen so many before, though she had heard about a time thirty years before when there had been a much greater display of falling stars. This one was such a beautiful sight that she woke us children so we could see it too. The stars were shooting and falling across the sky on all sides. I was just a little girl not quite six years old, but I shall never forget what a beautiful sight it was." We liked Mamma's stories.

Most carpet customers furnished their own rags already wound into balls, but occasionally they under-estimated, or Mamma supplied material for the entire carpet, at a price. The charge for weaving was sixteen cents a yard when it was woven with a solid color ground with interspersing stripes. Hit or miss carpeting throughout was a few cents less as it took less time both in the preparing and weaving. Rags of one color were sewn together, or white rags were wound into skeins and dyed the desired color to be used in the stripes. Hit or miss weaving permitted sewing any color of rags together, and took less time in the weaving since no time was lost in measuring or changing shuttles.

"Will you girls fill all those shuttles for me from the balls in the basket?" Nellie and I had come upstairs to see Mamma who was weaving a carpet for Mrs. Tulles.

"Does it make any difference which kind we wind from?"

"No, this carpet is all hit or miss. There aren't any solid ground or stripes," she told us. "She wants it for Stella's and Marie's bedroom."

Mamma had woven a new carpet for our front room, and it had just been put down. It had a pretty blue ground with colored stripes that extended across the room after she finished sewing it together. The floor had been padded with clean straw; then the carpet was spread out and stretched tightly, and tacked solidly close to the wall with edges turned under.

"Mamma, can I weave a little bit?" I had been watching her pass the shuttle back and forth through the warp. It looked easy.

"You wouldn't be able to weave tight enough," she explained as she crossed the threads with the foot treadle and pulled forward the frame which held a metal reed called a comb through which the warp was passed. It was brought firmly against the weaving with a solid thud to make a firm weave. From eight to ten yards a day was the usual amount that could be woven.

Building fences, getting land cleared and ready for sowing wheat, hauling water, looking after the stock and the multitude of other things out of doors filled Papa's time. He had the help of Jim, Headley and Otis. Headley was milking the three cows that had freshened that spring.

"The cows don't seem to be giving as much milk as they

should," Mamma observed. She may have suspected that Headley's quick temper had something to do with it.

"Well, when one of the cows kicks, he hits her," one of us chimed up, then perhaps afterward wished we had not been quite so quick to find a reason.

"Nellie, you and Laura had better take over the milking. We need to have them give down their milk or they will be drying up," Mamma instructed us. We girls had a strong suspicion he preferred work in other departments than in the cow nursery. The horses were more to his liking. But the yield did improve under our gentle ministration.

A large plot was planted to potatoes. They could be harvested in the fall, and those not needed for the family could be sold to help provide winter clothing for the family. But we made a discovery. Jack rabbits liked potatoes, too. They would slip into the patch from the sagebrush land around and enjoy the succulent tops; then after the potatoes had formed and become large enough to use, they even dug them. As the rabbits were there in great numbers they could do great damage to the potato crop. They usually came into the patch about dusk, so Papa would sometimes take a chair out into the yard to watch for and try to shoot the invaders.

On one occasion, while watching from the upstairs window, I had seen several rabbits come into the patch and start their destructive work. After some time, having heard no gun shot, I went down and joined him.

"There don't seem to be any rabbits coming this evening, Daughter," Papa remarked. "I haven't seen one yet." His eyesight was not the best.

Pointing to some I could see busily at work, I told him, "There have been several slip in that got past you."

When he heard that he raised the gun and fired in the direction where one had been pointed out. Rabbits sprang out in all directions and streaked for the brush at the sound of the blast. There were at least a dozen, but all lived to try again.

In preparing the seed wheat for planting, it was desirable

to give it a dip in blue vitriol solution to control rust, a disease that caused considerable damage to untreated wheat. The solution was put into a large wooden barrel set into the ground, and the wheat, a half sack at a time, was immersed in the solution until it was thoroughly saturated. It was then placed on an inclined surface to drain. This doubtless helped also to hasten sprouting when it had been planted.

As spring approached, the ground squirrels began to make their appearance in the fields of tender green wheat. Their long fast during their hibernation had given them healthy appetites. Large colonies of them, including a goodly increase of young during their stay under ground, made severe inroads in the stands of wheat if left to work unhindered. One of the methods of control for these pests was a generous helping of strychnine poisoned wheat left in little heaps around their holes and colonies. Otis had a method of his own to capture some of the young ones that had not yet become too worldly wise.

"Mamma, I caught a young squirrel out there in the field," he said, opening his hand to show her what he had. Mamma was always interested in the activities of her youngest child. "How did you catch it?" she inquired.

"I stalked it by first scaring all of them underground, then I laid down on the ground behind the hole so they would have to come clear out before they could see me." His face was all animation as he explained his trick. "I laid real still and pretty soon this young one got curious. It stuck its head out for a peep, but it looked toward the place it had seen me and I was behind its hole. When it came out a little farther, I grabbed it."

The old ones were seldom the victim of this ruse, but he often caught the inexperienced ones in this way.

One day when Otis had caught a young one, I pursuaded him to let me have it for a pet. The family couldn't see any point in my wanting to have it for a pet when Papa was putting out poison to rid the fields of them.

"You'd better kill it and not have anything like that around," was his comment. But none of their efforts to separate me from my pet had any effect. All day I tenderly watched over my new acquisition, taking it out to a patch of green wheat for its food. Someway, it seemed to make no effort to run away and I thought it liked me. More probably so much handling left it with little energy to run. At night it was placed in a cloth-lined box on a chair beside my pillow. I did not trust Nellie or Headley who had already made several efforts to get it from me. During the night I was awakened by a whistle close to my ear. There was the little squirrel on my pillow telling me it was lonesome for its foster mother. Several times during the night I was awakened by that whistle. I would hold it in the warmth of my hand in the box until it got cozy. It was still alive next morning, so I left it in the box while I went downstairs to breakfast.

"I am going upstairs and kill that squirrel," Nellie told me just as I had gotten my hands well soaped, and she headed for the stairway. There was not time to clean my hands of soap in this emergency, and with the cry, "Nellie, you leave my squirrel alone," I raced for the stairway, too.

She had found the box by the time I got up there, but not wanting to handle it, or perhaps just teasing me, she had not harmed it. With my soapy hands I grabbed the poor little thing making it a very bedraggled pet.

Another day it survived, and that night when I heard its whistle on my pillow, I took it into bed with me. It did no more whistling. The next morning I discovered it had whistled its last whistle. I had laid on it in my sleep.

We had no wheat harvest the summer of 1906, so Jim organized a crew to do custom harvesting.

"Dona, how would you like to go along to do the cooking?" Jim asked. "We will take the cook-house."

"Do you mean by myself?" she asked him. "I don't think I could manage it by myself."

"You would need someone to help you," Mamma told her. Jim had already been talking to Mamma about it. "Do you think Xerpha would be willing to go? She would be good help. You could ask her and see."

Mamma and Dona talked it over with Xerpha and her mother, and the arrangements were made. Xerpha wanted to go on to high school in Ritzville and this work seemed like a good opportunity to provide clothes and books for the school year up there. Billie was also joining the crew which had engaged to harvest wheat near Cunningham.

"Billie, what are you going to do about Mary?" Mamma asked him when she learned he was going. It was nearing the time for Mary's confinement, and Mamma was concerned about the arrangements he had made for that time. "Do you think she should be left home alone?"

"No, Mother, I am going to take Mary over to Cunningham with me where she will be near Dr. Tulles. Bristows have their new house now, and I can rent the old house for us to live in," Billie re-assured her.

"Could you and Mr. Tice (he always called Papa Mr. Tice,) and the children move over to our house to look after things while we are away?" Billie asked. He had built a new two-room plastered house that spring, but they were still using the original shack as a kitchen and dining room. "We will need to send for you when the time comes."

Mamma talked it over with Papa, and realizing it was just that much nearer to Cunningham when she would be needed, they consented to live at the new house while looking after things at both places.

Early one morning just as we returned to the house after milking the cows in the distant pasture, we found Will West waiting with an urgent message for Mamma. Nellie and I were not told what it was, but we knew from Mamma's quick preparations to go with Will it was something important.

"Nellie, you and Laura will have to be the housekeepers while I am away," she told us as she got her bag packed in readiness to leave. She and Papa seemed to understand what the excitement was all about.

A hasty breakfast was eaten, then the team and buggy taking Mamma, headed for Cunningham at a fast trot. We girls, ages ten and twelve, were to be the cooks while she was away.

Neither Nellie or I were experts in the culinary line. Dona had been of more assistance in that way; doing the dishes fell to us, but we had watched as the various foods were cooked so we felt we were prepared to take over the cooking. We knew how to make beds, wash dishes and sweep floors, so there was nothing new in that work.

Nellie could make biscuits, fry potatoes and make gravy, but she decided a pie would add something tasty to the menu.

"I am going to make a cream pie," she announced with aplomb a day or two later. That met with my immediate interest and approval. I thought she might let me have a finger in the pie, too, or at least the making of it.

"Do you remember how Mamma made it?" I had watched Mamma put one of those delicious offerings together many times, but now I couldn't be sure just how she did it.

With no apparent question in her mind about the first steps, Nellie got out the shortening, flour, salt, the rolling pin and bread board, and told me to get a pie pan ready. Mamma had made so many crusts she no longer needed a recipe. Nellie was not quite sure just how much of each ingredient to use, but put in what she thought was about right. She had not noticed that pie dough should be handled gently, and only enough to hold the ingredients together, so she gave it a good working.

It held together well as she put it into the pie tin and then pinched the dough around the edge to make a fancy design. Next, there was the filling to make. Setting the pan with the unbaked crust to one side, she got out the eggs, sugar, milk and vanilla flavoring, also a little more flour to act as thickening. She could not remember just how Mamma had combined these things. We talked it over and decided she must have mixed them right in the pie shell and then baked the whole thing together. It was difficult to mix all those ingredients in the unbaked crust which could hardly be called a crust yet, but it was accomplished with some going on her, the table and floor, and placed in the oven to bake. The results were not up to

**Threshing scene on the John McCulloch homestead — 1913.
Photo by Joseph H. Tice.**

Mamma's pie, but Papa and Otis ate it without critical comments.

On the next mail day a letter came to Papa from Mamma. It said, "We have a fine grandson, and they have named him James William May, Junior. Mary is doing fine. The baby was already born when I got here. Mrs. Bristow helped the doctor." Nellie and I looked at each other knowingly. Even though we had not been told, we suspected what the excitement and hurried trip was about. How thrilled we were now that we had a nephew! That made us aunts and Otis an uncle. We could hardly wait until we could see the baby. About ten days later Mamma brought Mary and the baby home in the buggy. Nellie and I were glad to resign as cooks to become baby tenders.

Following the cutting of the wheat came threshing. It was an exciting time for small boys and girls when the threshing machine with the big red separator in tow was seen headed toward the homestead with smoke pouring from its stack. The outfit included a cook wagon and thus entailed no extra work for the women in the house. She too, could enjoy the excitement. The results of the threshing would tell how many bushels to the acre the crop was running.

We missed this thrill that summer, but we were compensated by having the new nephew. Now I could compare notes with Flossie about our respective nephews on an even basis. She had become an aunt a short time before when a son had arrived at the Tipton home in Hatton. I had rather envied her as she told of the cute things her nephew, Ralph was doing.

Dust storms held up harvesting at times. The soil was light and dry causing it to blow whenever the wind came up, which it did frequently.

"Mamma, there is a dust storm coming," Dona called from the boys bedroom, where she was making up their bed. She had glanced out the window toward the northeast and noticed the dust coming with the gusts of wind.

"You had better close all the windows up there," Mamma told her. "If it gets bad everything will be full of dust. Nellie, you close the windows downstairs."

When these storms came up during the harvest season, the crews could only wait it out until the wind died down. Even on still days after hours in the field, so much dust collected on their faces the men no longer looked like the white race.

Hauling wheat to the warehouse in Cunningham brought more dust. So heavy was the cloud accompanying each wagon and team they were hidden much of the time, while deep chuck holes were worn in the roads by the heavily loaded wagons. Whirlwinds of dust devils could be seen here and there across the plowed fields. When a large one was seen headed toward the house, windows were quickly lowered and doors closed until it passed. When the weekly washing had just been hung on the line after having been rubbed clean on the washboard, a dust devil was most unwelcome to the housekeeper. The cooks in the cook house learned to drop the canvas down over the screened sides when the dust was flying, and even then the dishes and oil-cloth covered tables quickly had a layer of dust.

After harvest ended that fall, Dona secured a position as telephone operator in Cunningham through the influence of Doctor Tulles. The telephone office was in part of his building next to the drug store. When dust storms were blowing static electricity played on the wires around the room.

When time came for school to begin Mamma and Papa

62

thought it would be better for us children to return to Cunningham and attend school instead of going to the country school. The two and a quarter miles over rough ground seemed a bit too far for a crippled girl and a seven year old boy.

We rented a small three-room house next to the post office and store run by A. O. Lee, and moved in. The switchboard and telephone booth were also moved into the front room and became the office by day and a bedroom by night. The telephone company paid part of the rent for the office space. Papa and Mamma remained on the homestead with Jim except for visits.

Nellie and Headley were taken on as janitors at the school at five dollars a month for each of them; I was pressed into service as helper without pay to help Headley with the upper floor sweeping and dusting.

It was a two-story brick building with two class rooms, a small library and wide halls. Nellie swept and dusted the lower classroom and hall. Headley started the fires in both of the pot-bellied stoves in the early mornings and cleaned out the ashes in the evenings.

It hardly seemed fair to me that I should have to work at the same kind of work they were doing, when I was without remuneration and they were receiving a monthly pay check. I kept thinking about that and finally broached the subject to them about getting in on the pay as well as the work. "It looks like I ought to be getting pay for working the same as you two are doing," was my complaint.

"We were hired for the job, and you were not. Besides we are paying two dollars a month on the rent," was Headley's reasoning.

"You are not paying anything on the rent," Nellie reminded me. They made it sound like I should be satisfied with that free rent. But the three dollars they had left over after paying on the rent sounded like "clear gravy" to me. At least they had something over to spend as they wished while those rent receipts meant nothing to me.

One afternoon I decided to go on strike after giving some

63

hint of my intentions. Orders from Headley were explicit; "You stay here and help until the work is done." Instead, I waited until he went to the basement to empty the ashes, and then took off for home. Knowing it was best for me to get home to Dona before he caught up with me, I lost no time on the way. It was a two-block race, but I had a long headstart and made it with only seconds to spare.

Mamma and Papa came in soon after, and the case was taken to the higher court; Mamma sitting as judge, plaintiff and defendants each pleading his side. The plaintiff charged that she was putting in an almost equal amount of time and labor without cash benefit. The defendants contended they had been hired for the work; they were responsible to see that it was done, and in addition, they were each paying two dollars a month toward the rent, whereas, the plaintiff was not paying anything. Arguments were pro and con. The case was finally settled in favor of the plaintiff for the sum of fifty cents a month from each of the defendants. Justice had been done and harmony restored. The wisdom of a Solomon or a Portia was sometimes needed.

Christmas came with its break in school routine. We had parts in the school program, so instead of going home for the holidays, Mamma and Papa came in to spend it with us. Jim was left on the homestead to care for the farm animals and poultry. That week tragedy and loss took much of the cheer from the Christmas good times when a letter from Jim brought bad news. Pete, the best one of the farm team died in his stall one night. He had seemed entirely well at feeding time the night before, and there was nothing to indicate the cause of his death. This was a big loss that Papa felt keenly. Pete had been the steady dependable one even we children felt safe to be around. His companion in harness, Frank, was a nervous horse that needed Pete's calmness to balance the team.

A still greater loss came to the Adams family just before Christmas when Grandma Adams took sick and died. Men from the neighborhood got lumber and made a casket, then neighborhood women lined the casket and prepared the body for burial. There was a heavy snow on the ground and it was too far to go either to Lind or Cunningham for burial, so Grandpa Adams set apart one corner of his homestead for a cemetery. It was the custom for friends to come in and sit up with the corpse each night until the funeral to comfort and keep the family company. Mamma and Papa had helped there.

The snowfall was unusually heavy that winter as storm after storm kept adding to the increasing depth of snow. It lay on the ground for weeks creating new problems at the homestead when gaunt, starving range cattle broke through wire fences and invaded barn lots where the domestic cattle were fed. Morning after morning would reveal a bunch of them around or in the header boxes that had been taken from the wagons and placed on the ground from which to feed the cows. It was dangerous to approach these wild cattle on foot, and any attempts to drive them out except on horseback were futile.

"John McCulloch was chased into his own house by one of those range cattle," Mamma told us. "He had started to drive it out of the yard, and called his dog to help chase it out. But it turned on him. It would have killed him but his dog saved him by snapping at its head until he could get away and into the house."

Those cattle were wild, starving and dangerous. Some broke into a field where there was a straw stack, and in a starving condition ate straw until they bloated and died around the stack. Drumheller, who owned them, was notified of the conditions, but there was no way to get feed to them. Dead cattle were to be seen all over the flat.

Then came a warm Chinook wind that melted the snow so rapidly that the coulees became raging torrents. By that time the cattle were so weakened they mired in the soft mud and were unable to extricate themselves. When attempts were made to pull them out by the men on the homesteads, the cattle would turn on them and sometimes had to be shot down to enable their would-be rescuers to escape. The air was tainted with the dead carcasses. Farm dogs found themselves unwelcome around the kitchen door after visiting these sources of food, and coyotes fared well.

Another result from the Chinook was several new lakes in the Othello Potholes. Crab Creek overflowed its banks, bringing down sand, and ruining rich hay and meadow land belonging to Sam Hutchinson and Jim McManamon. Where they had formerly cut tons of hay from land along the creek channel, the creek now spread out into a wide sandy marsh where tules and mosquitos thrived. This land never again produced hay; but Crab Creek remained a place for recreation and outings.

One of the lakes in the potholes was given the name of Shiner Lake after a small fish belonging to the carp family. One odd thing about these fish was a little bend in the tail of every one, as if it had sometime been broken. It has been suggested that small deformity may have been a result of constant inbreeding. It was plainly seen in the spine, and so far as we ever heard, was peculiar to the fish in this lake. While boney, they were considered good picnic fare.

Chapter VII

Springtime

A SPRING RAIN was falling as we started for the homestead at the close of the school year in Cunningham. Billie came for us in the big header box. We thought of that long ride in the open wagon through the rain.

"We'll get wet in all this rain," Nellie told him.

"No you won't," Billie said, "I've got it fixed with a tent over most of the wagon. You'll stay nice and dry under there."

At first it seemed like a game to play under the shelter of the tent, sitting on the folded bedding listening to the rain hitting the canvas, and to the clop, clop of the horses feet as they plodded along the wet road. Occasionally, we heard the musical notes of the meadow lark, or the plaintive call of a turtle dove. There would be both out at the homestead. Then little drips of water began to penetrate through the canvas as little pockets of water formed on top. Canvas without a ridge pole will shed water only for a time, especially when poked from beneath. More and more drips developed. It became a problem to keep ourselves and the bedding from under the dripping water. That five hour trip seemed endless as we got more and more chilled. Home was a welcome sight.

We were as glad to see Mamma and Papa as they were to see us. "Mamma, I passed," Otis proudly held up his report card for her to see. "I'll be in the third grade next year." Our cards were brought out to show them we had all advanced to the next higher grade. Then we could forget school for the summer months.

It was fun to chase through the sagebrush again with feet freed from shoes. The uncleared land was gay with patches of pink phlox, blue larkspur, and a tall dainty, lavender-colored wild lily. The lily was similar to the Mariposa lily of California, only taller and larger. Its long botanical name, Calochortus Macrocarpus was unknown to us. We knew it only as the wild lily. Its pretty color showed up through the brush, standing straight and tall on slender stems, and we eagerly sought them to add to the bouquets of wild flowers we brought to Mamma.

Once when I was running to pick one growing up through a sage brush, I was just reaching down to pick it when a rattle warned me back, and a rattlesnake crawled out from under the bush and down a squirrel hole. Dona was with me and she stayed to watch the hole and prevent the snake's escape while I ran to the house and got Jim to bring a spade to dig it out. That was one less rattlesnake to watch out for.

New white lace curtains hung at the front room windows; they looked so pretty with the new rag carpet on the floor. Mamma liked pretty things, so I saved the money I earned for my part of the janitor work. She made up the sum I lacked to buy them, but let me select the design. Now they looked so nice at the big double windows!

We were anxious to see all the new things around the place. Several hens were setting, and some were already coming off with their batches of fluffy babies, requiring close attention from Mamma. She was chopping up hard boiled eggs and mixing in finely chopped green onion tops.

"This is the first feed for these new baby chicks," she explained as Otis asked questions. Into this she mixed grit.

"After they have had this for a day or two, I'll grind up some wheat in the coffee grinder for them," she said.

Since the flock of chickens was composed of a variety of breeds, the babies wore downy suits of different colors. Some were charcoal gray with touches of white.

"Mamma, what kind of chickens are these?" Otis didn't think they looked like any of the big chickens.

"Those are the Plymouth Rocks," she answered. "They will look like the mother hen when they get their feathers."

"What are these?" he asked, pointing to the cute little tan

and light brown chicks with the broad stripe down their backs. "Those are the Brown Leghorns like our pretty rooster," she said. "I hope most of these will be hens." We knew that the fluffy little white ones were White Rocks.

We were permitted to handle them gently, but occasionally some hen of the more nervous breeds proved fussy, and resented the possible injury to her family. With wings and feathers raised, she would dart at us and we were glad to retire from the vicinity. Dogs and cats were quickly routed by the hen, and learned to respect her rights.

The two young heifers belonging to Headley had their first calves, and our milk supply was increased so that we bought a cream separator and churn to care for the increased production. The chore of turning the barrel churn was at first considered fun.

"Mamma, can I turn the churn this time?" from one of us. "You turned it last time, its my turn this time," from another. "No, I didn't, don't you remember?" So the argument would go on while Mamma was putting the cream into the churn and fastening on the lid.

"You can each take your turn," she reproved us. "There will be plenty of time for all of you, and it will likely be an old story to all of you before long." She was right, and after a few churnings there were not so many volunteers.

There was a little round glass peep hole in the lid through which we could see when the butter came. When one of the boys got hold of the handle he would send the barrel spinning so fast the thick cream couldn't slosh from one end of the barrel to the other. Mamma would lay a gentle hand on a shoulder and say, "Now, Son, slow down. You won't make the butter come that way."

After the butter was removed to be washed we had our reward in a glass of buttermilk. If there was some freshly baked bread to go with it, it made a real treat.

"Papa, where did we get the sheep?" But Papa was busy at the moment and did not hear Otis. The sight that caused the question was three sheep running in the barn lot the next morning after we got home from school. One of them was a ewe; one was slightly smaller and the third was a spring lamb.

The summer before we had seen large bands of sheep numbering up to two or three thousand, being herded across the flat west of us, to new pastures. George Hendricks, Hans Harder and others ran sheep across the area at times. Accompanied by a herder and three or four dogs, the bleating flock could be heard for a mile or more away as they moved slowly along in a haze of dust.

The Barton girls had told us the herders would sometimes give a lamb away, and Otis and I determined to try and get one for a pet. More than once we raced across the flat to intercept the herder and his flock with the plea; "Mister, will you please give us a lamb?" Our requests were usually met with a stoical look, but no answer. We would keep pace with the flock for a short distance, repeating our request to be sure he understood. Whether the herder did not understand English, or there were no motherless lambs that would be too much trouble on the drive, we never succeeded. After a few times we gave up trying to get a lamb in this way.

Sometimes, as these bands went through the country, one or more sheep would be over-looked by the dogs, and become lost from the flock among the rocks and potholes. When this happened, the coyotes soon found them and had fresh mutton to offer their young pups.

This particular spring while Papa and Jim were renewing the supply of sagebrush for the kitchen range, they came across three sheep which had become lost from the flock. Not knowing who was the owner, or the destination of the flock that had passed early that day, the sheep were brought home and turned loose in the barn yard. Now we had a lamb.

Along with the sheep came new problems. At first they were too shy to stray far from the barnyard, but gradually, as they became more familiar with their surroundings, they grazed farther out into the brush. Several times a day someone would go upstairs to look out across the brush to get sight of the sheep.

If they strayed too far beyond what we considered safe territory, one of us would be sent to drive them to safer ground.

One day while we were seated at the dinner table, someone happened to glance out the window to see the sheep racing madly for the barn yard. Two coyotes, one on either side, were chasing them, snapping at their throats in an endeavor to pull them down.

"The coyotes are after the sheep!" was the cry as we jumped from the table and out the door, yelling to frighten them away and save the sheep. Headley grabbed a gun from the wall, but before he could get outside the coyotes had fled to safety.

After that for a time, we kept a more careful watch than ever. Then, one day Mamma said, "Girls, have you been up to see where the sheep are lately?" We had forgotten them for some time. When we went upstairs to look, there were no white woolly backs to be seen anywhere.

"Mamma, we don't see them anywhere," we reported. "Do you think they might be at the barn?" We hoped they were, but investigation showed no sheep were around.

"Nellie, you and Laura put on your bonnets and go look for them. They may have wandered down over the hill, or the coyotes may have gotten them." We knew she might be right.

We spent hours looking through the brush, down into the big flat, among the rocks, even back to the deep coulee a half mile to the north where we suspected the coyotes had their den, but without getting a trace of them. The coyotes had gotten them. That ended our sheep raising.

One night when Mamma and we three younger children were the only ones at home, we had been asleep only a little while when we were brought wide awake by the wild chorus of coyote yells so close they seemed almost under the window. It was coming from right below the barn near the pig pens, and Mammas' first thought was of a sow and her new litter of pigs which had just been farrowed that day. Mamma was on her feet instantly, and taking the lantern with us three children following, she went to find whether the coyotes had snatched any of the baby pigs.

Anxiously, Mamma hung the lantern over into the pen while she counted the little piglets lying snugly around their grunting mother. They had not been disturbed, and we went back to the house to lie wide awake after the sudden interruption to our sleep.

While we were calling back and forth from the upstairs bedroom to Mamma's room on the ground floor where Otis had been granted the privilege of sleeping with her while Papa and Headley were away, the whole sky was suddenly lighted up as though a flaming fireball had been thrown over the house. Nellie and I were startled by the bright flare of light.

"Mamma, what was that bright light?" we asked. "It lit up everything out of doors. What was it?"

"It must have been a meteor," she told us, "But I never saw one that made such a bright light all around. I wonder if it struck anywhere near here."

"What is a meteor?" we wanted to know. She explained how they come from space and burn up when they strike our atmosphere. We had seen many shooting stars at night, but never when they came close enough to light up the earth as this one had done.

Henry Gable's spring round-up brought his wranglers racing across the hills and through the potholes as they rounded up the range horses and started them back toward the home corrals at Skootenai Springs. Young stock were branded before being turned out on the range again. Every homesteader for miles around was acquainted with Gable and bought horses from him, and they would be looking for horses to break for the summer work. Some of ours were from his herds.

It was exciting to watch the round-up of the horses. Riding at break-neck speed as they tried to head off some wild cayuse that was determined to escape, was rough work. Once the riders came to our barn lot for their noon lunch, and to rest and water their mounts. We were especially interested in the outfits they wore since we had come from Missouri only four years before.

Chaparajos, always called "shaps", were of leather, covered with long wavy wool or goats hair to protect the legs of the rider in brush and rough country. Some of the shaps were white, others black or orange. High heeled boots on which they wore spurs, faded shirts and pants, a blue or red kerchief about the neck, and a beat-up old hat that would stay on in hard riding, completed the attire. Probably one reason for the beat-up appearance of the hats was caused by being used to "fan out" some bucking bronc they were breaking for the saddle string. Headley and Otis were fascinated with the shaps, and were permitted to proudly try them on by the obliging cowboys. Otis was sure he wanted to be a cowboy when he got big.

Sometimes horses which had been broken in and returned to Gable could be bought, but usually they were wild unbroken horses direct from the range; then came the job of breaking them to harness and farm work. Most of them gentled without too much difficulty, but again, some did not follow the usual pattern of horse temperament. We bought two such horses from Gable, a strawberry roan and a buckskin.

These two, with several others purchased by Papa and Billie, were hazed along to our place and driven into the barn. They had never been handled except for branding, and were wild young things, scared of man, and they fought any attempts to control them. By careful manuvering, the men managed to get a lasso around the neck of each one and they were drawn up close to the manger and held securely while a halter was slipped over the head of the horse and buckled. A halter chain was fastened to the halter and the horse was fastened into a stall in the barn to become used to the men feeding them. They would strike out with their front feet at the person so indiscreet as to enter the stall, or snort and pull back the full length of the chain when anyone appeared at the opening outside their stall.

The men found that getting the harness on these wild horses was a problem. The first time they tried to harness "Roanie" as he came to be called, he fought the attempts, trembling with

73

belonging to Drumheller, rounded up and placed under fence over on Crab Creek. Drumheller and other stockmen had run stock on the open range for years, but the hard winter had brought serious losses to the cattlemen. Open range land, too, was becoming more scarce as more and more homestead people took up land and fences were built.

Ralph Barton homestead shack — about 1905. L to R: Ralph, Mrs. Barton, Bonnie. Courtesy Mrs. Orley Sanders.

Chapter VIII

Railroad Construction

THE RAILROAD CONSTRUCTION was coming nearer, and when we heard it was only a few miles way Papa thought it might be interesting for the family to see it.

"How would you like to go up and see where the new railroad is being graded?" he asked Mamma. His suggestion met instant favor with all the children, and Mamma thought it would be of interest to some company we had at the time. Papa borrowed a two-seated rig called a hack in which he could make the trip.

We had gone only a short distance when Mamma became ill. "Papa, I am getting so sick. I don't think I'm able to make the trip," she told him. "Could you take me home?" Papa could see she was suffering intense pain.

"Is it the same you had a few weeks ago?" he inquired.

"Yes, it is just like that other attack I had," she replied. The horses were turned around and started toward home at once. Though in intense pain, she urged him not to give up the trip and disappoint the family, but none of us wanted to go without her.

Within a few weeks, however, we could see signs of activity on a large scale about two miles northeast of our place where one of the construction camps was being set up.

One Sunday the three younger Barton girls came riding over to invite Nellie and me to go with them to see the new camp. It was being located only a short distance from their home, and they had already become acquainted with some of the workers. After getting permission, we soon got our horses saddled, and with a clatter of hoofs, and a lot of chatter, we were on the way to see what a railroad construction camp looked like.

Hancock and McArthur were the sub-contractors on that

stretch of grading. A vast amount of equipment was being assembled for the work. Fresno scrapers and horse drawn shovels in two sizes for moving the dirt, water tanks, wagons, and a large assortment of hand tools were lying around. A number of men were at the camp trying to get things organized to begin the work. Large tents to be used as sleeping quarters for the men, another for the mess hall, a small shack for the timekeeper's office, and a small tent for the foreman's living quarters were already up. There was a round metal tank in which to water the horses, and temporary feeding racks were being put in place. Feed and hay was being hauled to camp. From a discreet distance we watched the activity that was to produce a railroad.

A similar camp under Contractor Tom Hancock, was set up on a corner of our land shortly after. With this one, especially the kitchen part, we younger children were glad to form a closer acquaintance. Those huge sugary doughnuts fresh from the kettle, slices of left-over pie, passed on to us in response to the unspoken wish in our eyes, (we had instructions from Mamma not to ask for things to eat), won our admiration for the cook's ability as well as his understanding of children's appetites. For this reason we were always happy when Mamma went to make a neighborly call on the contractor's wife. While she visited Mrs. Hancock in the small tent, we made a friend in the mess hall.

Work progressed rapidly as the camps were placed about two miles apart. Another camp was located one mile north of the little town just coming into existance. Wilson and Wells were the contractors in that area. The railroad yards were laid out; a large tent hospital with a small tent beside it for the doctor's office, was erected to take care of construction workers who might be injured or become sick on the job. The depot was later built where the hospital tent had stood.

The hospital was one large ward with beds placed down each side, and a wide aisle down the middle of the tent. White mosquito netting covered the two foot opening which extended the full length of the ward on each side, and a canvas fly on the outside could be raised or lowered over this opening to shut

78

out sun and dust. It provided the necessary medical care. The railroad-employed physician in charge was Doctor J. S. Judah. We had reason to become well acquainted with him a little later.

Since the number of patients did not require the doctor's full time, he was often called to some farm home to deliver a baby, or to attend any sickness requiring more than home remedies. He drove a team and buggy, or rode horseback to make his calls.

Dust flew as the dry earth was torn up in building the road bed. Sweating horses and men toiled under the hot sun as shovel after shovel of dirt was moved to build up the grade to the proper height. The smaller shovels were drawn by two horses; the larger ones by a four-horse team which required two men to fill and dump. Intermingled with the rasping sound of metal against rocks as the shovels bit into the rocky ground, and the jingle of harness, were the shouts of the drivers giving rebuke or encouragement to their teams. It was rough cruel work for the horses, and hard work for the men. Men and teams spread out for a quarter to a half mile, depending on the terrain through which they were working. In some areas cuts were made through higher elevations where blasting was necessary.

It was exciting to watch from a distance as the blasts were set off, sending the dirt and rocks high into the air. The railroad passed about one quarter mile from our house where a cut and considerable blasting was needed. This afforded us almost a ringside seat. When men and teams had gone back to camp after work hours, we frequently gave that gash an unofficial inspection. It lay directly across the trail leading from our house to that of the Mays.

A mile south of Othello the grade swung in a long curve across the flat to the base of Saddle Mountain, and then followed the mountain due west to where it crossed the Columbia River. Throughout this stretch, much blasting was needed because of rock formation. Here, too, they blasted out great dens of rattlesnakes which were a constant menace to men and teams.

One man, an Italian laborer, was bitten and taken to the hospital for treatment.

79

"Why didn't you jump out of the way?" one of his fellow workers asked. "Didn't you hear him rattle?"

"He no ringa da bell," he told his questioner.

Several miles west of Othello was a natural ice cave at the base of the mountain known to the early settlers. One construction camp which was located near the cave, made use of it after boarding up the inside and placing a door at the entrance. It was used as a refrigerator in which the cook kept the meats and perishable foods while the camp was in the area. The temperature might be soaring above a hundred just outside, but two or three paces inside the breath showed white in the cold current of air coming down through the rear of the cave.

Meanwhile, a townsite was being laid out and streets surveyed on what had formerly been the R. M. Chavis and Ed Lee homesteads. The Milwauke Land Company of Spokane was the investment company which had bought the townsite; lots were selling at high prices. In a letter to Dona who was still with the telephone company in Cunningham, Mamma wrote, "The forty-acre townsite brought $83,000 so we heard. Guess we'll not invest our money in town lots." That did seem a bit high for that dry sagebrush land.

Each time Papa or Headley went to town they brought home reports of new buildings and more businesses. Piles of lumber appeared near the road leading north from the main road running east and west.

"Papa, you know where we saw all the piles of lumber as we started out of town the other day? There are two lumber yards going in there. One is the Potlatch and the other is the Crab Creek Lumber Company." Headley had gone to town after the mail, and had been looking around the new town.

"There will be a lot of building going on now," Papa said. "I saw some freight wagons full of lumber being hauled out the other day from Cunningham. They were using a six-horse team with two wagons hooked one behind the other.

"What are some of the new businesses that are being brought in?" asked Mamma.

"Tipton is transferring his store from Hatton to Othello. He bought that old house that was standing just across the road from the Adams cemetery. You know, the one we saw standing empty in the section he bought just east of McCulloch's place. He is having it moved to what they say is Fourth Avenue, north of the main road. The post office is going to be in his store, I heard.

"There is another store going in near where Hibbard is building a hotel," Headley added. "Did you know that Billie has the contract to do the plastering on the hotel?"

Two or three saloons appeared, the first of which received the name "Irrigator Number One," indicating it was there to slake the overmastering thirst, and wash the dry throats of the laborers. Herman W. Krause was the owner. Mike Cummings opened up another thirst quenching emporium. R. M. Chavis built a hotel, a livery barn and a real estate office a block north of Main Street opposite the lumber yards. These were all of frame construction with false fronts. Another hotel down nearer the railroad tracks was soon built and given the name of The Milwaukee Hotel. All the hotels had bars as an inducement to patronage.

Struppler's General Merchandise, Crockett's Hardware, (the latter was built by L. W. Habel and operated as a grocery store, but soon sold to Crockett), Tulles Drugs, The Othello State Bank with J. W. Webster the first cashier, and Mentzell's Meat Market soon followed. With the exception of Struppler's, which was a block south of Main Street on First Avenue, these were located along the main street which was actually a country road with a foot trail along one side. Later a wooden sidewalk extended for three blocks on the south side of Main Street from Broadway to Third.

"What are they doing for water?" Mamma questioned. The ever present problem of water was in her mind. "They will have to drill wells to supply the town, won't they?"

"The Land Company is having one drilled east of the new Hibbard Hotel, and the railroad is having one drilled down near where the railroad will go. They will both have high tanks to give pressure."

"How deep will they have to go before they find plenty of water?" Mamma knew the McCulloch's had found water at about four hundred feet.

"I heard they have gone down nearly four hundred now. They should strike water pretty soon."

Several homes were being built, and Othello was on the way to becoming the largest town within miles. At such times various rumors often get started which cause some uneasiness in certain circles. The following exchange of letters indicate just one such rumor.

Othello, Wash.
Jan. 23, 1908

Milwaukee Land Company
Spokane, Wash.

Gentlemen:

In the interest of the people of Othello I am writing to enquire as to the location of the division point of the Chicago, Milwaukee and Saint Paul Railway.

There are a number of rumors afloat that Lind, or some other town is being considered as a possible location, and this has led to considerable disturbances in the line of business here, and has hindered investments to quite an extent.

Trusting we may be favored with an early reply, I am,

Yours respectfully,
L. W. Habel.

To this inquiry the following answer was received.

Spokane, Wash.
Feb. 7, 1908

Mr. L. W. Habel
Othello, Wash.

Dear Sir:

I have your favor of the 23rd of January, wherein you enquire as to the location of the division point on the Chicago, Milwaukee and St. Paul railway.

I have to inform you that Othello is the only town in eastern Washington announced by the railroad company up to this time. All improvements incident and necessary to a division point will be installed there. There will be no other division point in Adams or Grant Counties.

Yours Very Truly,
G. W. Morrow
G. T. and L. A.

This doubtless set the minds of many at rest as to the future development of the town and its prospects. Othello was to have the edge over Warden, its rival some thirteen miles to the north.

As soon as a section of grading was completed, the camp was moved and set up again in another location farther toward the coast. Farm teams and men from the homesteads returned to their homes to take up needed farm work again.

Chapter IX

Homestead Visitors

LOOKING OUT THE KITCHEN WINDOW late one afternoon, Mamma noticed a young man turning in at the front gate.

"I wonder who that is coming here," she said to Dona who had returned from her telephone work in Cunningham. "Why, that looks like Ottie!" Together, she and Dona hurried to the door to welcome her nephew Archie Wood from Saint Louis, Missouri. Mamma had received a letter from her sister Ellen that Ottie was coming out to Seattle to work on the New Washington Hotel. Ottie was a marble setter, and Seattle was getting ready for the Alaska-Yukon-Pacific Exposition that was to be held in 1909. This was bringing workers and visitors to the west.

"Hello, Aunt Susie," was Ottie's greeting as Mamma threw her arms around him.

"Ottie, why didn't you let us know when you would get here so we could have met you at the train in Cunningham?" She could see he was tired and dusty from his long walk. "Come in, we are so glad to see you."

"I caught a ride for a few miles with someone in a buggy out this way from Cunningham. These roads are sure dusty." Ottie was used to paved streets.

The name Ottie had stuck with him since his childhood when his brother Cleveland, only two years older, had found that this was the nearest he could come to saying "Archie." Ottie was a favorite with all of us, and his coming was a happy time for all the family. When we found he would be with us for several days we determined to show him a good time.

Ours was a family which liked to take over-night camping trips. Trips had been made to Palouse Falls the first year or two we were in Washington; we had taken a camping trip to the

85

Columbia River at White Bluffs, but we had only gone for daytime picnics on Crab Creek. Ottie had lived most of his life in a large city and we thought a camping trip would be a pleasant experience for him.

"Ottie, how would you like to go camping?" Otis was sticking close to this new cousin he couldn't remember having seen before. "Do you like to fish?"

"Where would you find enough water to fish out here?" Ottie's eyes had a teasing gleam in them as he swung his adoring cousin off his feet.

"There's fish in Crab Creek. We've caught lots of them there. There are crawdads there too. We use them for bait," Otis assured him.

"Do you mean to tell me that a fish would bite a crawdad? A fish wouldn't have any teeth to bite through its shell." He winked at Dona as he noticed she was listening to the conversation that was going on between him and Otis.

"Aw, Ottie! We don't put a whole crawdad on the hook; we break off their legs and use the meat on the inside." It seemed plain to him that Ottie had never fished with crawfish for bait.

The idea of a camping trip appealed to all of us including Papa and Mamma. Wheat harvest was ended and other work well in hand when he arrived; the nights were warm and there was a beautiful full moon to give light for camping, so plans were made.

"We'll take the wheat rack," Papa preferred it to the header box for a trip like this. "Headley, you and Ottie can put the side boards on the wagon, and put a couple of boards across for seats for Mamma and the girls." Mamma saw that those boards were padded with quilts to soften some of the bumps we found on the rocky roads. Springs under the wagon were a minus quality.

She also saw that plenty of bedding, food that could be cooked over a camp fire, a heavy skillet in which to fry fish should any be caught, and other necessary dishes and pans were packed into the wagon.

A twenty-two rifle and fishing lines were put in by the boys, for they and Papa planned to have some fish cooked over the camp fire for supper. Grain was added for the horses, though there was grass for them to graze along the creek; and straw to put under the bedding on the ground.

The place selected was at a small falls on lower Crab Creek about twelve miles from home. We followed a road that meandered out across the sagebrush in the general direction of the creek, digressing to avoid badger holes or outcroppings of lava when necessary. These heavy folded quilts on the board seats softened the rough road only a little, but we were used to this mode of travel.

"Do you want to drive?" Headley liked to do the driving, but this time he relinquished the lines to his cousin, and Ottie who seldom had the opportunity of driving a team, took the reins for the drive to the creek. There were only slight brakes to the wagon, a rope led back to a pole that was attached to a block of wood. By pulling on the rope, the block was tightened against the metal rim of the wheel and provided some braking power. Going down a hill, the horses were held back against the neck yoke on the front end of the wagon tongue which was fastened to their collars by leather straps. If the hill was short the horses were allowed to run to keep out of the way of the wagon.

We had just passed such a short hill when we came to a slight turn-out in the deeply rutted road. Thinking it was only a by-pass, Ottie kept on in the more traveled road. Suddenly, the wagon was brought to an abrupt stop; we were thrown from our seats, and the boys on the high front seat were nearly thrown over the front of the wagon onto the horses. Confusion prevailed for just a moment! Then Ottie was back on the seat in control, and we learned the reason for the by-pass. The ruts in the road had worn deeper and deeper in the dry earth until a large rock in the middle of the road had caught on the under frame of the wagon, bringing us to a jarring stop. No harm was done, and we were soon on the way again.

It was about four o'clock in the afternoon when we reached

the selected spot to camp beside the falls. Ottie had taken a short cut the last half mile after getting directions to just follow the creek, and showed up at camp with a rabbit he had shot.

The horses were unharnessed and staked out to graze. Things were unloaded from the wagon and straw spread on the ground on which to make up the beds. We would be dependent on the moonlight when night came on, so it was well to have the beds ready when the outdoors made us sleepy.

Ottie proved quite adept at improvising. With Otis watching his every move, he took a gunny sack and rolled the top down to form a bag about fourteen inches deep. He then ran a wire around the top to hold it open, and attached another wire to make a bail to which he fastened a long willow pole.

"What is that for?" Otis questioned. He didn't think that was going to be a very successful method of catching fish, but he thought it wouldn't do to let Ottie think he was a greenhorn.

I was more direct. "Are you going to catch fish in that thing?" I was skeptical about it, too.

"Don't you think this is a good way to catch fish?" Ottie's answers were very confusing as we watched him wide-eyed. He was enjoying keeping us guessing. Next, he skinned the rabbit and wired it into the bottom of the bag and lowered it into the water at the foot of the falls. Even when he lowered it into the water our questions were still unanswered. It certainly seemed an odd way to fish, but then he was brought up in the city, we thought. Some half hour later when he drew it up, we had our answer and he had about a dozen crawfish neatly trapped in the bag to use for fish bait. Our admiration for him increased.

Papa scouted around for dry willows with which to build a fire for cooking supper; Mamma, Dona and Nellie had made up the beds. Headley was looking for suitable willow poles to be made into fishing rods while Otis and I were trying to see everything, and exploring the willows that lined the creek. It was shallow above the falls, just right for us to wade.

Again, Ottie showed his ingenuity by assembling several flat

88

rocks as he saw Mamma starting to cook over the small open fire.

"Here, Aunt Susie, let me fix it so you won't get your clothes on fire."

Digging a trench he left open at both ends, he placed long, flat, narrow rocks on edge on either side of the trench. With two thin flat ones laid across the top with a narrow opening between and the fire placed in the trench, it made a convenient outdoor stove. We were learning our city cousin had a lot of know-how when it came to camping out.

"Ottie, that is a big help," Mamma commented.

Meanwhile, Headley found a favorable spot for fishing where he was joined by Papa and Ottie. Now and then a cork float bobbed under the water as some small perch sampled the craw-fish bait and was caught. The three lines soon had enough to fill the skillet, and were cleaned for Mamma to fry.

Potatoes were frying on the improvised stove while a pot of beans, brought ready-cooked from home, was warming, and it wasn't long until the scent of frying fish on the evening air carried to the hungry family.

"Come to supper," came the call that needed no repeating, and we gathered around the cloth spread on the ground on which had been placed homemade bread and butter, and a dried apple pie. As we bowed our heads, we were again made aware of the Giver of Good Things as Mamma quietly offered thanks.

Slowly dusk came on as the sun disappeared and the stars began to appear. The sound of "Cuckoo! Cuckoo!" came softly from the small owls we knew as cuckoos, sitting on the mounds beside old badger holes. Night hawks, which we called bullbats, were sweeping back and forth across the evening sky, uttering their distinctive call, or making long swoops which ended in the peculiar roar as the bird ended its dive and started back up into the sky. (At one time, before I learned what was making the sound, I had imagined it was the call of some wild animal.) Small birds were twittering among the willows as they found places to perch for the night. The full moon edged up over a long row of cliffs to the east, and the coyotes called to one another across the waste land. Nature was at peace, bringing a sense of well-being to the human family.

The men returned to their fishing by the light of a bonfire, and it soon guided us to where they were, still getting some nibbles and an occasional catch. But the excitement of the day, the pleasant evening air and the glow of the dancing flames soon put weights on our eyelids. Mamma took us back to where the beds had been made ready and tucked us in for the night.

It was almost as light as day in the dry air. The Milky Way spread like a wide shining highway across the heavens; the Big Dipper, and Orion, that wonder of the sky, with less familiar constellations, drew our eyes heavenward for only a few minutes. We were soon sleeping soundly and knew no more until a bright sun shining in our eyes awakened us in the morning. A few itching bumps on exposed areas were proof that we had been visited by blood-thirsty mosquitos in the night.

Breakfast was soon over. Fish were on the menu again. Mamma and Papa were doing a little fishing above the falls but without success. After a little coaxing she let me take her fishing pole to try in a deeper place. For some time the pole dangled without response from anything; then suddenly a crawfish darted out from the shadows after the baited hook so quickly it startled me into jerking it wildly into the air. It had barely gotten its claws clamped onto the bait when it came flying through the air to land at my feet before it could release its claw, for my first success in fishing. There is a question which was the most surprised. Nor have I ever had much greater success at that sport. It was added to the can containing the other crawfish.

"Dona, have you ever eaten lobster?" asked Ottie as we were preparing to gather the things for going home.

"No! They are such horrible looking things I don't think I would ever want to try," Dona grimaced at the thought.

"Well, they are quite a choice dish in some of the better restaurants in St. Louis," Ottie was teasing her. "These crawfish look a whole lot like lobsters. I wonder if they wouldn't taste about the same. Suppose we take these home and cook them. Would you help me try eating some to see what they are like?" Ottie grinned. But Dona turned the offer down.

It was early afternoon when we headed for home, and again Ottie took a slightly different shortcut up the creek with the rifle to meet us at a bend in the road.

"What do you think I saw up there in the creek?" he asked as he joined the wagon again. He had a teasing light in his eyes as he asked Dona the questions.

"Was it a rattlesnake?" she asked. But that wasn't it. Others guessed "Coyote?" "Rabbit?" but none of these were correct, and after some quizzing he told us.

"There were the skeletal remains of a dead cow lying in the creek just above where we were getting water to use." Dona looked a bit disturbed by this bit of news. Ottie was enjoying the reaction he was getting. "It had probably been well washed by the time we got water for the camp," he chortled. We philosophically decided the sand and sun would have acted as a good purifier.

Another visitor to the homestead that summer was Estella Tulles. She was the daughter of Doctor Tulles who officiated at the birth of babies for miles around, even as far away as Othello. Papa had purchased the section of land near Cunningham from him. Stella's brother Carl had opened a drug store at Othello, but she was a student at Pullman College.

Stella had always been interested in rocks, crystals and minerals, and found the cliffs and rock formations new and interesting to her. It gave her an idea.

"Dona, do you know what I would like to do?" she asked, "I'd like to capture some scorpions to take back to college with me."

"What would you want with them?" Dona had always considered scorpions were something to leave alone.

"They would be interesting specimens for our biology

would be much of the time when he would be away from home.

"How about one of Uncle Joe's hounds?" Cleve knew his mother was not an admirer of the hounds, but he liked to tease her a bit.

"You know I wouldn't have a hound on the place," she retorted. "I'd like a little dog."

A few days later he came home with a pair of small fox terriers, to her delight. The puppies grew rapidly, and their frisking around the cabin was just what she needed to keep her company. They were her constant companions on the walks she took, and sometimes warned her when she was near a rattlesnake.

Then one day, a real tragedy happened. The little female was bitten on the head by a rattlesnake under the cabin. Its whole head swelled badly, and it was beyond anything she could do when she discovered it next morning. After that only one little dog remained to keep her company. Despite the loneliness, she stayed on until she could get title to the land, then traded it for a house in Cheney where she could keep students who were attending the Normal.

Another event took place in our family in July 1907. Jim seemed to have developed a great fondness for our cousins, Lottie and Millard Morgan who lived on a homestead a few miles from Washtucna, near the Delight farmhouse postoffice. A young lady named Iva Flint worked for Lottie, and Jim's frequent visits up there and his interest in the mail had us guessing at the reason for the visits; but he met all our teasing with only a good-natured grin until one day he came to Mamma with some questions.

"Mamma, could you get a minister to marry Iva and me?" Mamma had arranged for Elder B. S. Pate of the Primitive Baptist church at Dayton to perform the marriage ceremony for Mary and Billie. His question was no surprise to her, but she was pleased that he wanted her to arrange for the minister.

"Yes, Jim, I'm sure I can get either Elder Pate or Elder Barnes from Touchet. Elder Barnes comes up to visit the Adams family since his daughter is married to their son Frank. Have you set a date yet?"

"Iva wants to be married around our birthdays the last of this month," he answered. "We'll be married at Millard's."

"Where are you going to live?" Mamma knew that though Jim was working on the railroad grading down near where the new town of Othello was getting a start, there would be little possibility of finding anything to rent.

"Could you make room for us here for a while?" he asked. With only the two bedrooms upstairs this was not going to be an easy problem to solve. She couldn't see moving either the boys out of their bedroom, or the girls from theirs.

"If I divide the girls room by running a long curtain down the center, could you manage to use one side of that for a while?"

"Yes, that will be all right. We'll be here only until we can find a place to rent." So it was settled. They would live with us for a while.

We younger children had an ulterior reason for giving our new sister-in-law a big welcome; she liked horses and riding as well as we did. She was bringing along her riding horse, a white pony she called Snowball. A little later when Jim and Iva moved to the small one-room shack one mile north of Othello, belonging to Ada Fuqua, Snowball was left with us to our great joy. Unlike the other farm horses, Snowball was always available for our use.

Our cows had discovered the new green wheat fields as the wheat began to grow after the fall planting. Our fields were too near home for them to long enjoy eating there unmolested, and they started sneaking away to the Barton homestead. The Bartons were away for a while. It was not long until we learned of this when going to round them up at milking time. Nellie and Iva went after them a number of times and one day came back highly elated at a discovery they had made.

"We found where Bartons have their watermelon patch." They were giggling over something they had done. It was evident there was more to the story.

dishpan to your father. He will need it in which to place the livers and hearts."

Resting on halter chains which had been placed over the vat, the carcass was turned and rolled in the scalding water until the bristles pulled loose easily. When they were considered sufficiently loosened the chains were brought to the platform side and the carcass pulled to the platform for scraping. Every inch of the skin was scraped free of bristles, dirt and scales; afterward, a strong pointed stick was run through under the tendons in the hind feet, and a chain with a strong hook attached to the stick was used to hang the carcass head down to the high timber. The internal organs could then be removed, and we could see the internal anatomy of a hog.

"Papa, what is that light pink thing you took out just now?" He had already removed the heart and liver, but this was a light spongy-looking mass from under the ribs. Otis was standing where he could see the different organs as they were removed.

"That is the lights," Papa told him, "That is the same as our lungs," he added as he placed them in the tub with the offal which would be discarded after the fat was removed from inside the carcass, and the fat stripped from the gut to be brought to the house for rendering into lard. The rest of the carcass was left hanging until the next morning to cool.

In Missouri Papa used hickory smoke to cure the hams and side meat, but no hickory wood was available on the homestead, (it is doubtful if sagebrush smoke would have given the desired flavor,) so the meat was heavily salted to preserve it.

Lard was rendered in a large dishpan on the kitchen range after being cut into one or two inch chunks. Rendering could be quite hazardous if a few drops of water were accidently dropped into the pan of seething fat causing it to spatter onto the hot stove. The fat was strained through a cloth to remove the cracklings and poured into pails to cool. The cracklings were saved and combined with other waste fats to make lye soap for the laundry and dish washing.

One evening while Mamma had a large pan of fat rendering

on the stove, someone brought in some wet sagebrush and placed it in the oven to dry for starting the fires in the morning. It was temporarily forgotten while Mamma was busy caring for the pan of fat when suddenly, smoke was noticed coming from the oven. As the oven door was opened, the whole mass of brush burst into flames that shot up past the pan of liquid fat that was seething at the front of the stove. Near panic engulfed the family as we realized the danger; if that hot grease caught on fire nothing could save the house.

"Keep back!" Jim shouted to Mamma as he saw what had happened. "Open the door!" And as she swung the kitchen door open he seized the whole bundle of blazing sagebrush with his bare hands and rushed to fling it far out into the yard where it burned out harmlessly. It was done so quickly he suffered only minor burns.

After the harvesting was over, the cook-wagon was brought home and set off the wagon frame onto the ground near the back door to use for a food storage place. It provided a good place to store the meat as the days became cooler. There were numerous holes in the lumber with which it had been constructed, most of which had been covered with tin. But a small one had been overlooked.

One crisp morning when Mamma stepped outside to get something from the cook-house for breakfast, she noticed one of the pet kittens seated up close to the cook-house on a table that had been placed there on which she could air and sun the milk pans. She thought nothing of it until she went inside the cook-house, and there was the cat's head without any visible body. It startled her until she realized what had happened; the smell of fresh meat had enticed the cat to try the knothole entry to its own undoing. It was held fast as in the stocks, unable to extricate itself until Mamma sent one of the boys to rescue it.

October days brought great wedges of Canadian geese on their migratory flight from the far north. Papa would catch the sound of their musical honking as he was working out around the barn lot, and coming to the kitchen door he would say,

"Geese!" That was all that we needed to have every one rush out of doors to watch the flight of the big "honkers," sometimes several great V's of them calling to companions in flight. It was always a thrill to watch them.

At times the geese would circle and land in some wheat field to feed and rest before continuing their flight. They would land in the fields by the hundreds in the early morning hours, and if left unmolested would feed for several hours. Sometimes their feeding was interrupted by the blast of a shotgun or rifle, and some bird failed to respond to the call of the leader as the flock took off. Then there would be fattened goose on the table of some homestead family.

Ottie came over from Seattle to make a brief visit that autumn, and was eager to try his skill with a gun among the feeding geese. There was a small deserted homesteader's shack in one field where the geese were coming to feed much of the time. The shack would serve as a blind.

"Mamma, wake us up about four; we want to get there before the geese start coming in." The boys were quite excited about hunting the big Canadian geese, and though getting them up at that early hour at any other time would have been a problem, they were on their feet as soon as she called.

"We'll ride Roanie and Bert," Headley told Papa, "then we can tie them out and they won't alarm the geese. They might not alight if they saw a rig there."

With the first streaks of dawn came the sound of "honkers" circling the field and coming in to land. Soon the field was alive with the great flocks. Ganders were stationed here and there to keep watch for signs of danger; but that deserted shack gave no sign of the hidden danger within its walls, and the beautiful birds fed on with no suspicion of the avid eyes watching them.

"Look at them come," whispered Headley to Ottie.

"Yes, there must be at least two or three hundred of them," came back the whispered answer. Ottie had never seen such a sight before.

Then a rifle shot rang out; the flock arose in confusion, their

100

wings beating the air to put distance under them, but three could take no part in the flight.

"You got some! You got some! That was a good shot, Ottie." The cabin door was hastily opened and the boys raced to where they could see a wounded bird endeavoring to fly and dropping back to the ground. Two had been killed and a third winged by that one shot directly into the flock of feeding birds. After an exciting chase after the dodging, wounded bird, the boys were at last able to capture it and returned home with their trophies. One goose was served up on our table; another went to the Mays, and the winged goose was placed in a small wire-enclosed chicken pen to await its turn on the Thanksgiving table. From the enclosure it hissed in scorn at us children as we watched it from the safe side of the fence. It seemed a pity that such a magnificient bird should come to this sad end.

Rising Star School—April 1906—Last day of term. L to R Back Row: Roy Lee, Bruce Hayden, F. L. Barton, Emma Langworthy, teacher, Mrs. F. L. Barton, J. W. Tice, Mrs. J. W. Tice, "Grandpa" Francis Adams. Middle Row: Elmer Moore, "Grandma" Hayden, "Grandma" Frances Adams, Mrs. Gorsuch, unknown, Mrs. John McCulloch, Baby Marion Lee, Mrs. John Lee, "Grandpa" Hayden. Front Row: Ruth Barton, Kenneth Gorsuch, Johnny Lee (white blouse), Marian Moore, Jennie Barton, Grace Moore, Flossie McCulloch, Nellie Barton, Clarence Showalter. Seated in front: Ethel Lee, Xerpha McCulloch.

Chapter XI

Country Schools

"How are we going to take our books and things to school this morning?" Nellie asked Mamma as we came down stairs for breakfast about half past six. It was the first day of school.

"Papa will take you in the buggy this morning because you will have so many things to carry," she told her. We were glad to hear about the ride for in addition to our school books, we had slates, pencil boxes containing our pens, pencils, erasers, extra pen points, besides our lunch buckets. (Dona was fixing our lunches in small lard pails.) All books and supplies for each child were furnished by the parents and were passed down to the next child the following year.

"Mamma, there is only one bottle of ink; Nellie has that one." Only one bottle had been purchased when we got our tablets, pencils and spelling tablets. "What am I going to do for ink?"

"You won't need ink as much as I will." Nellie was in the eighth grade, and some of her compositions and papers would have to be written in ink. I was two grades behind her, but even a sixth grader might have to have ink occasionally, especially in our copy books.

"You and Nellie can share this bottle. There will be a little ink well in the top of your desk; that way you won't knock the bottle off and spill it," Mamma told us.

She had made new dresses for us to wear the first day of school. She made them of percale and gingham, and they reached half way between our knees and the tops of our high-topped shoes. Nellie's was a plaid gingham with lots of red in it since Nellie favored red. Mine was made in Mother Hubbard style, (we didn't call them mu-mus,) gathered onto a yoke and joined to the dress with a ruffle around the yoke. It had long sleeves, and hung from the shoulders without interruption to about eight inches below the knees where it too, ended in a ruffle. My shoes were the button shoes which required a button hook to fasten. Often the buttons pulled off and left gaps. Nellie had advanced to laced shoes. Black stockings of coarse ribbed cotton, and new hair ribbons completed our attire. Otis had a new blouse and bib overalls like the other homestead boys were wearing, but he preferred to go barefooted until the weather turned colder.

The Rising Star School where we attended, was two and a quarter miles from our home. It had been organized only about four years before we started to school there.

Schools became a necessity as homesteads were taken by men with families. The Billington district, located about five miles east of Othello Post Office, was formed from the Cunningham District in 1902. It included a wide area which was later divided to form five districts since it made too great a distance to accomodate children living on the homesteads farther west.

In organizing a school district it was first necessary to hold a trial term of a few weeks to ascertain how many children would be attending, since state funds for a new district were based on the pupil-day attendance. These trial terms were usually held after the regular five or six months term in some other school had closed in the spring. Children from other organized districts were urged to attend the trial term in order to increase the state aid for the new district in process of organization.

In the spring of 1903, a school called the Lee School after Aaron E. Lee, who first promoted it, was held in the James B. Price home one mile north of the present town of Othello. It afterward became the Othello School District No. 74. The trial term lasted for twelve weeks with Laura Irvin as the first teacher. She had just completed a regular term at Providence, a small town on the Northern Pacific railroad south of Lind.

The Price house was a plain one and a half story building, with a lean-to on one side that served as a shelter for the horses, and a storage for feed. The lean-to became the school room. The school room was about fourteen by twenty feet with bare walls of shiplap siding, and heated by a sheet iron stove in the middle of the room. The sagebrush that was brought in to use for fuel sometimes brought in sage ticks that later might be found on some child's neck, getting ready to settle in for tasty living. It would be picked off and crushed or dropped on the hot stove.

Sloping shelves, built along the wall on one side served as desks, and the pupils sat on backless benches that paralleled the shelf. The teacher's desk was a box mounted on four legs with a kitchen chair for a seat. The recitation bench was another backless bench. These may have developed some good strong spines for the rugged life on the homesteads. The blackboards were provided by painting smooth boards black, possibly with stove blacking since it would not make a slick shiny surface.

Two girls in one family who attended this trial term, walked nearly three miles across unfenced sagebrush land. Fearing the girls might become lost in a dust storm, their father hitched up his team to a plow and made a straight furrow across from their homestead to the school; then turning back he threw another furrow the other way making a smooth path to follow. The girls were instructed never to leave the trail during a dust storm.

After the organization of the school was completed and approved by the school authorities, land for its location was donated by Harry Gregg in the northwest corner of his homestead. On this corner a small frame building was constructed, and a regular term of school opened in October of 1903. John W. Hicks was the teacher for that first full term. This was the school where Mary taught in 1905.

Sometimes discipline in the way of a good old-fashioned whipping seemed necessary; but how to administer it to a lad who was as big as the teacher was a poser. One day some of the older girls, who were in their teens, came in from a visit to the small building in the corner of the yard during the noon hour. Their whispering and excited giggling and actions suggested to the teacher that something unusual had taken place.

"What is all the excitement about, girls?" she enquired. An embarrassed look from one girl to another, and a fresh burst of giggles met her inquiry. They seemed a bit reluctant to answer.

"Is there something you should tell me about?" she again questioned. "You girls just came from the toilet, did you not?" Then a thought struck her mind. "Has it anything to do with the conduct of some of the boys?" Again the girls looked at one another. Finally, one of them answered, "Yes."

"Were any of the boys over around the girls' toilet while you girls were in there?" Again, came an abashed "Yes." Then it came out. One of the oldest boys had been peeking in through a crack at the rear of the privy while the girls were inside. Reluctantly, they named the lad who had stepped out of line.

The boy was called in, and admitted his guilt. Now it was up to the teacher to decide. Here was a boy as tall as she, but if she let him get away with it her control over the school would be jeopardized. She knew she could not whip him if he resisted her, so she gave him a choice.

"You may either take a whipping, or I shall expel you from school," she said. "I will leave it to you to make the choice." He may have thought she could not lay on a whipping very hard, but he should have taken a second look at her red hair and the determined look in her eyes.

"I'll take the whipping," was his choice.

Mary stepped out to where her horse was tied, loosened the riding quirt from the saddle horn. Returning to the school room she proceeded to administer a thorough whipping. He respected her for her decision and gave no more trouble.

Now that this school was successfully launched, another district was formed four and a half miles northeast of there in 1904. The trial term of twelve weeks which began in February, was held in the John F. Lee home with Pliny Hayden as the teacher. Byron Hayden, Charles Showalter and Lee were directors in the organization of this school. Showalter donated land on the southeast corner of his land for the new school building which was constructed by neighborhood men. This was the Rising Star School, District No. 77.

The school building was a frame building about thirty feet

square made with a hip roof. (This hip roof had a way of diverting the ball the wrong way when we played anti-over.) The building was never painted either on the inside or the outside, and was taking on the dull gray appearance that blended quite well with dust that so often was raised around it by the wind. The inside, which was sealed with a beaded siding, had taken on a smoke-tinged yellow under the influence of the pot-bellied stove which stood near the center of the room.

One small building stood off in one corner of the yard for the use of both boys and girls. It had an extra wooden button on the inside to insure privacy. Most schools provided two such buildings in opposite corners of the yard as more in keeping with acceptable custom, but either the builders ran out of time or lumber as the first one was completed, or we were considered to be one happy family; only one was ever built at Rising Star.

Papa deposited us with our books and school supplies beside the barbed wire fence in front of the school building as Nellie Phillips was vigorously ringing the hand school bell to call her pupils from the game of pom-pom-pull-away they were playing in the front yard.

"Alberta, you and Nellie may sit together as you are both in the eighth grade." Mrs. Phillips was assigning more seats to those who had come later. "We have no seventh grade this year," she continued, "But we have two in the sixth grade. Irma, you and Laura may sit here." Alberta and Irma Rice were sisters who lived in the opposite direction from the school, and we had not previously met either of the girls.

Two rows of double desks and seats were lined up on each side of the stove, facing a long blackboard made of oil-cloth covered board extending across the front of the room. The part of the blackboard which was used most frequently, gradually lost its slick surface, but the chalk slipped over the more seldom used portion without leaving much trace. Another shorter board at the side of the room contained the carefully worked out schedule of classes for the day. Since most of the grades from first to eighth were represented, the time had to be carefully budgeted.

The desks and seats were graduated in size from the larger ones at the rear of the room to those for the first grade children at the front of the rows. Mrs. Phillips had taught here the previous term and was engaged again for the 1907-1908 term. She and her husband were living on the Byron Hayden place.

The era of slates and scratching slate pencils was nearing its close, though still in use in country schools. They came in various sizes from 8 x 11 to 12 x 14 inches; a smooth piece of slate framed in wood with a strip of red felt laced around the edge. A mistake in arithmetic or spelling could be easily corrected by a mouth-moistened finger, or a damp rag kept in one corner of the desk. After the work was inspected and graded by the teacher, the whole surface was cleaned off by the damp rag which sometimes acquired a peculiar odor from the constant re-wetting by the particular house-keeping little girls. Small boys, who could not be bothered with such fussy ways, used the spit and sleeve method.

Equipment for the school was very limited, but included a small bookcase containing a small assortment of books, a set of Geographic Readers, one on each of the five world continents to be used for reference reading, a large dictionary, a pump organ, the teacher's desk and captain's chair and a backless recitation bench. Wasn't it one of the old philosophers who expressed the idea that to obtain an education, all that was needed was a log with a good teacher on one end and a pupil on the other end of the log? Times and ideas change, and good equipment helps. Later, as a result of an enterprising teacher and pupils, a set of world maps in a wall case and a world globe were added. The schools were also provided with a good-sized national flag which was flown on special days. A short bench on which was the water pail and dipper for quenching thirsts, and an enamel basin stood behind the door. On the wall behind the pail hung a mirror with comb on a chain, and with a roller towel conveniently near. From time to time the towel was replaced by a fresh one laundered by some homestead mother.

"Miz Phillips, can I get me a drink?" Lydia Lang was the

little six year old Russian girl, who with her two brothers, Willie and Johnny, had just begun school at Rising Star, and was still having problems with the English language. Their mother had brought the family from Russia only a few years before, and was living about three miles north of the school.

"You may get a drink, Lydia," the teacher consented, then learned that the gray pail was empty.

"John, you and Otis may go after a pail of water." The task of carrying the pails of water from the Showalter yard an eighth of a mile away, was usually assigned to some of the boys. Waste water was thrown into the bare yard and helped to settle the dust around the door.

A ten minute period for opening exercises was allowed in the morning and again at noon. Sometimes we sang to the accompaniment of the old-fashioned organ played by one of the girls who had learned to play a few songs by ear. With no knowledge of sharps or flats, the songs were not always played in the right key, but the singers were not too critical as they entered heartily into singing patriotic songs.

At other times we were called on to recite favorite memory gems, and responded with some old favorite:

"To do to others as I would that they should do to me, will make me honest, kind and good as children ought to be."

"Politeness is to do and say the kindest things in the kindest way."

"If a task is once begun, never leave it 'till it's done; be thy labor great or small, do it well or not at all."

The times we liked best were when the teacher read to us from some new books from our small library. Among the favorites were Beautiful Joe, Five Little Peppers and How They Grew, Helen's Babies, (this last one with plenty of expression,) or one of the Louisa M. Alcott books. The boys preferred some of the Horatio Alger series or the Rover Boys stories. That ten minutes given to reading seemed all too short as it so frequently brought the story to some exciting point where we were left until the next morning to learn the outcome. It was doubtless a good way to insure we would be on time for school.

"Otis, what is taking your attention there in your desk when you ought to be working your arithmetic problems?" The teacher had caught some grins passing between him and Johnny Lee, and which seemed to have something to do with some object Otis was holding below the desk top.

"A ground squirrel," he told her, grinning sheepishly. "Its a young one," he added, bringing the squirrel out into view. Now the attention of the whole school room had been gained.

"Where did you get it?" Teacher knew those ground squirrels were pests to the farmers, but she was stalling for time while she decided whether to suggest it be killed or turned loose. "Bring it here," was her next request. Perhaps she suspected it might have been found in her desk a little later; and that is just what the mischievious lad had in mind when he brought it to school.

"What are you intending to do with it?" The teacher knew boys.

"I caught it on the way to school," answering her first question first. "I just want to play with it. I'll take it home tonight."

Feeling the problem could be settled without any big decision on her part, she gave him an empty chalk box in which to keep it on her desk. "Now get to your arithmetic problems right away," she told him, then called the next class to the recitation bench as the school room settled to studying after the diversion.

March was a time of flying dust, for when the wind blew it picked up the light soil from the plowed fields surrounding the school, filling the air with the fine dust. At times the air was so filled with the smothering dust it prohibited outdoor games; then we had only a half hour at noon and were dismissed earlier at the close of the day.

Walking home was difficult. Eyes were squinted to shield them from the dirt, and we often turned to walk backwards across the Adams' plowed fields where the heavier gusts caused clouds of fine dust to swirl around us. Hair, eyebrows, lashes, nostrils and clothing were filled with the powdery dust. Little globules of tear-filled dirt gathered at the corners of the eyes where they had been washed by tears. When the dust storms were more dense than usual, Papa would sometimes come for us in the wagon. But dust storms were not considered sufficient reason to skip a day of school.

The school serving the families in what later became the Corfu area was first called the Wilsie school. The first teacher was Grace Sinclair; and as janitor she learned how to start fires on cold mornings with the most available kindling, sagebrush, which had been provided by the homestead men.

Roxie Gillis taught this school from 1910 to 1913. Not only was she the teacher and janitor, but at times she drove the "school bus," a buggy or cart pulled by a pinto pony. When the snow was deep, a homestead version of a sleigh was substituted. Coyotes sometimes appeared and followed them until Roxie started carrying a gun. After that no more coyotes showed up.

One morning as they were on their way to school with a full cart load, they were startled by the shotgun blast of an early rabbit hunter near the road. Instantly, the pinto wheeled and took off across the sagebrush at a furious pace with Roxie trying to "sweet talk" their excited steed into calming down. Roxie's hat was the only thing lost in the excitement.

Another pioneer teacher was Teresa Motheral who taught near Quincy in Grant County. She came out in 1909 to teach the school at Low Gap. Already having had some experience in teaching pioneer schools in other areas, she landed in Quincy and learned that the stage to take her out there was already booked to capacity by other teachers who had been attending a Teachers' Institute at Ephrata.

Learning of a homestead woman who wanted to go in the same direction, the two got together and engaged a buggy and team at the livery stable to take them to Low Gap in search of the school clerk who had written to her from that place. Teresa had been accustomed to living in wooded country, and when mile after mile of nothing but desert sand and sagebrush was to be seen, she began to query the driver.

"Mister, when are we ever going to get to Low Gap?" The noon hour was past and she was getting hungry and tired from the long dusty ride.

"Why, Ma'am, that there's Low Gap, right there, that-a-way, see it?" What she saw was a little knot of shacks off in the distance.

"Will there be a place to rest and get something to eat there?" she wanted to know.

"Rest? They ain't no place to eat there, Ma'am," he told her.

"But where does the Low Gap school clerk live?" At least they could inquire, she thought, as the driver pulled the team to a stop beside one of the small unpainted shacks the driver had pointed out to her.

"Oh, he lives on east a piece," they told her, "Mebbe twenty miles, mebbe more. He jist comes here ever' now and then for his mail."

She finally found refuge with the kindly homestead familiy for the night, and word was sent to the school clerk by a rider who chanced to pass that way.

Most of the early day teachers lived in the various homes in the school district during the school year, and soon Teresa was an interested part of the homestead community. She had learned you could file on a quarter section of land, build a shack on it and live there for a while, then prove up on it and your fortune was made. She began to think of filing on a homestead claim for herself. She heard that eventually irrigation was bound to come, and with the big wheat crops and other crops that could be produced on that rich soil, you could sell out for two to five hundred dollars an acre. Like many others, Teresa envisioned something that was yet far distant.

After picking out what looked like a good piece of land, she filed on it, and soon had a small shack under construction. There was only a shell by the time the hot days of summer came and she found the heat so intense she deserted the homestead for cooler weather on the coast until time to return for the next school term.

Literary societies offered opportunities for homestead people to get together from time to time, and one was organizd by Vesta Bush to include several schools for miles around. One program with a supper was held each month.

One Saturday night the men were to cook and serve the supper; this caused a good bit of speculation among the women on how tasty the food might be. The highlight of the supper came when the surprised women were served cream puffs for dessert. Unknown to them, one of the men had been a chef. Needless to say, the men were quite elated over their success in keeping their women in the dark; nor could they be pursuaded to divulge the chef's secret unique way of getting the cream inside the puffs.

Some of the teachers were accused of having matrimonial designs on the bachelors living around that section of the country. Several matches were made, so the rumor may have been justified.

Chapter XII

Typhoid Fever

IT WAS NEARING THE END of October; the wheat fields were showing green from the fall planting. Ground squirrels had long since gone into hibernation, and homestead men were repairing the roads which had been deeply rutted by the heavily loaded wagons of wheat and tanks of water hauled over them during the hot dry summer. Repairs were made by spreading old straw from the previous year's threshing along the road where deep chuck holes had been worn, and fine dust arose in a cloud whenever disturbed by a passing team. Each homesteader was supposed to be responsible for the road that ran past his piece of land, though sometimes it was left to the wind and weather to gradually fill in the ruts.

"Mamma, I don't feel good, my head aches." Otis had come downstairs one morning near the end of the first month of school with a flushed face and a feeling of lassitude. "Do I have to go to school today?"

Placing her hand upon his forehead and cheeks, she could tell he seemed to have some fever. It might be a case of biliousness which a generous dose of castor oil would clear up in a few days. "No, you'd better stay at home today. You may get into the bed in the front room." The next day he was no better, and for the remainder of the week he remained at home with no improvement.

At school it was time for the written end-of-the-month examinations. It took two days to cover all the studies of the previous weeks; two days of anxiety on the part of the pupils. By noon of the second day my head was throbbing from what I supposed was concentration on the questions. I was glad to be getting through with the last question, and that this was Friday.

When I showed no appetite for supper, Mamma sent me upstairs to bed. Otis was still feeling miserable. When neither of us showed any improvement the next morning, Mamma knew it was something more serious than biliousness.

"Papa, we'd better take these children down to the doctor," Mamma was getting anxious about us. The only doctor in town was the one employed for the railroad hospital.

"All right, Mamma, I'll get the team harnessed. We shall have to go in the header box," he added as he went to the barn to harness the team.

Full of curiosity in spite of our physical feelings, we followed the doctor back through the rows of beds to the small tent in the rear which served as his office. Our experiences with doctors had been rather meager up to this time; Mamma had seen us through measles, mumps and other childhood diseases.

"How long have they been sick?" asked the doctor as he began to study our flushed faces.

"Otis has been sick since last Monday. He has been out of school all week. But Laura came home from school not feeling well yesterday. Neither seem to have any appetite," she went on.

Following several more questions from the doctor on the symptoms, he examined Otis carefully. The doctor seemed to be looking for certain tell-tale symptoms. Next, he put me through the same procedure, then he turned to Mamma.

"These children both have typhoid fever," was his diagnosis. "Did you say the boy has been sick for a week?"

"Yes, I have kept him out of school all week," was her answer. The doctor's next remark surprised her.

"The girl's symptoms show she has been coming down with it for over two weeks. Take these children home at once and put them to bed." Knowing we had come to town in the header box he added, "Do you have something you can spread on the floor of the wagon? They must not stand up going home. Give them no food except liquids. I will see them on Monday."

Perhaps we had just a little feeling of importance that our sickness was something more than a case of biliousness, which

116

In 1910. Main Street looking east from Broadway to Fourth Street. From left — Irrigator No. 1 (Krause's Saloon), Cummings' Saloon, Shamrock Cafe, Othello State Bank, Mendel's Meat Market with volunteer fire bell just beyond, barn near Tiptons Store at 4th. From right— McMillian's Pool Hall, Tulles Drugs, Crawford building, Crockett's store, Hibbard Hotel, Tipton's new store, city water tank (wooden).

might have called for more castor oil, but if we entertained any such pride we lost that feeling when we learned we were not even to be allowed to stand up and look around at the new town. Coats were spread on the floor of the wagon, and we rode the three miles back to the homestead prone, and without benefit of springs under the jolting wagon.

The front room was turned into a sick ward by the addition of a cot, and Mamma took on the duties of day and night nurse to two feverish, fretful children. The kitchen became the living room for the rest of the family, and Papa moved upstairs to sleep.

Doctor Judah had said, "No foods, except liquids," and although we had shown little desire for foods before the call on the doctor, now that only liquids were permitted we began to feel hungry for something more solid. That subject was to loom big in our thoughts for the next several weeks.

On Monday, the doctor came to see us and to give Mamma further instructions for our care. He appeared to be in his early thirties; he was of medium height and wore a Van Dyke beard. He may have worn the beard to add dignity to his youthful appearance, but more likely it was to protect his face from the biting cold as he frequently rode horseback to make the calls on his widely separated country patients. Carrying a small medical satchel which, when opened, revealed an intriguing assort-

117

ment of little bottles of pills in varied colors, and wearing a heavy fur coat, cap and mittens, he made his rounds.

Temperatures soared. Cold sponge baths were ordered to bring them down. His suggestion that ice water be used met with no favor from his patients. How we hated those cold sponges! Mamma listened to our pleas to leave out the ice, but she disregarded our suggestion that she add a little warm water, too.

The doctor came every other day to check our progress. He would show up with a twinkle in his eyes, and a face quite rosy from the cold winds; and after divesting himself of cap, coat and gloves, would warm his hands over the heater while passing on news of the latest medical cases to Mamma. We were not the only victims of the typhoid germ in the neighborhood. After getting a verbal account of our progress from Mamma he would turn to inspect the medical chart which was pinned to the wall. He had shown her just how to keep a medical chart for each of us.

Next came taking the temperature, pulse and respiration and percussion of the abdomen. Heart and lung action was carefully noted by placing his ear to back and chest. His Van Dyke may have given protection to his face in the cold wind, but my thin-as-gauze shirt worn under my gown was no protection from those short side whiskers. They penetrated like a stiff bristled brush.

Days ran into weeks. We were starving for something besides that thin liquid diet of strained soups and gruels.

"Mamma, ask the doctor if I can have some creamed potatoes, or some turnips," I begged her. "I'm so hungry."

"Ask him if I can have some beans," was Otis request. We could smell the odors coming from the kitchen, and we always had a list of foods for Mamma to ask the doctor about adding to our diet. Patiently, she would ask to please us, knowing the answer in most cases would be "No."

"No creamed potatoes or turnips, but you may strain some bean soup and let them have that," the doctor conceded on his next trip. Otis got the modified form of his request, but my

118

desire for those delectable creamed potatoes like Mamma fixed had to go unsatisfied. It seemed like an unfair world.

One evening after school, Nellie came in from the kitchen eating a large slice of pumpkin pie. Oh how good it looked!

"I wish I could have some pie," was my plea knowing it would be another unfulfilled wish. Nellie always had a good, (though I thought a sometimes misplaced) sense of humor and liked to tease.

"I'm going to write that down on your chart for the doctor to see," she threatened. My sense of humor was at very low ebb just then.

"Mamma, don't let her," I appealed to Mamma.

"I was only joking," Nellie assured me; but when the doctor read my chart on his next visit, he noticed the item placed there by Nellie, "Wants pie!" and turned to me with a quizzical look.

I stood somewhat in awe of the doctor and apologetically tried to explain I was only expressing a wish; at the same time wishing she had choked on the pie.

By Thanksgiving Otis was up and well on the way to recovery, but I had a relapse. Another three weeks went by under Mamma's careful nursing as my temperature soared and climbed higher than ever. More cold baths! More strained soups and gruels! Finally, it started down until the doctor pronounced it safe for me to sit up for brief periods.

The momentous day finally arrived when I was permitted to eat breakfast with the family. For the first time in six weeks I looked into the kitchen mirror; a bony skeleton scarecrow with large, hollow startled eyes stared back at me.

From time to time we learned of other neighbors who had also been victims of the typhoid germ. Our teacher, Nellie Phillips, had taken sick soon after we became ill. Ralph Barton was another victim, and the doctor mentioned other cases he was attending in the area around Othello. Either some water source had become contaminated, or there may have been a typhoid carrier among the migrant workers.

I had seen Otis making faces when he took the tonic the doctor

119

prescribed for him as he was convalescing; now it was my time to learn how bitter it was. The Christmas holidays were past before I was able to return to school. Louise Pape had been employed to finish teaching the term.

Chapter XIII

Homestead Christmas

HOMESTEAD CHILDREN had few of the outward trappings of Christmas, but the children looked forward to it with as much eagerness as do children where brightly colored lights and toy-filled windows enlarge their wants and visions of what to expect from Santa. No shops being available to whet our desires, we were satisfied with more simple practical gifts.

The decorated fir Christmas tree was seen only at such gathering places as a school, or the church, after the town came into existence. The tree came by special order. No scent of fir challenged the odor of the sagebrush burning in the kitchen stoves; but some families solved the Christmas tree problem for their children by scouting for the largest, best-shaped sage brush they could find, and decorating it with strings of popcorn, cranberries, bits of tin foil and chains of colored paper. A dash of flour gave a semblance of snow.

The Don P. Estep family who had homesteaded three and a half miles east of Othello several years before the town was started, brought the festive spirit into their home by this method. Another family brought in a wheel from the buggy one Christmas, and set it on a frame in a horizontal position. The rim and spokes were wrapped with green and red crepe paper; colored chains were draped around the rim, and candles were placed where each spoke joined into the rim.

We never had a Christmas tree in our home. Instead, we hung our stockings behind the living room stove, (there was some question on how Santa could be expected to make his grand entrance through the stove pipe; we'd had a large fireplace in Missouri), and set our plates at our usual places on the dining table. Christmas morning we found Christmas candy, nuts and oranges in the plates. Unwrapped gifts were either in the stockings, or if too large for those, they were placed beside the plates.

Christmas eve was a time for popping corn and making popcorn balls. If we had sorghum molasses, we made sorghum candy, but on the homestead it was more often made of the things on hand. Afterward, we sat around the front room stove and listened to Mamma's stories of when she was a little girl.

One Christmas Mamma felt she had run out of stories. She said, "Get your father to tell you a story."

Rarely could we get him to tell stories, but this time when we clamored for a story from him, he laughed and replied, "I'll tell you a story of when I was a boy." We settled to listen.

"Brother Doug, (Uncle Doug became a doctor in St. Louis), and I had gotten a deck of playing cards. We kept them hidden from Mother because we knew she did not approve the use of that kind of cards. She would promptly have destroyed any she found.

"One day we found just the place where we could play without being found out. A well was being dug on the place where we lived and the ladder was still standing in the hole. The water hadn't been reached, but the men were not digging that day. We descended the ladder to the bottom of the hole and proceeded to our game. The only one we knew how to play was one called 'seven-up.' One of us had just succeeded in taking all four tricks, and forgetting to keep the voice down, shouted, 'High, low, jack and the game.' " Papa was laughing at the memory now.

"The elation was brief. From the top of the well came a well-known voice 'Come up here my Sons, I'll high, low, jack and the game you.' "

We could just picture the boys climbing sheepishly up the ladder to hand the cards over to Grandma.

"Papa, did she whip you?" (She had lived with us in Missouri). But Papa's memory seemed to have left him a bit hazy on that.

Christmas morning we younger children were awake early and

anxious to get downstairs to examine our gifts; but now that there was no longer sickness in the home the fires were allowed to go out at night to save fuel, and the house was cold. Finally, after what seemed a long time to us, we heard Papa get up and start the fires. With new fallen snow on the ground, and the temperature registering about ten degrees above zero, we would have been sent back up stairs to wait until it warmed up down stairs. With permission finally given us we raced down the stairs in our night clothes to examine our gifts. They gave us the same pleasure an assortment of toys would have brought.

Otis found a harmonica, which we called a mouth harp, in his stocking. He spent most of the morning blowing on it in the house until sent out of doors where he discovered the dogs would howl an accompaniment to his blowing. Nellie and I were thrilled when we each found a small bottle of perfume and other small feminine articles in our stockings. Story books were other gifts we welcomed. In my stocking that year was a tiny box. Mamma had seen me studying the mail order catalog during my convalescense, and had seen me look longingly at a little ring set with three small amethysts, which was my birthstone. Mamma understood little girls.

Earlier, Mamma and Mary had gotten together on plans for the Christmas dinner. Mary had raised turkeys that year.

"You and Billie and little Willie must come over and have dinner with us. Jim and Iva will be home from Seattle, and Ellen will be here, too," Mamma told her. "We'll all be together again."

"Let me furnish the turkey, Mamma. There is an extra young tom that I won't need," Mary offered. "Maybe you could send Laura over on the horse after it a couple of days before Christmas." That was my first ride since October, and the turkey rode home fastened to the horn of the saddle.

That Christmas was a happy one for all of us. The siege of sickness was past, and all the family was together. Though Mamma was rather tired from the long siege of nursing, anticipation of having all the family together again had been a tonic to her far more pleasant than was the bitter tonic prescribed for the convalescents. Now as her eyes rested on the food filling the table, her heart was full of thankfulness that all the family was home and safe. Reverently, she expressed those thanks as we bowed our heads; then passed our plates for the favorite piece of turkey. Little Willie found the drumstick was about all his small hands could handle even after most of the meat was removed. Sucking on the bone soon had his face and hands well smeared, to Mamma's great delight. The day was a success for all.

When the weather turned colder we awoke in the morning to find the bed covers stiff with ice where our breath had congealed as we snuggled deep in the feather bed. Beautiful frost patterns formed on the windows during the night, delicately picturing ferns and winter scenes to our active imaginations. Reluctantly, we crawled out from under the warm covers and hovered close to the stoves to dress while breakfast was being prepared.

"The pump froze last night; I'll have to thaw it out before I can pump water for the horses," Papa explained as he appeared at the kitchen door with the pitcher pump and some eight feet of pipe. Although the water had been drained from the pump the night before, the slight amount left in the valve had frozen.

"You get the horses harnessed," Papa instructed Headley who had remained at home from the high school in Ritzville to help Papa after Thanksgiving. "You will have to warm the bridle bits here at the oven before you can bridle the horses," he added; "We'll have to haul up some straw to bed the animals since it is turning colder." A large brass kettle of cooked wheat was steaming on the back of the stove to feed to the hogs.

"Breakfast will soon be ready," Mamma reminded them as they donned wraps and pulled the inner flaps of their caps down over their ears.

"We'll be in by the time the biscuits are out of the oven," she was assured. "We won't stay out any longer than we have to in this cold wind."

Snow covered the wheat fields and showed jack rabbit trails leading to the hay stacks from all directions. At times it looked

124

like a flock of sheep had been feeding there, making heavy inroads into the feed intended for the farm animals. Circular patches, a hundred feet or more in diameter were trampled down in the freshly fallen snow where hundreds of rabbits had frolicked during the night. These jacks were not easy for the dogs to catch, but occasionally, Headley went hunting with the rifle to bring some of them to feed to the dogs. He set traps along coyote trails and caught several coyotes on which a bounty was paid. Coyotes did little calling during the winter, but now and then a hen was missing from the flock.

1907. The Chavis buildings were among the first in Othello. The small building between the lodging house and livery barn housed the first newspaper, The Othello Times.

Chapter XIV

A New Venture

THE LITTLE TOWN of Othello was continuing to grow and to attract various kinds of business. Following the opening of grocery and general merchandise stores by Homer Tipton and W. A. Struppler, a bank was organized with John W. Webster as the first manager. B. Keeney opened a harness shop but later sold it to Charles Showalter; a meat market, barber shops, the Shamrock Cafe and real estate offices were soon doing a good business.

The small weekly newspaper in Cunningham, called The Cunningham Gazettte, had discontinued publication, and O. E. Pape bought out the equipment. Pape was a school teacher. He taught at the Cunningham school the last year we attended there. It was his sister Louise who was teaching at the Rising Star School after Nellie Phillips took down with the typhoid fever.

Shortly before Christmas Mr. Pape made a visit to our home. He was a most interesting story teller, and his stories of saber-toothed tigers, mammoths, and other prehistoric animals had us younger children enthralled with the supposed adventures of the cave men. His visit was not primarily intended to tell stories, however.

"Dona, have you thought over the proposition on starting a newspaper in Othello?" he asked as Dona and Mamma came into the front room after supper. "What do your mother and father think of it?"

"I've talked with Mamma and Papa about it, but I would like for you to tell them more about it." Dona had not reached any decision.

"Mrs. Tice, Dona has no doubt told you that I bought out the equipment of the Cunningham Gazettte when it discontinued publication several weeks ago," Pape said, "And I think Othello would be a good place to start a weekly newspaper." He continued, "What I am suggesting is this, that we start the paper with Dona as the editor, and she and I as co-owners."

"But Mr. Pape, you know Dona has never had any experience in newspaper work of any kind," she told him, "How would she know how to run a newspaper?"

"Mrs. Tice, I have every confidence that Dona will do a very good job as editor of the paper. She has had some contact with the public in her work as a telephone operator at Cunningham," and he added, "She has a good education and is conscientous in whatever she does."

"How would she finance her part of it?" Papa inquired. He knew that the doctor's bills which had accumulated recently made it impossible for him to finance a venture into newspaper publishing.

"Her work as editor would cover part of it," Pape said, "And your son-in-law, Billie May, has offered to put up one hundred dollars as a loan to Dona for her part in the equipment."

"What is the equipment, Mr. Pape?" inquired Papa.

"It includes a Franklin hand press, a small job press and several cases and fonts of type in various kinds and sizes for newspaper and job work." Mr. Pape gave them a pretty good idea of the amount of the equipment.

"Would there be heavy work involved in operating the press?" was Mamma's next question. She wanted to be sure Dona did not take on more than she could handle.

"I will help her get started, and then come out once a week to operate the press in running off the paper," he assured her.

Dona went to Cunningham for a few days instruction from the editor of the defunct Gazette to learn how to set type, make up the advertisements and lock the forms; in other words how to get out a newspaper. He showed her how to operate the little job press as she could expect occasional jobs of that kind. Some points were given on how to get the news, but on how to get along with some of the peculiarities and idiosyncrasies of the people she would meet in her newspaper work was left for her to learn as she went along.

The first issue was published on January 10, 1908; and the first few copies came out under the name of The Gazette. Shortly, however, the name The Othello Times was selected for the new paper. Until the paper was admitted as second class mail each individual paper was wrapped, addressed and stamped by hand before being carried to the post office. Nellie went down to help with the tedious job of wrapping and attaching the stamps.

After a short time Pape sold his interest in the paper to George Allen; then Allen sold his interest to Dona leaving her the sole owner and publisher. She then employed E. L. Sheldon, a young attorney who was just getting started in law practice, to operate the press and carry the regular monthly statements to the advertisers. One advertiser became so incensed when his monthly statement was handed to him, which he considered a dun, he discontinued all further advertising. Wrathfully, he stated he had never been dunned before in his life. Thus the idiosyncrasies began to show up to the young editor.

News items were gotten in various ways. Sheldon was a good news gatherer as he got around among the business people of the town. People from the country areas who were pleased to have a means of learning what was being done by their neighbors, sent in items on their own activities. The following news items were reported in one of the early editions of the paper.

"The Milwaukee expects to begin laying track out of Lind the first of March." This was welcome news after seeing the bare graded roadbed stretching for empty miles in both directions for several months.

"Mr. and Mrs. F. Bagwell, Mr. and Mrs. J. F. Lee, Mrs. McCollom and son Charles all visited at the home of F. L. Barton and wife on Sunday." Such items of what the neighbors were doing always proved interesting, and encouraged others to report their own social activities.

"Leland Lucy has just returned from a trip to Missouri; he

reports everything there at a standstill." Leland was a bachelor living east of Othello who had originally come from Missouri. His sisters, Pattie and Phoebe had taken the trip with us to White Bluffs and the Columbia River three years previously. His homestead adjoined his father's, and he had developed it some years before, but he had not yet acquired a wife. These little personal news accounts of neighborhood doings were the first items to be read.

Sometimes an item appeared that aroused a different response. Among the news sent in by a woman from one section of the community was one containing some nice complimentary remarks about a neighbor of hers. The next week another woman came into the newspaper office as mad as the proverbial wet hen; she had an item of her own she insisted should be printed. It contained some very uncomplimentary things about the previously complimented woman. It was quite evident she wanted to counteract the influence of the previous remarks. Editor Dona was on the spot; this called for diplomacy. Quietly, she pointed out that she could not print anything like that in the paper. When she continued to refuse to print the article despite the woman's insistence, the woman's spleen was vented on the editor. Dona learned the truth of a statement made by Mr. Haas, editor of the Lind Leader when he called to get acquainted with the woman editor: "You are in a man's work here, and you will have to take a man's knocks."

Another item appearing in the paper in January told of a box supper to be held at the Rising Star school. Money obtained from the sale of the boxes was to be used to buy some equipment for the school. The young teacher may also have found teaching a little country school of homestead children was a bit lacking in social opportunities, and proposed to make a change.

A program was prepared to demonstrate the supposed talents of the children to their parents; but the high point of the evening came when the decorated boxes were auctioned off to the highest bidder. No one was supposed to know the identity of the owner until after the box was sold.

When the big evening came, the dimly lighted room was filled with folks from the surrounding homesteads and town. Four coal oil lamps in high wall brackets had their light only slightly increased by the mirrored reflectors behind each lamp, but they gave enough light to show the keen interest of everyone. The railroad doctor and some of the young surveyors who were working for the railroad company, heard of the social event and came to help enliven the evening. The school room was crowded to capacity.

The bidding started moderately with the young surveyors and doctor, who were standing in a little group near the door, putting in a bid now and then to liven things up. Then a more artistically decorated box was passed over to the auctioneer.

"Ah! Look what we have here, boys. Now the one who gets this box will be a lucky fellow." The auctioneer was warming up in his sales talk. He hardly had time to get it up where it could be seen when the bidding started. It soon became evident that someone had tipped off the young men who were standing near the door as to the ownership. Suspicion fell on John McCulloch, at whose home the teacher was boarding.

The surveyors and doctor took a quickened interest in that particular box and there was a sudden upsurge in the bidding. Higher and higher rose the bids. Local boys and men dropped out of the bidding leaving the doctor and surveyors to compete for the honor of eating with the teacher. Up and up went the bids until it reached nearly sixteen dollars, and the bidding slowed to a stop. "Are you all through?" called the elated auctioneer as the bidding stopped. "Going, once! Going, twice! Do I hear any more bids? Sold!" and one of the surveyors went forward to claim his prize. Louise had been standing behind the curtain from where the boxes were being handed, convulsed in laughter as the bidding went higher and higher.

The little weekly newspaper had helped to spread the news whereby the school funds profited.

Another item appeared shortly after that showed some of the transportation problems.

131

"Strayed. 1 sorrel mare 820 pounds, 1 dark bay mare 820 pounds, both had halters with ropes tied to the halters. Reward of $10.00 for their return, or for information leading to their recovery. Signed D. Judah."

A comment from the editor of The Othello Times hinted that this might have made quite an awkward delay if it should have been at a time when the aforesaid sorrel and bay were needed to transport a fair member of the gentle sex from Cunningham when romance was in the air. Louise had a sister Mamie who was teaching school there.

Chapter XV

Sickness Strikes Again

THOUGH PAPA was twenty-three years older than Mamma, he relied on her counsel, whether in financial matters or in making the garden. He was prone to fret and worry when things got difficult, and he needed Mamma's calm encouragement to reassure him. Papa's brow would wrinkle up and he became quite agitated when confronted with some unexpected expense. The doctor's bill from our long sickness added nothing to his peace of mind. Mamma was more apt to be thankful we were all well again, and to assure Papa they would find a way to get it paid in time.

Papa liked to know Mamma was near even if it was only in planting the garden. Many of the tasks were shared. Papa dug and raked the ground at gardening time, but Mamma planted the seed. Washing clothes for the family on the homestead was a hard all-day job. There was no electric motor on the wash board. It took a good bit of what was sometimes called "elbow grease" to get the overalls, work shirts and children's clothes ready to wear again. He carried the water and filled the boiler to heat on the kitchen range; then filled the tubs. They had bought a hand-operated, dolly type machine to make wash day easier for her, but when it was loaded with the heavier garments it was heavy for her to operate. When his outdoor work permitted, he would work the machine for her. He always saw there was plenty of sagebrush for the stove with a wheelbarrow load ready at the back door.

Papa had gotten his right hand crushed in a pump where he worked in Cunningham, and it left his fingers stiff. Mamma became his barber; but before she could start on the week's growth of beard with the old-fashioned straight razor, some preliminary work needed to be done.

Sunday morning after breakfast Papa would call, "Daughter, are you going to wash my neck and ears?" He meant not only his neck and ears but his hair and beard as well. He wore a mustache and chin whiskers.

I felt flattered that he depended on me for this delicate work, and assembled the basin of warm water, wash rag, (we did not have the modern type), soap and the roller towel. The job was done to the accompaniment of comments on the amount of soil in his ears.

"Are my neck and ears dirty?" he would ask, knowing it had been a full week since the last thorough cleansing.

"Papa, we could plant a good crop of potatoes in your ears," I would tell him. It tickled him to be told there was enough dirt to raise a crop of potatoes, and he would chuckle over the remark. When this was completed, Mamma took over to trim his hair and shave his neck and cheeks. When we got all finished and he had finished cleaning up and changing clothes, his blue eyes and Roman nose gave him the look of a Southern gentleman.

We had only one comfortable rocking chair. Papa might be sitting in it when he had a little time to rest, but if Mamma came in to sit down he immediately got up to give her the comfortable rocker. He considered it his chair only when Mamma did not need it.

Mamma continued to have trouble with the soreness high under the lower ribs on the right side. Sometime earlier, after a severe attack, she had gone to a doctor in Cunningham for advice. A small bottle of laudanum was given her to keep on hand for times when the pain became intense, since it was a long distance to the doctor. That little bottle was hung high on the kitchen wall where the red skull and crossed bones warned us it was poison, and only to be used in an emergency.

More of the same attacks came. In late January Mamma became so sick that Dr. Judah was sent for. He was out of town. Mary came to apply what home remedies she could, but nothing alleviated the agonizing pain. After a day and night of suffering, the doctor returned to town and got the message to come. His diagnosis was gall stones, and he advised that she should be taken to a hospital in Seattle for surgery at once.

The nearest railroad point was Cunningham. That would be a long hard trip over the frozen ground for Mamma.

"Mamma, do you think you can stand the trip?" Papa was almost beside himself with anxiety.

"Anything, Papa, anything to relieve this suffering. I don't think I could stand to go through suffering again like I have been having," she told him.

The doctor was going along with them; and she was well wrapped up with heated bricks at her feet. Nellie remained at home to help get her ready for the trip; but two children, one openly weeping, and both with an unspoken fear bottled inside, started for school the morning Mamma and Papa were to leave.

A few days later we received a post card from Mamma. It read: "Seattle, Wash., Feb. the 6th. Dear Ones: Arrived here all right on time. Am now at the Seattle General Hospital. Suppose they will operate on me tomorrow at 10 o'clock. Have a private room at $17.50 per week, was the best we could do. Dr. Judah will stay over until tomorrow. The boys are still here, (She meant Ottie and Cleve). Expect them to call on me this evening. Papa can stay with me nearly all the time. Will write you tomorrow and tell you where to address. Lovingly, Mamma.

This card was dated three days earlier so we knew the operation was over. No other word came and we began to look forward to having Mamma and Papa at home again. He had written, but because the mail was still being brought out to Othello three days a week, it had not reached us.

One evening as Nellie, Otis and I came down the hill after leaving Miss Pape and Flossie at McCulloch's corner, we saw Billie's team and buggy coming from our house. Instead of coming on to pass us, he made a short turn and remained waiting just beyond the railroad grade. That seemed odd. He would ordinarily have met us with a joking remark, but this time he seemed strangely silent as he waited for us to get into the buggy, then headed the team for our house. In a moment he said quietly, "I don't know how to tell you children, but your mother is dead."

That evening the family gathered again in the home knowing this time that there would always be one missing at the family gatherings. Along with the telephoned message from Papa were directions to arrange for the burial at Cunningham.

A thin covering of snow whitened the frozen ground as we started for Cunningham to meet the train bringing Papa and Mamma. The news had been carried around the community, and the depot platform was crowded with friends waiting there with us when the train came slowly to a stop and Papa stepped off alone.

In the bare little church a few simple arrangements were being made. A neighbor had taken the blooms from her few house plants to make a floral piece of callas and pink geraniums. It lay on the casket as we took our places near the front of the church, and waited with faces heavily veiled in black crepe for the services to begin. Elder Eaton, a minister of Mamma's faith had come from Cheney to conduct the burial service.

There was no funeral coach available, but a light wagon from Harry Snead's store was used to carry the casket to the cemetery. The cemetery was located on the hillside overlooking the town. Slowly, the light wagon led the way followed by horse-drawn rigs at a slow walk, with many following on foot to the grave side. A heap of bare earth lay beside the open grave.

Gently, the white flakes fell into the opening as the casket was lowered by means of long driving lines to the bottom of the grave. They continued to fall with the shovels of earth as former neighbors stepped forward, relieving one another in filling the grave and heaping it over Mamma's resting place. Reluctantly, we turned away to take up a bewildering life without her.

After nearly twenty-eight years of marriage, Papa now seventy years of age, must carry on alone with the five children who were yet at home. The problems seemed staggering. Dona's work as editor required her to continue on with the newspaper work, so a decision was made over the week-end that fun-loving Nellie, aged fourteen, would remain at home to keep Papa company and do the housework for the remainder of the school term.

Nellie brought her books home to continue her studies, and prepare for the eighth grade examination at the close of the school year. This she passed with high grades even though the last six weeks were spent without supervised study.

With the school year ended we were ready to watch the next phase of railroad construction.

Chapter XVI

The Railroad Comes

WE HAD BECOME used to the bare grade during all the months since the construction camps had moved on, leaving the graded road bed to settle and pack down during the winter months. It would have made a beautiful highway for buggies and horseback riding, straight and direct to Othello, but we had instructions from Papa to stay off the graded road bed. So far as I recall, no such tracks marred its surface. We used the rough rocky road that ran parallel to it along the right-of-way, which had been made during the construction.

Ours was a personal interest in that railroad. We had seen the surveyors at work; they had eaten at our table. We had seen the construction crews at work, and had visited the camps and gotten on good terms with the cooks. Homestead men with their teams, had worked on the grading, or hauled supplies for both horses and men at the camps. Some of our land had been sold to the railroad company. It was our railroad; any news of its progress was talked over and passed on. Then had come word that the tracks were being laid past Lind.

One day shortly after the school term was out, Otis came into the house in great excitement.

"There's smoke up there around the curve by Thorp's. It looks like train smoke!" All other activities were suspended while we went to see what he was talking about. Sure enough! There was smoke puffing up occasionally from some thing that was out of sight around the curve.

"Do you think it could be the train laying the track, Papa?" We thought it might be, but we hoped he would verify our hopes.

"Yes, *it* looks like that could be the work train laying the track," was his confirmation. He soon went back to his work, but we children continued watching to see who would be first to catch sight of the first train. Hardly daring to take our eyes off of the curve, we watched the puffs of smoke edge nearer to view.

"There it is!" we shouted a little while later as we saw loaded cars inch slowly into view, pushed along by the puffing engine. Our railroad was coming! It would cross our homestead and we felt almost a part of it. We hardly had time to play as we watched the work train come on around the hill, and start across McCulloch's land; there we could get a better view of the operation. Men swarmed around the train like ants around an ant hill. Eagerly, we watched.

First, was a flat car loaded with ties. Men working on top of the car moved the ties forward to the end of the car where they were grasped by other teams of men on the ground, and carried forward to be laid parallel with the ones already laid. Like an endless belt, the workers paired up to receive and lay the ties. When enough were in place, other men with long iron bars carried the rail forward and placed it on the ties. Then we heard the pounding of the heavy sledges as the spikes were driven, and the clank of metal when the angle bars were placed and bolted to connect the rails to make immovable joints. Cautiously, the train moved onto the newly laid track. Only a few miles of track could be laid each day as man power alone was used in laying the track.

How odd it seemed to see the short train gradually working its way across the fields where never a train had been before! As the day ended, the train now loaded with men instead of ties and rails, cautiously made its way back over the newly laid rails to where the rest of the work train had been left, leaving the track clear for a closer inspection on our part. Our house was about three eighths of a mile from the nearest point of the track.

"Papa, can we go up now and see the railroad?" Otis had been wanting to go before, but Papa thought it best for us to stay away from where the large crew was working.

"It won't hurt anything now for us to go," I added my plea,

just as eager as was Otis to see the new track. When Papa gave his consent we were off on a run to inspect and try to hold our balance on the new-laid rails.

Soon after the tracks were laid through Othello, construction of the round house and depot was begun in confirmation of the word that Othello would be the division point. A manually operated turn-table for turning the engines around was installed. This one was replaced a few years later by a longer power-operated one to accomodate the big Mallet engines, and new stalls were added to the round house. A water tank, freight sheds and side tracks were built. The first depot was a very crude affair, but before the railroad was put into operation with passenger service, a real depot with a lunch room inside opened for business. Various local town and homestead girls worked at "The Beanery" from time to time.

Much remained to be done before the railroad could start running trains, and regular passenger and freight service begun. Heavy freight wagons continued to haul building supplies and other freight from points on the Northern Pacific railroad. We saw the work trains passing back and forth at moderate speeds as the track was settled more firmly in preparation for the cars heavily loaded with gravel for ballasting the road bed.

1908—1910. The railroad yards looking north from the roundhouse, showing turntable in foreground, water tank, train. Center: Steam from engine obscures ice house, freight house and depot. Square white building at right was the Milwaukee Hotel built in 1907.

A side track was laid a half mile from our place where the railroad crossed the section line road between McCulloch's and Bartons. After passenger service started the train could be flagged there to take on passengers though no depot or other buildings were located at that place. We could buy tickets to Novara, the name given the siding; a ticket from Othello to Novara cost a dime. Sometimes there was a slip-up like the one that happened to one passenger on the short run.

I was working in town and wanted to go out home for a short stay. Rather than walk the three miles out home, and wanting a little train ride, I went to the depot, bought a ticket and boarded the train for Novara. I showed my ticket as I got on, but after the train started, the conductor was a bit slow in taking up the tickets. It was only a seven or eight minute ride to my station, and he had gotten interested in two young women a bit farther back in the coach; the train was getting nearer and nearer to my destination. We were within half a mile of where I was to get off when he finally got to where I was inwardly stewing. I gave a sigh of relief.

After taking my ticket he passed on out of the coach, and I expected the train to slow to a stop and let me off. It never paused. The next stop would be Warden, thirteen miles further. The situation for a fifteen year old girl with only twenty-five cents in her pocket, was quite disturbing. There would be no more trains going toward home until next morning. I knew then his mind had not been on his work when he punched my ticket.

A brakeman came through the train a few minutes later. "Mister, my ticket was to Novara," I timidly told him. "You've carried me past my station." He checked the stub beside my seat, whistled, and said, "Sure enough," then passed on out of the coach.

"What is the conductor going to do about this?" I asked the brakeman as I got off the train at the next stop. "I haven't enough money to keep me over night at Warden."

"Go into the depot. The conductor will take care of it."

Inside the depot, the conductor was talking to someone on the phone. When he hung up the receiver he turned to me.

"I have ordered a rig to take you back home," he said. "It will be here in a little while. You wait here."

When the driver of the buggy heard the whole story on the way home, for he had been curious as to why the conductor of the train had ordered the rig, he had a hearty laugh over my ten cent ride which cost the conductor several dollars. It was nearly ten o'clock when I got home from what should have been a ten minute ride. Papa was asleep.

The night passenger trains going west from Othello were not giving quite the same personal service to the girls living around Corfu and Smyrna. No. 17, later called the Columbian, left Othello about 2:30 in the morning, and stopped at these small stations farther west toward the river only when flagged, or for mail and express. This created a problem for the girls living on the homesteads who wanted to attend the occasional dance or social event in Othello. They could come to town on the late afternoon train, but there was no way to get home afterward.

One day Orton Gilbert was notified there was an express package for him at the express office. He was handed a gunny sack containing something which seemed to be carefully wrapped with straw to prevent breakage. He had come to town on horseback, so without stopping to unwrap the object, he loaded it onto his horse for the ride home. Carefully, he unwrapped it. It contained only straw.

"Wal, I'll be a horned toad! Now who could a done that?" he exclaimed as he scratched his head in perplexity. The mystery continued to puzzle him until a few days later when he met one of the girls.

"Did you get the package we sent you Orton?" she asked, and laughed.

"You sent me that package o' straw?" he questioned. "Why? I don't need no straw." Then he learned what was behind the mystery. The girls, contriving a way to get home had arranged to send the dummy package knowing the train would have to stop for express delivery, and they could get off.

1908. Nellie on Snowball with Anna Chavis. New building at right is Crawford building at First and Main. Mendel's butcher shop far right. Picture looking north from near Broadway and Hemlock. Building at right, Ogden building.

Chapter XVII

Development and Dust

"HELLO, TIP! Has that sprocket come that you ordered for me?" Mac was shouting into the phone since the reception was not clear.

"Hello, Mac!" Tipton shouted back into the extended mouth piece to make himself heard at the other end of the line. "Yes, it came out today. Is there anything else you need to get that machine to working?"

J. H. Tipton had joined forces with his father-in-law in expanded farming, and the first telephone to be installed in the neighborhood was put in at the McCulloch homestead.

The telephone line consisted of a single strand of wire, fastened with small insulators to two by fours which in turn were nailed to fence posts along the section line road. It joined the main line, which was of similar construction, a half mile east of Othello. A crank on the side of the phone box was used to call other parties. With poor reception, Mr. Mac would shout his message into the mouth piece and in turn, Tipton, at his store in Othello, would shout back again until the conversation became public knowledge throughout the store.

In explaining the combined set-up, Tipton was heard to say jocosely, "I furnish the money and Mac does the work." Whatever the arrangement, it brought new activities around the McCulloch homestead. A large barn and haymow was built to accomodate the greater number of horses which were now needed. A separate barn to house the big black stallion was set off inside a strong board fence in one corner of the barn lot; here he reared and romped in excitement when the barn lot was filled with horses, the sun bringing out the highlights in his glistening coat.

"Flossie, when you are hunting eggs and nests, you must never go around the stallion's barn," her father told her, "He might trample you to death."

A cattle barn was built, and two more strands of barbed wire were added to the one strand fence to enclose the herd of cattle. The herd was being increased, and a herd sire had been added to the herd. That field was the one we crossed when going over to the May's, but after the bull was put in the field, no one had to caution us to stay out of the field. We went around.

Tipton bought the section of land lying east of McCulloch's homestead, and it was put under cultivation by Mr. Mac with the help of two hired men. He also leased the section of land north of our homestead; it contained the small lake where Otis and I got our supply of poliwogs.

Along with the plowing and harrowing came dust storms as more homesteads were denuded of the sage brush and bunch grass, and the light soil freed to be picked up by the wind. Women on the homesteads found their housekeeping problems increasing, and unless they could adopt a philosophical attitude, somewhat discouraging when the morning's cleaning was all undone in the afternoon as wind-borne dust filled the air and formed a film where the children could write their names and draw pictures on every flat surface. Sometimes the dust storms were very dense.

One day in the late spring, we noticed one coming from the northeast, a rather unusual thing as they more frequently came from the southwest. It was a high wall of boiling dust that swallowed up the landscape, and shut out the view of houses and other landmarks as it advanced. It appeared to be three or four miles in width, and extended high into the air. From its density, it was easily seen that anyone caught out in it might be smothered to death.

About the same time we noticed the coming storm, we also saw a team and buckboard coming on a dead run from toward McCulloch's corner. It was evident the driver had seen the fearful danger, and was making every effort to reach the safety of our

146

place before the storm struck him. Word was sent to Papa who was working in the barn and had not seen the wall of dust, nor the rapidly approaching team and wagon. Quickly, he went to open the barnyard gate to admit Charley Morgan who lived on west of us. Together, they unhitched the team and hurriedly led them into the barn; then they ran for the house, getting there as the storm struck.

"I was afraid I wasn't going to make it," Charley said as they stood panting in the kitchen. "This is the worst I've ever seen."

"You could have been smothered to death in this, Charley." Papa shook his head as he looked out the window.

The light of the sun dimmed, and was shut out; the interior of the house darkened as the dust engulfed us. Everything outside was blotted out, and the air inside the house began to get hazy from the fine dust nothing could keep out. A kerosene lamp was lit to dispel the gloom. We could only gaze in awe at the windows beyond which nothing could be seen but the boiling dust.

For a half hour it continued without let-up. Suddenly, a ball of mud struck the window to be followed by more. Mud-streaks began to gather on the glass as raindrops fell faster and faster. The rain shower lasted only five minutes, but when it stopped the windows were clean; the air was sweet and clear with no trace of the turmoil which had filled it only a few minutes before. The men went on with their customary duties. Inside, the fine dust gradually settled gently onto every surface to wait for the housekeeper's broom, mop and dust cloth.

The population in Othello increased rapidly as the railroad drew some of the people from the areas surrounding the town who had proved up on their homesteads and were looking for more adequate sources of income. Some went to work for the railroad, while others went into business, or worked for others already established.

Jay and Ollie Kellenberger moved into town from their place near the Estep homestead east of town, and Jay went to work in Tipton's store. M. E. Morgan and his family from south of town did the same. Harry and Essie Gregg built a house in the northeast part of town and moved from their homestead, and Don P. Estep, with his large family of nine children increased Othello's population when he went to work on the rip track. Another family who came early to locate in Othello was the J. W. Reynolds family from up toward Warden. J. W. and his son Loren went into the feed and grocery business together. Over the years Mrs. Reynolds came to be known as Grandmother Reynolds for her wide interest in the activities of the town and its people. Earl K. Reynolds and his brother Loren, whose father lived on a homestead south of town, became a part of the progress the new town was making.

Later, Jim and Joe McManamon, who with their brother Tom had been early settlers and cattle and sheep men along Crab Creek, either built homes or went into business in town. All felt that Othello had a bright future; but it is doubtful if they reckoned on the number of years it would take. At that time the coming of water for irrigation was still a dream of the future. Other increases to the population came.

"Gaynell's baby was born last night. It is a boy, and the first baby to be born in Othello." Mrs. Chavis had come in to the newspaper office one morning when Dona came to start the day's work, with this bit of news.

The son of Seth and Gaynell Tiffany Smith, arriving in December of 1907, had won over all contestants for the honor. A few months later, on May 30, 1908, the first baby girl, Inez Hamilton made her entry, to be followed the same day by another boy, Joseph Perle Tice. He came to make his home with Jim and Iva. The same doctor, J. W. Tulles, with the assistance of Lottie Mason (who afterward married Will Chavis), officiated at both of these later entries.

All babies were born right at home, usually with the help of the doctor (if the team got him there fast enough), and some woman from the neighborhood. Occasionally, the doctor lost out in the race and arrived minutes late to find a crying baby and a flustered nurse.

The doctor made a tardy appearance at the May home two weeks later when a second boy was born to Mary and Billie. A phone call was made to Cunningham for Dr. Tulles, and a woman who often assisted with such cases was brought out from Othello. Something was done before the doctor got there that started an infection. When a high fever developed the doctor was called back to find his patient with a serious case of septicemia. It called for quick emergency action; an operation was necessary and the nearest hospital was at Spokane, too far away to take the patient. The railroad doctor and hospital had moved on and the trains were not yet running.

"Bill, we shall have to do a curettment; it is the only way we can save her life," the doctor explained. "Is there any good woman near here you could get to assist me? Do you know of any nurse anywhere around?" he asked.

"Could we send to Spokane for a nurse?" Billie asked anxiously. "I don't know of any nurse around here."

"It would take too long for a nurse to come from Spokane. This must be done as quickly as we can get her ready."

"Then the best person I know is Mrs. McCulloch, our neighbor just north of us." Then turning to Nellie who had been helping with the housework during Mary's confinement, Billie said, "Nellie, you help the doctor until I get back. I am going after Mrs. McCulloch."

The dining table, extended to full length and covered with a sterile sheet, would have to serve as the operating table; and with the careful assistance of a kind neighbor, the doctor was able to do the necessary remedial work. When it was over and the patient was again returned to her bed, the doctor gave further instructions while washing up.

"Mrs. McCulloch, I greatly appreciate your assistance. Now can you stay on until I can have a nurse sent down from Spokane? I will phone for one at once, and bring her out from Cunningham as soon as she arrives." Doctor Tulles knew that now it depended on the most careful nursing to bring his patient through after he had done all he could.

149

"Yes, Doctor, I will stay. How soon will the nurse be here?" Mrs. McCulloch's quiet voice assured the doctor.

"I will phone from Carl's Drug Store in Othello, so we should have a nurse down on the late evening train," he told her as he prepared to leave.

The nurse arrived on schedule and immediately excluded everyone from the sick room permitting Billie a brief visit once a day at first. Mosquito netting was put up to cover the windows to eliminate flies while permitting plenty of fresh air. A cot was moved into the sick room for the nurse's use, though she never removed her clothes to sleep for nearly two weeks. Those were anxious days. Edith Whittaker knew her patient's life hung in the balance, and day or night she was on her feet at the least sound until the crisis finally passed. Mary's fever went down and gradually she returned to health.

Tears dimmed the eyes of both patient and nurse when the moment of parting came; they had been drawn close in the battle they had fought together.

We saw very little of the new baby during the illness of his mother, though now and then we saw the nurse sterilizing bottles and preparing the formula since the natural source of his food had failed. He had been given the name of Phillip Tice May, combining the name of Billie's father and Mary's family name.

Nellie stayed on with them during this time to do the cooking and care for Willie who was just under two years old. At home, Dona cooked the morning meals while still continuing the newspaper work in town. She left right after breakfast. This left the dishwashing and lighter work for Otis and me to do during the day, though sometimes play and outdoor adventures saw the dishes still waiting until late in the afternoon. We did not particularly enjoy doing the dishes when there were so many more enjoyable things we could do outside, but along late in the afternoon, the knowledge that Dona would soon be coming home sent us to the house where a hurried splashing of dishwater averted the deserved censure.

"Laura, would you like to take these little turkeys home to

raise?" Billie had seven little newly-hatched baby turkeys in a box he was holding out to me. Would I! Then I wondered if he meant I could keep them.

"Do you mean I can keep them?" I asked, thrilled at the prospect of having those baby turkeys.

"Yes, if you take care of them and raise them, they are yours," he assured me.

Mary had been raising turkeys that spring, and a small setting of them hatched out while she was sick. Something had happened to the hen, and here were the babies needing TLC which Billie had no time to give. His offer was eagerly accepted.

I brought them home and made an improvised nursery in one corner of the kitchen. Two of the weaker ones died and were given burial with appropriate rites; the others grew rapidly and the shallow box which was their nursery soon had to be replaced with a deeper one as their wing feathers grew and their jumping powers increased. They became so tame from all the handling they received they could be picked up anywhere. Even after they were transferred to the chicken house for sleeping quarters at Papa's insistance, they seemed to think the kitchen was their proper residence, and hung around the kitchen door, on which there was no screen, and came in at every opportunity.

After we finished the noon meal one day, and Papa had pushed his chair back from the table to take his after-dinner nap, some of those six-weeks old turkeys entered the kitchen to pick up stray crumbs under the table. Before I could scare them out, or pick up the broom to sweep out the crumbs, Headley grabbed one, rushed to the back door and tossed it high into the air.

"Don't do that; you'll hurt them," I yelled at him as it came fluttering down in a heap. I tried to stop him, but another and another was snatched up and given the same treatment. Alarmed for the safety of my pets I took after him, but he was having a hilarious time by then. Nellie joined in the fun, setting one on the broom to flip it high into the air. By that time my temper was triggered, and with gritted teeth I went after them. Around the house they ran and in through the front door, with me furiously trying to catch them and avenge the mistreatment of my pets. They paused as they raced through the kitchen just long enough to pick up and toss another of those silly turkeys which kept coming back into the house again.

Frustrated because they could run faster and I could not catch them or stop their fun, on the third round through the kitchen, I jumped to a chair and reached for the loaded twenty-two rifle. Desperately I thought, "If I can't stop them in one way, I can another."

"Papa, Papa, Laura's getting the gun!" they yelled in alarm. That brought him awake to see what was going on.

"Laura, Laura, what are you doing with that?" he asked as he saw my hand on the rifle.

Amid sobs, I told what had happened. Sternly he rebuked them and brought an end to their fun. It was easy to get me mad and crying; and that often made me the butt of their teasing. My sense of humor needed developing.

Othello School—1910. 7th and 8th grades. Teacher, D. L. Haile. Front Row L-R: Helen Wade Crabb, Nora Estep, Hazel Pebbles, Lora Estep. Rear Row: Fannie Phillips, Florence Ogden, Dewey Crabb, Iva Billington, Ina Tiffany, Lillian Hatfield. Courtesy of Mrs. Walter Krause.

Chapter XVIII

Adventures

IT WAS TIME for school to begin again and we were as eager for it to begin as we had been for it to close in the spring. Rising Star expected only ten pupils this term since some had completed the eight grades and others had moved away. The Rice family had moved away so Alberta and Irma could have better educational advantages.

Ethel, Xerpha, Nellie and Nellie Barton were ready for high school, having completed the eight grades of the country school. Xerpha was going back to Ritzville for her second year and Nellie, too, was starting high school there. Ethel decided to go to Cheney and prepare for teaching, and the other Nellie went to stay with a married sister in Myrtle Point, Oregon. Most homestead girls found it necessary to work for their room and board while attending high school.

The two-story brick school building in Othello was nearing completion. Grace Grantham was employed to teach the thirty-six weeks term there. That school had grown as more people moved to the new town, many of them from the homesteads.

Our teacher at Rising Star was pretty, pink-cheeked Emza Hiday, a Quaker girl with soft brown eyes and a smiling face. We immediately fell in love with her. Not only was she a good teacher in helping us to acquire book learning, but she shared our play on the school ground at times, and planned special events outside the regular school program. A Thanksgiving dinner at school to which each child brought something; an interchange of visits between our school and the Billington school, were some of the things to be credited to her. She was only a few years older than her oldest pupil, but we felt she loved every one of us. One of her interests was elocution. She

Deadman's Bluff.

had won several silver and gold medals when speaking in Temperence contests in her home state of Indiana. These added to our admiration for our teacher.

Always in the autumn, came a week-long vacation for the pupils when the Teachers' Institute was held in Ritzville. When word came that several contests would be held in connection with the Institute in which representatives from the schools could participate, Emza's interest centered on the declamatory contest. A gold medal was to be awarded the winner. Near the close of one school day, Emza brought the subject up to her school room.

"The Superintendent of Schools has sent word there are to be several contests at the Institute this year," she informed us. "Each school may send a contestant to one of the contests."

"W-w-what kind of contests, M-m-miss Hiday?" asked Flossie. Flossie was in the sixth grade, and a very studious girl.

"There will be contests in spelling, arithmetic and a declamatory contest," Miss Hiday replied, and added, "I would like for our little school to be represented in one of them."

"What's a declam, or what you said that other contest is?" asked one of the children, puzzled by the long word.

"A declamatory contest? That is where you speak pieces or give a recitation," she answered, smiling.

Our enthusiasm began to build up as she told us of the honor it would be to represent our school. Representatives from the third, fourth and fifth grades could take part in the spelling and arithmetic contests, but only sixth, seventh and eighth grade pupils might enter the declamatory contest. All expenses to and from Ritzville, as well as room and board while there, would be paid.

"Wouldn't it be nice if we could bring the gold medal to our school?" our teacher continued after telling us what prizes were to be awarded in the various contests. "I believe we could."

We had no eighth grade that year; Edith and Flossie were in the sixth grade, and I was the only seventh grade pupil. Those who were in the fourth and fifth grades wanted no part in the

155

spelling or arithmetic contests, but as the girls in the two eligible grades listened to Emza outline a plan for the declamatory contest our timidity began to melt away.

"If we should decide on the declamatory contest," Miss Hiday said, "only Edith, Flossie and Laura would be eligible to go to Ritzville, but we would have a program here to decide who should go, and you could all take part in that." The school lost no time in deciding that should be the contest to enter.

She further outlined a plan for the girls taking part. "You may each select a reading you like and that you think would be interesting to give; then commit it to memory. It must be letter perfect so it will come automatically, no matter how scared you may feel when you get up to give it."

She promised to rehearse us, give us pointers in diction, expression and clearness in speaking. "It will be good for you to practice before the home folks and before the mirror when you are alone so you can get used to the sound of your own voice, and watch your expression," she explained.

Flossie selected, "Asleep at the Switch," a touching piece with dramatic possibilities. Mine was a humorous tirade against a tobacco-chewing husband that Dona had once given, called, "An Old Woman's Complaint." The decision on who was to represent the school was to be made on the local level at a program and box social planned for the evening of our local contest.

The crucial evening came, with some very excited girls wondering who would win. Edith had been late in starting to school that term and it seemed that either Flossie or I stood the best chance to win.

While waiting for the crowd to gather and the program to begin, Flossie turned to me and said, "Let me wish your ring on." It was game we often played.

"All right!" My ring was promptly handed to her, and my finger held out for her to replace it as she made a silent wish. The ring was supposed to remain in place until such time as she designated; if taken off before the designated time, it would break the wish.

"Take it off in the morning," she directed.

The question kept recurring to me; "What would she be most likely to wish at this time?" Quietly, I slipped the ring from my finger and replaced it without being seen. Self-interest was going to take no chances in any little gimmick causing me to lose; at least I thought so.

There was a grave doubt in my mind which I had voiced to her, whether I should be able to go to Ritzville even if I should be the winner at our school. It was a matter of clothes. Since Mamma was gone my clothes were getting quite limited, especially anything suitable to go on a train, or appear before a large group of teachers.

Before the evening was over, Mary and Dona had put their heads together and decided they could manage to make me presentable for the occasion.

"That gray wool skirt we made for Mamma to wear to Seattle on the train would be enough to make Laura a dress, wouldn't it, Mary?"

"I am sure it would be. You know Mamma had us make it with pleats instead of gores." Mary was remembering quietly. "Do you suppose she thought possibly she might not need it again?" That would have been another example of Mamma's forethought. "I'll make a jumper dress out of it."

Dona lengthened a white dress Mamma had made for me the previous summer, and did it up carefully. These few things were carefully packed in a small canvas telescope for the trip.

The Institute began on Monday and continued all week, but the contest in which I was to enter came Wednesday evening. That made it necessary for me to go up alone, something I had never done before. It was a thirty-five mile trip, and the first part was by stage to Cunningham and change to the train there. My train ticket would have to be bought at that point.

The stage operated by Chavis from Othello to Cunningham was a three-seated open hack. It left Othello at seven in the morning to arrive at Cunningham in time for the noon train. I stayed over night with the Chavises in order to be there early enough in the morning.

My trip nearly ended in Cunningham when the ticket agent paid no attention to my timid face at the ticket window. He evidently thought I was just a child with someone else. The train pulled in and stopped for the short period it took to take on passengers and discharge the small amount of freight.

Nearly frantic, but too timid to speak up and interrupt his conversation with another man, my heart was rising higher and higher into my throat in a sob when Dr. Tulles came into the depot. He seemed to immediately take in the situation and briefly asked if I wanted to take the train. I nodded mutely.

"Here, Agent," he said with quick authority, "This little girl wants a ticket." It brought quick action, and I got to the train just as the porter was starting to remove the little step. The train was beginning to move as I went up the steps. Had the doctor "just happened" to come into the depot at that particular moment, or had the One who takes note of the little sparrow seen my need, and taken care of it in His own way?

My teacher was waiting at the depot in Ritzville, and was at the train to slip her arm around me as I came down the steps. A big weight slipped from my shoulders. I had wondered if the train would stop at Ritzville to let me off; or if she would be at the depot to meet me; or if I should be able to find her in the large crowd I saw waiting as the train slowed to a stop.

A quick introduction to another teacher who had come to the train with her was followed by a question and suggestion.

"You haven't had your dinner yet have you?" asked Emza. "It is a little late for us to go up to where some of the teachers are boarding. We haven't had our dinner either, but we can go to a restaurant down here in town." That would be another new experience for me, and soon we were seated at a small table.

"You may order anything on the menu that you like," she told me. I looked at the menu on which were listed the kinds of

The author as an 8th grade graduate in 1910—wearing the gold
medal won at the Teacher's Institute in 1908.

159

meat dinners at thirty-five cents. The only ones I recognized were beef steak and pork chops.

We spent the afternoon at the institute, then went for our supper at the teacher's boarding place where I was the only child among the many teachers. Then it was time to get ready for the contest.

With freshly brushed and braided hair on which Miss Hiday tied a new hair ribbon she had purchased for me, we made our way to the church where the contest was to be held. She gave me an extra hug to give a lift to my courage, and left me to go sit with the modest sized audience. Many of the teachers preferred an evening at the skating rink, or some more entertaining recreation after weeks spent with children in the country schools.

I was taken to a small room where two other girls about my age were waiting for J. H. Perkins, the County Superintendent to announce the rules, and numbers on the program.

In turn, with rapidly beating hearts, each contestant ascended the two steps to the center of the stage and spoke her piece, then returned to the small room to await the decision of the judges. Heart beats came back to normal as we wondered who would win. It was no longer in our hands. Soon Superintendent Perkins came to the room where we waited.

"When I announce the name of the winner," he said, "I would like for her to come onto the stage again to be presented to the audience and receive the award." I thought he talked a bit more directly to me as he explained the next step; but did that mean anything? With a few preliminary remarks he announced the name of the winner. My teacher was as thrilled as her pupil that the representative of her school won.

The next Monday the gold medal was taken to school so all the other pupils could see what our school had won; then it was back to fractions, parsing sentences and learning history dates as usual. The brief moment of glory could not be allowed to interfere with school work.

One evening when we got home from school we found Papa had company. It was a bit unusual for Papa, and he was just a

160

bit apologetic as he took us aside to explain the circumstances. The guest was Joe Quinn, a bachelor homesteader who had a homestead farther over in the rimrocks northwest of our place. Joe was in an inebriated condition, and in process of becoming more so. Sometime before, he had sent a large packing box of groceries to our place to be left until he came; then he with his groceries could be taken to his homestead.

"When I was down in town today, I ran across Quinn," Papa told us. "I saw he had been drinking a little, but when he asked me to bring him out home and then take him on to his homestead tomorrow, I couldn't very well refuse. He was so good to Headley this fall." Papa continued, "I didn't know he had another quart of whiskey with him, but I felt obligated to him." That obligation had come about following a hunting accident.

John and Rupert Chavis, with Headley, had gone duck hunting on some lakes over near Crab Creek. They left the team and buggy at the south end of Crescent Lake, and used an old raft to convey them to the upper end. A low strip of ground lay between Crescent Lake and Deadman's Lake on which they saw some ducks.[1] Leaving the raft, they managed to get a shot at the flock of ducks on the upper lake. One duck was killed and dropped into the water, but the rest took flight. As the ducks showed no disposition to alight and give them another shot, they decided to go back to the raft to recover the duck they had shot.

Headley laid his gun down against a grease-wood bush, forgetting to uncock it. They had gone only a few steps when they saw the flock had returned and was preparing to settle on the water near by. Turning back, he hastily grabbed up the shotgun, catching the trigger on a twig and firing the gun. The full load of shot missed his chest and plowed across his upper left arm below the shoulder muscle, taking the flesh and laying bare the bone.

The boys were stunned by the accident, and scared. They were

[1]Originally, the lake lying north of Crescent Lake, and reaching to the north end of Deadman's Bluff was called Deadman's Lake. It is now called Morgan Lake. A lake south of Crescent Lake has now been given the name of Deadman Lake.

miles from home, and some distance from where they left the team. Then they remembered that a family by the name of Brown lived above another lake just south of Crescent Lake. They might get some help there. Leaving his gun where it had fallen, they headed back to the buggy and the Brown's homestead, with blood saturating his clothes.

Mrs. Brown did what she could in the way of first aid before the boys started to find a doctor.

"There isn't any doctor at Othello now," Brown told them, "The nearest one is at Warden. You boys better head for there."

"Should we go by home and tell Papa what has happened?" Headley was white-faced from fear and loss of blood.

"No, that would be farther and out of the way. It is seventeen miles from here," Brown explained.

"Rupert, you go by and tell Mr. Tice, and I'll drive to Warden with Headley. You can explain what has happened," John was the older of the boys.

Headley had remained in Warden to be near the doctor, and had boarded and roomed with Joe Quinn who had a restaurant there. Joe would never take any pay for the two weeks Headley stayed with him. Now Papa couldn't refuse to entertain Joe.

That was a hilarious evening for the boys. To see that fat, partially bald-headed man dancing around the kitchen, quoting Shakespeare, and attempting to display his histrionic ability, was the funniest sight they had seen in some time.

There had been some problems in the preparation of the evening meal. Joe was a good cook. He wanted to be helpful, especially with the biscuit making. I met Dona at the horse-trough. "Dona, don't eat any of the biscuits; Old Joe helped me make them, and he didn't wash his hands before sticking his fingers in the dough."

Those biscuits were light and fluffy, but Dona and I abstained. Papa and the boys seemed to think them superior to the ones I offered them. Doubtless they were, in lightness.

After supper Papa withdrew to the front room, inviting Quinn to join him there. But Joe was enjoying his more appreciative audience in the kitchen. He was still imbibing from his bottle but Papa had turned down all of Joe's offers to "have a drink" from the bottle which was rapidly becoming emptied with no other help.

"Miss Dona, you're a great elocutionist, and I am a great historian," Joe extolled as he quoted Shakespeare. Dona and I took refuge upstairs as soon as the dishes were put away.

Next morning, when the effects of the drink had been slept off, he was a most embarrassed man. He apologized to Papa, and sent his apologies to "Miss Dona." Though his apologies were accepted he was too ashamed to come in for breakfast. We never learned whether his embarrassment reformed him.

Dona Tice, editor, The Othello Times, 1908.

Chapter XIX

Another Year Passes

SEVERAL INCHES OF SNOW fell just before Christmas, insuring at least a Christmas setting. Then the weather turned clear and colder. The snow squeaked under our feet as we walked, and the wagon wheels made musical sounds in the cold exhilarating air. Diamond lights sparkled on the snow in the sunlight, giving off iridescent colors of the real gems. At night, the full moon cast bluish tints over the landscape and straw stacks now wearing their winter ermines. Stars twinkled with greater brilliancy through the dry cold air. Christmas vacation was nearing when the girls who were away in high school would be coming home for the holidays.

This Christmas would be different, but we still felt that Christmas was a happy time. It must have been difficult for Papa as he contrasted this Christmas with the previous one. We had often come home from school in the late afternoon and seen him wiping tears from his eyes as we came in the kitchen door, but he made no mention of his loneliness.

"The Christmas program is going to be at the Othello school," Dona told us one evening when she came home from work. "All the people living around Othello will be included in it."

"Can we go, Dona?" We had not gone to a Christmas program since the winter we were in Cunningham, and Otis and I were eager to go.

"I don't think so," was her disappointing reply. "John will take Nellie and me, and there won't be room in the buggy for all of us." John was Billie's brother who had come out from Missouri. But Dona had not heard a suggestion John had made to Headley.

"Headley, why don't you ask Miss Hiday if you can take her

to the Christmas program? You can take her in the buggy." Headley was nearly seventeen and John knew he had never gone with a girl. "I dare you to ask her."

Under pressure of John's dare, Headley decided to ask her to go. But when he suggested it to her, she countered with a suggestion of her own.

"That is kind of you Headley, but why don't you get a larger rig, or hack, and we can take your sisters and the McCulloch girls, too. That would be fun if we all go together."

"At least she can sit with me on the front seat," he told us at home. "I will be driving the team. I'm glad she didn't turn me down."

Christmas eve came. From some source the two boys had secured the use of a topless two-seated hack in which to go. Headley was elated to have Emza and Xerpha ride with him on the front seat, with Nellie, Dona and John occupying the second seat. A small space back of the rear seat in the bed of the hack served as a rumble seat for Flossie and me.

"You'd ought to sit between the two girls and let them keep you warm, Headley," teased Mr. Mac. It tickled him to see Headley color with embarrassment as he helped the girls to the front seat.

"Be sure to keep well wrapped up," Mrs. McCulloch cautioned us, tucking in the edges of the quilts and blankets we were using for lap robes. "It is going to be cold riding. Flossie, are you going to be warm enough?"

"Yes, Mamma, we shall be real warm back here," she assured her mother.

The moon and every visible star seemed to turn on its brightest radiance for the occasion. The Pleiades, with its seeming small cluster of stars, was using its "sweet influences" to calm the night, while the astral hunter, with his belt and sword, stood out boldly as he stalked the heavenly meadows.

The crowd was beginning to gather at the little one-room school building which had been moved into town. Its windows were all alight as we approached after the four mile ride in the biting air behind the trotting team.

Several reflector type kerosene lamps fastened to opposite walls shown down on the rapidly filling room. The odor of fir greeted us as we entered the door and caught our first breath-taking glimpse of the decorated tree at the front of the room.

Long strings of popcorn and cranberries with glittering tinsel strands were strung in festoons all over the tree. Colored balls and wax Christmas candles in a variety of colors were tied or clipped to the tips of the branches, wherever they could be displayed to the best advantage on the tree. It reached nearly to the ceiling. The candles would be lighted just before the program started.

There was a pleasant confusion from the group of children as more hurried to join their little friends near the front of the room where they could see every thing to advantage. Adults hurried back and forth carrying mysterious packages to add to the growing pile beside the tree, or to place the smaller ones among the boughs. These would be distributed later when Santa Claus arrived to help. First, came the program which had been prepared to include many of the children. Someone on the program committee had sent out a long poem for me to learn just two days before it was to be given. Since this insured me a chance to go if I would learn it, I made sure I learned the piece. Nor have I forgotten "The Legend of the Christmas Tree."

Songs, recitations and dialogues had been carefully rehearsed. If some shy child in the excitement of its first appearance before such a large audience forgot some line, and stood twisting a lock of hair, or corner of a dress until given prompting from the side-lines, the applause was no less generous for the effort made. Parents beamed with pride when their child spoke up clearly and finished without a hitch.

A few minutes of suspense ensued after the last part of the program was concluded. The children began to stir excitedly as a jingle of bells was heard outside and someone shouted, "Here's Santa now!" Every head was turned toward the door, and many of the children stood up in the excitement of the moment to catch their first glimpse of the white-whiskered, red-suited visitor.

"Hello, Santa!" "Hello, Santa!" came the greeting from all sides in answer to the "Merry Christmas, children!" of the merry old saint advancing down the aisle with a large bag of candy and nuts slung over his shoulder.

In the usual regalia of Santa Claus, Don P. Estep made a good saint though some extra padding was needed to round out his normally spare figure.

Gifts were distributed to those whose names appeared on the outside of each package; bags of candy and nuts from Santa's sack were passed around to each child. Then, with a "Merry Christmas, everybody," he was gone and we heard the sleigh bells jingle once more.

Though the names of our family had slight mention when the gifts were distributed, we returned home singing songs as the team jogged along to the sound of the wheels on the crisp snowy road. Snuggled down among the quilts behind the rear seat, Flossie and I were nearly asleep by the time we got home.

Thick ice formed on the lakes. Young people from town and the nearby homesteads converged on Dill Lake, now sometimes called Owl Lake, lying about two miles northwest of town. The lake took its name from the Dill family whose homestead lay beside the lake.

"Nellie, come on and go skating with us?" John and Headley were getting ready to go during the holiday while the ice was in good condition for that sport.

"I don't know how to skate. Besides, I don't have any ice skates," she replied, then added with an interested gleam in her eyes, "I'd sure like to learn." Nellie had been the first girl to ride Roanie while he was still a bit skittish, and from then on shared that fun with Headley when she was at home.

"Mary used to have a pair of ice skates," Headley remembered, "I wonder if she still has them. We can go and see." The boys had skates of their own.

The skates were hunted out and soon Nellie was having her first lesson in trying to stand erect on those thin blades. The sport of skating is not learned in one setting as she soon learned after several times finding her seat on the ice, but before the week was out she was doing a creditable job of swinging around the lake with the others. Then New Year's Day passed taking us all back to school again.

Early car in Othello in 1912, with the author posing at the wheel, beside the Hibbard Hotel. Shows conditions of the dusty roads.

Chapter XX

A Growing City

THE CONSTRUCTION CAMPS had long since completed the work of grading and moved on; the ties and rails had been laid through the area and on toward the coast, though there was still much ballasting of the road bed to be done. Work on the railroad buildings and the round house was nearing completion.

On March 29, 1909, word came that the last rail had been laid, completing the railroad to the coast. The report stated that train service would soon begin.

One of the new sights in Othello about this time was Josh Billings and his mules. Having once seen Josh and his long-eared team, you never again thought of them as separate entities; they seemed to belong together. The horse had long been the only means of transportation for man or his freight in that area, but Josh started a dray and transfer business using mule-power. It created an interesting diversion. They moved along at a slow easy-going pace that nothing seemed to fluster or hurry. Hitched to a covered van with open back, they meandered along, and if they were ever urged to trot all record of it is lost.

Everybody knew Josh, and liked him. He was of sturdy build with such a short neck he almost had to turn his body to look behind him. A twinkle in his eye belied the usual gravity of his rather staid expression, so his regular good humor may have been the reason for his name rather than an abbreviation of the Biblical Joshua. It is doubtful if anyone ever saw him or his mules out of humor.

The mules were a trim-lined team whose well-groomed coats glistened in the sunlight. Red felt trimmings with bright nickel adornments on the shiny black harness showed the pride and devotion of Josh toward his mules. Their long ears turned first one way than another like antennaes to catch any sounds or directions from their boss-partner.

Even though Josh was loyal to his mules most of the time, he was the first to drive an automobile down Othello's Main Street. The car was said to be an early EMF which Josh said stood for "Every-morning-fixit." The local teacher concluded Othello was a modern city with its first "Ah-tum-beel."

Josh needed another partner to keep things going at the livery barn while he was taking care of the transfer work. He found such a partner in little Billie Bartelt. Billie was short, probably not over five feet two or three inches tall, with a pronounced Dutch accent. His square rugged features were always ready to break into a wide smile whenever someone spoke to him. But Billie always carried the aroma of the livery stable with him wherever he was, possibly for lack of a wife.

Another early addition to Othello was a town marshall in the person of Rufus Pugh, another homesteader whose homestead lay southwest of town. Rufe was a tall man with a strong-boned frame which could handle any infraction of the public peace; not that there were many calls of a serious nature in those early days. Othello was a peaceful country town most of the time.

The town people were shocked one morning to hear that some stranger had been found murdered in a box car sitting on the side track. He apparently was a hobo who was taking a free ride on the train, but who was responsible for his death could not be determined, nor when it happened. Rufe had the help of the railroad detectives in investigating the murder since it had apparently happened on railroad property.

Another case, less serious, which Rufe cleared up in a short time, concerned another knight of the road.

It was the busy noon hour at the Shamrock Cafe, with only one waitress to fill the orders at the rapidly filling tables. One customer who had drawn her attention as she took his order, was a grimy individual whose clothes looked like they had been slept in. His whole appearance was that of what was usually termed a tramp, and a stranger in the area.

172

As the waitress went to the cashier's register to take payment of meals from some of the customers, she noted the stranger's place at the table was empty. He had slipped out through a side door without paying for his meal while she was getting another order from the kitchen.

"Mrs. Simonson, that tramp didn't pay for his meal," she informed her employer who was also the cook. "He must have sneaked out through the washroom."

"We'll send word to Rufe," and turning to one of her smaller boys she sent him on a run for the marshall. Rufe lost no time answering her call.

"Can you give me a description of the man?" he asked the waitress. She told him of his grimy appearance and his trampish looks.

Some half hour later, the marshall again came into the kitchen of the cafe with the stranger carrying a bed roll on his back.

"Is this the man?" Rufe wanted her identification of the man he had picked up down near the railroad preparing to board a freight train being made up to leave.

"Yes, this is the one," the waitress assured him.

"Why didn't you pay for your meal?" the marshall asked.

"I'm broke," was the answer from the man who had been apprehended.

"Do you think you can find some way of earning thirty-five cents for your meal before you leave town if I don't lock you up?" again questioned the marshall. "You can leave your bed roll here until you come back with the money."

A bit later in the afternoon the stranger again showed up to pay his bill and reclaim his bedding. Then instead of leaving town, he remained for some months to reveal he was quite an artist in painting scenic pictures. Some of his paintings were purchased by two of the saloon owners for their thirst-quenching emporiums. Doubtless some of the purchase price was taken out in trade.

Another unique character was a little old white-haired violin player. He lived all alone in a small shack below the railroad tracks. At one time he had played with some of the finest orchestras on the east coast, but his addiction to drink had ruined his career and now he was occasionally hired to play for some of the local dances. Even though frequent trips to his bottle, cached outside, during the evening found him swaying in his chair in an endeavor to keep upright, he never lost a beat in the music until he passed out.

Tipton's new store at the corner of Third and Main Streets was carrying on a thriving business in competition with Struppler's general merchandise store on First Avenue. Struppler had come up with a new way of giving better service to the housewives of the town who had no telephones yet with which to telephone their orders for groceries. One of his clerks, was sent around to each home right after the store opened in the morning, to receive their orders for the day. The order would then be delivered before noon in a little red cut-down car Struppler had put into delivery work.

Tipton did a large credit business, not only for those living in Othello, but for the surrounding farms and homesteads until he had thousands of dollars standing on his books. At times he carried debts from shortly after one harvest until the next year's harvest.

By the end of 1908 about forty families had come to make Othello their home. The town covered an area about six blocks from north to south and five blocks from east to west, with the houses somewhat scattered.

It was also in 1908 that the first Presbyterian church was organized in Othello.

Their first pastor was Reverend E. M. Landis who came from Connell every two weeks to conduct the services.

To reach Othello, Pastor Landis came to Cunningham by train, but there was no way of getting the rest of the way except to walk. Nothing daunted, he rolled up the cuffs of his trousers to start the seventeen mile hike to his appointment. Now and then a passing buggy would give him a lift for a few miles of the dusty road. Perhaps some thoughtful member took him home to

174

have dinner with them before he began the long trek back to catch the train going to Connell.

"Papa, the railroad is going to start through freight service pretty soon," Dona brought the news when she came home from the newspaper office one evening.

"Where did you hear that?" he asked.

"I heard them talking about it up at the post office when I went up to mail the newspapers."

"Did you hear them say when it would start?" Papa did not get to town very often to hear what was going on.

"I understood it will be around the 4th of July," she answered as she prepared to start supper.

As the report had said, train service was soon to start. On June 11, 1909, the first passenger train began service from Seattle to St. Maries, Idaho. This enabled those living along the railroad route to visit the Alaska-Yukon-Pacific Exposition which had started in Seattle the day before.

Such a happy occasion as the first passenger train would doubtless have seen all of Othello's people at the depot to witness the long-awaited event, but a terrible dust storm came up that day. The train could hardly make its way through Othello, and was compelled to stop for a while near Warden because of the density of the dust.

The storm extended to the A. O. Lee farm several miles east of town where a new cistern had just been cemented. Mrs. Lee and the three children, Helen, Lucille and wee baby Charles, climbed down into the cistern for safety. Johnny Chavis, who was carrying the mail from Cunningham that day, came along and got down into the cistern with them.

The wind was so strong the header boxes were moved around; chickens were blown away and lost, and plaster fell from the ceiling of their home. But when the storm was over and the dust settled, the sun shone serenely from a clear blue sky and meadow larks were singing from the fence posts in the clean sweet air.

Chapter XXI

Difficult Times

Times were getting more difficult at our house. The long siege of sickness with the typhoid fever, followed so quickly by Mamma's sickness, her operation, death and funeral expenses, had left Papa deeply in debt. Without her counsel he was at a loss to know how to manage ways of paying off his obligations, or planning for the future.

To satisfy a pressing debt, the two younger cows were sold, leaving the older cow to supply us with milk and butter. Since Nellie was away in school and not around to help with the milking there was no mourning on my part when the two cows were sold. But when Old Cherry dried up in preparation for her next calf, I found that eating biscuits without butter, and making both gravy and biscuits with only water, to go with the boiled potatoes, left much to be desired. We still had some sow belly to season the dried beans.

After the newspaper was gotten out on Friday, Dona's weekends were spent trying to catch up on the house cleaning, washing and ironing. There was little time or money for mending or replacing worn or outgrown clothing. It helped out when the warm spring days led the hens into making a greater contribution to our living, so fewer hens were set and we had fewer baby chicks that spring.

Now that winter was past, Dona was again riding a horse to her work. To save on hay, Snowball was turned out to graze after he had been fed in the evening. It was the chore for Otis and me to go out to the pasture and bring him to the barn before breakfast.

"Laura, Otis, its time to get up and go after the horse," we would hear Papa call about six o'clock in the morning. Dona was already up and starting down stairs. After two or three calls from Papa, we would get our eyes opened enough to get up and slip into our simple clothes. Snowball had to be fed and saddled for Dona to leave right after seven.

One spring morning we started out to the pasture after the pony, which was about a quarter of a mile walk from the house. We always carried a bridle with us so we could ride back to the house after we caught him. We had gone only a short distance when we came upon a rattlesnake which had crawled out of a ground squirrel hole to warm up in the morning sunshine. It was a bit sluggish but it managed to crawl back down into the hole when we threw a clod at it.

Knowing our first responsibility was getting the horse, we proceeded to push the hole in after it, first with clods, then by trampling it tighter with our bare feet.

"Now, Mr. Snake, we'll come back after breakfast and fix you," Otis told the snake.

"We can dig him out then, and kill him." I seconded the project.

Snowball was obliging that morning and let one of us get hold of his mane while the other stayed in the background with the bridle until the capture. (Sometimes he was not so co-operative and we had to walk back driving him before us.) Helping each other, we climbed onto his bare back for the ride home. Riding past the place where we had imprisoned the snake we found it just as we had left it.

"Papa, we found a rattlesnake out in the field past the pig pen," Otis told Papa at the breakfast table.

"We threw clods at him, and he crawled down a squirrel hole," I hurried to add to the story. Papa was listening as soon as he heard us mention seeing a rattlesnake. From time to time he found and killed them.

"We threw clods and dirt into the hole and trampled it in real tight," we were both trying to talk at once. "We're going back out there after breakfast and dig him out and kill him."

"You'll never see that snake again," Papa told us, "He'll be

178

a long way from there by the time you get back out there." That didn't sound like he was optimistic about our being able to carry out our designs on the snake. We hoped he was wrong.

Right after breakfast, armed with spade and hoe, we started opening up that hole. The second spade full of dirt turned out the snake. He didn't have a chance against two homestead children armed with such effective weapons, and soon we had the dead snake draped around the hoe and on our way to the barn to show Papa. It was the first time we had killed a rattlesnake, and we felt quite proud of our valor.

Mamma had promised Headley a rifle if he would not smoke before he was eighteen. She probably felt if he did not smoke befc ⸲ he was that age he would have sense enough to never start the nabit. But he was only sixteen when she died, so he saved what money he could earn and bought a 25-35 Winchester rifle. He was very proud of it and warned us younger children never to touch it.

One day when Otis and I were at home alone, we saw a coyote sauntering along out a little way from the chicken house, evidently looking over the flock with sinister intent. No dogs happened to be around the place at the time, possibly the reason for the coyote's boldness.

"Let's get the rifle and kill him!" Otis shouted. "It'll get one of the chickens!" I watched from the upstairs window while Otis ran to get Headley's cherished rifle.

"You know Headley told us never to touch his gun," I reminded Otis as he came back with the rifle, but privately as anxious to try the gun on the coyote as he was. "What will he say if he finds out we have shot off his gun?"

"I don't think he will care if we use it to kill a coyote," Otis reasoned. "We will keep it from getting one of the chickens."

"Besides, he can get a bounty for the scalp," I concurred. Hurriedly, we tried to throw the cartridge from the magazine into the barrel only to have it jam so it could neither slip into the barrel, or be ejected.

Whether the coyote got the chicken or not, we never knew.

We were more concerned now with restoring that gun to its original condition and place before we had to make explanations to Headley. We were not successful.

Another day Papa was working down around the barnyard while Headley was working in the field. Otis and I were supposed to be doing the dishes and indoor work. We had gone to the front room to make up the bed there when our eyes were attracted to the two shot guns leaning in the corner of the room. We each picked up a gun. They were loaded. The one he held was a twelve gauge hammer gun; the one I had was a ten gauge hammerless.

"This one doesn't have any hammers. How do you cock it?" I asked Otis. He knew more about guns than I did.

"You push that little thing toward the barrel," he showed me. "That cocks it." I cocked it. But now that I had it cocked, how could I uncock it without pulling the trigger I wondered.

Otis had his gun pointing out the window resting on the sill as he pretended to be shooting a coyote.

"How do you uncock this gun, Otis?" I was standing a little way behind him with the gun barrels pointing toward the floor. Still with his gun pointing out the window, he tried to explain another way to uncock it without pushing the little button back again. It was rather obscure to me as I stood three feet behind him trying to follow his directions.

Suddenly, there was a blast as my finger came in contact with the trigger. Two white-faced children looked at each other in consternation. What if that gun had been raised just a few inches from the floor! Standing there dumfounded at what had happened, we suddenly heard footsteps coming from the barn on a run.

"What's that! What's that!" It was Papa, calling as he ran.

Two thoroughly frightened children hastily put the two guns back into the corner, and fled upstairs to hide under the bed. We heard Papa rush into the house and on into the front room. He did not know what he might find. All was quiet. The two guns had slipped down to the floor from the corner where they had been so hastily thrust, but no children were in sight. A hole was through the floor where no hole had been before. It did not take Papa long to surmise where we had fled. Coming to the foot of the stairs, he called, "Laura, Otis, come down here." At first we were too scared to answer. But Papa's voice grew sterner. "Laura, Otis, come down here right now." Reluctantly, we crawled out from under the bed to take what we knew we deserved. In his relief he gave us only a stern warning.

When high school was out in Ritzville, Nellie came home again to help with the house work. Sometimes one of us went to town with Dona in the morning to bring the pony home again so it did not have to stand all day. This gave us the opportunity to see the new things happening around Othello. The mail was now brought in daily by train, and the freight service eliminated the long hauls to Cunningham.

"Headley, you'd better haul water tomorrow and fill the cistern. We will be starting to cut wheat in a day or two." Papa was thinking all the horses would be needed to pull the header and header boxes. Besides, he would be short-handed, and Headley would drive one of the header box teams.

"Who all are you getting to help this year?" Headley asked. Although we had less acreage in wheat that year, and it looked like the crop would yield less to the acre, Papa would need help.

"McDonald offered to come over and help us," Papa answered. "Billie and John and Buster are coming to help. We'll be short-handed but we'll have to make out." (Buster was another boy from Missouri who was staying at Billie's place).

Dona looked at Nellie and me, "You girls will have to get the dinners and start the suppers," she told us. "The men will go home at night, but they will have to eat dinner and supper here." Nellie had been doing most of the cooking after she came home from high school, but only for the family.

"What shall we do about bread?" Nellie asked. It would be beyond her skill to make light bread, as we called bread made with yeast, and it would take a large pan of biscuits to feed six hungry men twice a day.

181

"I will make a big batch of bread Sunday, and you can use that for the dinners. We will make biscuits for supper," Dona planned.

We were glad the men were not coming for breakfast; it would not be quite so bad to get up at five o'clock to get breakfast for the family with Dona's help. Nellie was to be the cook with me as kitchen aide. No fancy dishes were offered or expected, so we managed with no casualties resulting.

As the time approached for another school year, other changes were made in our home life. One evening when Dona came home from the newspaper office, she told Papa, "I have a chance to sell the paper. I would like to go back to school again."

"Who is it that wants to buy it?" he asked her. "Someone from out of town?"

"It is some people by the name of Ogden, Will Ogden and his son Guy. They recently came to Othello," she told him.

"Where would you go to school?" was his next query.

"I'd go to Cheney and attend the Normal so I could prepare to teach." Dona had never been able to complete the high school grades, and by going to the Normal she could get a teaching permit after two more years of school work. She could not see any future in the newspaper field in Othello; and the life of a school teacher seemed preferable to that of an editor for her. The sale was made and with the modest amount left over after her accounts were satisfied, she packed her trunk and took the train for Cheney. She too, would have to work for her room and board as so many girls were doing.

This arrangement left me as chief biscuit maker for Papa and the two boys who were at home. One try at making bread with yeast on my own produced such weighty results I returned to biscuit making. They were the lesser of two evils from the standpoint of the critics.

One small advantage for Otis and me came as compensation; Snowball was no longer needed to carry the editor back and forth to town, so now we could ride to school. It took less time getting back and forth to school leaving more time for home work not in any way connected with school studies.

Snowball had one annoying little habit. He seemed to think he knew better than we did whether he should be called on to take us where we wanted to go. At times he balked. It may have been because at one time he had some success as a race horse, leaving him with a slightly swelled ego, or he may have considered two homestead children had something more to learn. The most probable reason for his stubborn streaks, however, was his reluctance to leave the barn and well-filled manger to stand hitched all day at school in all kinds of weather. This was good reasoning even for a horse.

We would get on, riding double and carrying our lunch pail, (containing cold biscuits, sans butter and left over from breakfast, hard boiled eggs and a small jar of apple butter or cold beans). Snowball would start his protest by turning around in circles. At our insistence that he go forward instead of in circles, he very determinedly continued to back and turn. If we became more insistent by using our heels or the reins, he would jump his hind feet off the ground a little as a sort of threat that he would scatter us and our belongings over the ground if we persisted. It was doubtless just a threat to buffalo us. He never bucked. Then Papa would come to our aid and lead him out the gate, heading him toward school with a parting slap. Sometimes when we got to the corner of the McCulloch homestead and found Flossie had gone on to school on her little white pony, Snowball would decide that instead of going to school he preferred to turn south toward Billie's place. He may have been disappointed that he would not have Pearl's company on the way. Again, we would argue the point without success.

"Otis, you will have to get off and lead him a ways past the corner," I would remark resignedly. It was easier for Otis to get back on again.

"Come on, Snowball, we are going to school," and Otis would take the bridle reins to lead him about fifty feet past the corner.

After that there was no further trouble. This was not a daily occurance, just when he felt tempermental.

We had another horse with some tempermental qualities; this was Bert. Though he was only a work horse, Papa sometimes rode him to town or on errands. Usually Bert was quite well behaved, but now and then at widely separated intervals, perhaps to put the rider off guard, he reverted to his frisky days. It was always when you were least expecting it.

One night at the close of wheat harvest, Papa showed up at the kitchen door, and with a sheepish grin asked, "Did Bert come home?"

"I thought you were riding him," replied Nellie, surprised at the question. We knew he had ridden away on Bert. Then we noticed that his clothes looked rather dusty.

"I was, but he bucked me off," Pappa confessed with an embarrassed laugh. Bert trotted on home leaving Papa to walk the last half mile, and was waiting at the barn to be unsaddled.

There were only nine pupils starting the term of school at Rising Star that fall. Ruth, Jennie, Flossie, Otis and I were riding, but the three Lang children and Johnny Lee still walked. Clarence Showalter's family had moved to town so we kept our horses in their empty barn when the weather was stormy or cold.

It turned cold in the early part of the winter; so cold it was hard to keep warm when the fires were out at night. Frost and ice made the covers stiff around our faces from our breath. I slept between two feather beds, trying to keep warm.

"It was ten below zero last night," Papa told us when we went downstairs to hover around the stoves. We children thought of the two and a quarter miles to school; with no mittens or overshoes, and no warm winter clothing, it promised to be grim. The last few days as the weather turned colder, we had arrived at the school house with fingers and feet numb and blue from the cold, then aching as the blood circulated back into them.

"Papa, do we have to go to school today?" we asked anxiously.

"No, you had better stay at home. It is too cold for you to be out when it is this cold," and added, "You couldn't take the horse and let him stay tied all day in the cold, either."

Other children were kept at home for the same reason, and the school at Rising Star stayed closed for two weeks while the mercury remained below zero. Our thermometer registered to ten below zero and never got above that for a week, but some of the neighbors reported it was twenty-five below on theirs.

Frost collected so thickly on the windows we could scarcely melt a small circle on the glass through which to look out. The pump at the cistern froze. Horse trough and chicken watering basins froze solid and had to be thawed with boiling water so the farm animals and fowl could get water twice a day. Even the water pail in the kitchen froze almost as solidly as did the horse trough outside. Unless the eggs were gathered within a few minutes after being laid, they froze and cracked; even the hens did little cackling over a newly laid egg at ten below zero, so the eggs were well iced when we found them. The family stayed close by the fire unless necessity took us outside; modern plumbing had not yet come to the homesteads so some calls to the small house in the corner of the yard were put off as long as possible, then taken with much shivering.

A short time before this cold snap, Headley had brought a letter home from the post office. It was from Jim. After reading it Papa said, "Jim's work will be closing down for the winter there at the mill. He wants to come down and spend the winter with us." Jim had been working at one of the mills in Hunters, north of Spokane where the deep snows interfered with lumbering and mill work.

Papa passed the letter on to Headley to read. Otis and I listened as they talked. That was good news to us. I had found the job of keeping house for Papa and the boys was no easy one, and to have Iva's help would be very welcome. Their nineteen months old baby, Joe Perle, was going to be a happy addition to our lonely home.

"Jim wants me to bring the team and wagon up after their things," Headley commented.

"Do you think you could find the way up there?" Papa asked. "It must be all of a hundred and fifty miles. That would take you all of three days to get up there."

"I can take some bedding and food along and camp on the way." Headley was excited at the adventure of going that distance alone, and fully confidant he could find the road. There would be no road maps, paved roads or signs to direct him.

"You'd better get ready to leave tomorrow," Papa directed, "We could have a cold spell any time, and that is quite a ways farther north." The caution was well taken for it had been only a few days later that the cold weather hit. Fortunately, he had made it to Hunters before it turned so bitterly cold. Then as the weather moderated again the return trip was made in safety, permitting them to camp two nights on the road without undue hardship.

Along in January, after an exchange of letters between Dona and Mary, and with Papa's consent, it was arranged that I, too, should go to Cheney to complete the eighth grade. A place was secured for me to work for my room and board in the home of J. R. Forden, one of the Normal instructors. I was glad to go for I was missing my school chum, Flossie, who had collapsed at school and under the doctor's directions was compelled to remain out of school for the rest of the school term.

But both Nellie and I found that going away to school had its problems. To begin with, our clothing was quite limited. Shoes have a way of wearing through on the bottoms. One method Nellie used as a means of keeping her stockings from doing the same was to shape a piece of cardboard to fit into her shoes. It had to be replaced daily, and of course the cardboard kept out neither snow nor slush. Colds and lagrippe followed.

My shabby shoes become so noticeable that one day my name was called in chapel with directions to come to the office of the Dean of Women. I went wondering why I was called. My arithmetic teacher, Miss Craig, had bought a pair of new shoes for me. How we missed Mamma! She would have realized our needs and found a way to fill them; but Papa, now in his seventy-third year, was helpless to supply the necessary things.

The night of the eighth grade graduation brought mixed feelings. The program was a pageant of America with each member of the class having a part. It was not the learning of the poem assigned to me that was my great difficulty, but what was I going to wear? The girls in the class had discussed the subject of what we were to wear, then voted that all should wear white dresses with white stockings and black patent leather slippers, and for the remaining weeks I heard descriptions of the new dresses their mothers were making or buying for the important night. I took my problem to Dona, knowing she had no spare money to supply the things I needed. She remembered a dress Nellie had worn the summer before, and wrote to request the use of it. Back came the skirt, but she wrote that the waist was worn out. Dona's employer offered the use of a woman's white blouse with long sleeves. By turning the sleeves up inside to the elbows and basting some wide white lace to the bottom, it was made to do. The problem of patent leather slippers and white stockings seemed insurmountable until Pearl Shearer, a junior in the Normal, offered me the use of some she had used the summer before. Thus outfitted, I sat on the platform with my classmates and went forward to receive my diploma.

It was well for my peace of mind that the other graduates were too occupied receiving congratulations, flowers and gifts of family and friends to detect the lump in my throat as I passed the flower and gift laden table, and went to join two elderly aunts at the rear of the room. I knew there would be no gift for me.

"Don't feel badly," they told me, "You have your diploma the same as the others, and that is what counts." They must have read in my eyes the hunger I felt for the things like the other girls had.

Nellie returned home at the close of the school year to keep house for Papa and the two boys. Jim and his family had left early in the spring after helping to sow the spring wheat. I continued to work for the same family where I had been working, to earn money for my train fare home, and to have a graduation picture taken. Dona took a position as telephone operator in Cheney for the summer.

Again it was time for harvesting the wheat, and again the crew was very limited; so limited in fact, that part of the time Nellie was left to do the cooking alone while I climbed into the header box to load wheat. From time to time the header was stopped while the driver shifted the wheat into more compact form.

"There won't be enough wheat that we could get a threshing crew to thresh it this year," we heard Papa say. "The horses will need most of it for hay," he added, "We might be able to let Tipton have a few loads on the store bill."

Often at night after we children had gone to bed, we could hear his steps pacing back and forth down stairs, and occasionally a groan of perplexity. Nellie had obtained a job helping Mrs. Godsey during the harvest season at their home near Lind, and Headley joined a harvesting crew near Cunningham. It was getting to be a lonely place at home, and doubtless Papa felt his inadequacy to solve his problems as well as the loneliness. The cohesive quality of our home was gone.

Otis and I were still finding interesting things and adventures amid the sagebrush. Sometimes it was a meadow lark's nest cleverly hidden on the ground in a field of grain. The little cuckoos were still to be heard at dusk, but we never tried twisting the head off by walking in wide circles around and around it as Headley had tried to do shortly after we moved to Washington. He had been told this was possible, and spent most of one morning in the endeavor without success. Somehow, he missed the quick movement as the bird turned its head back to watch him as he made the circuit.

On one of our exploring trips into the sagebrush down in the big flat below our house, we jumped a little rock rabbit near a ledge of rocks. It eluded our efforts to catch it for a time, but it was so tiny it could not run fast and Otis got between it and its haven in the rocks and caught it.

"Let's take it up to the house and keep it for a pet, shall we?" he suggested as we stroked its soft fur.

"It would make a nice little pet, but what would we feed it?" I was just as anxious as he was for a pet rabbit but I did not know much about the feeding of rabbits.

"We can pull grass for it; or it can eat wheat and straw. There is nothing but dry grass for it to eat down here." His reasoning sounded logical, at least it fitted right in with our wishes, so we took turns carrying and stroking our new pet on the way back to the house.

"What have you got there?" Papa asked as he saw our absorbed interest in a box we had fixed for it.

"It's a little rock rabbit we caught down in the flat," we told him. "We're going to keep it for a pet." We showed him how tiny and cute it was.

"It won't live in captivity. You'd ought to take it back down to the place you found it and let it go." After listening to his reasoning, we reluctantly came to see it would be better for the rabbit to have its freedom. But evening was drawing on and we were still more reluctant to go back down into the lonely flat again that late in the day.

Then we thought of a place nearer the house on top of the hill where the green grass was more plentiful. We would take it there. With care we built a shelter of dry sagebrush sticks in a nice patch of green grass; in it we placed the little rabbit, assuring it we would see that it got plenty of good things to eat.

"What did you do with the little rabbit?" Papa inquired when we go back to the house.

"Out there," we said, pointing to the sagebrush northeast of the house.

"Some dog or cat will get it there," was his disturbing answer. "It needs the rocks to hide in."

We hoped he might be mistaken once more. To reassure ourselves, we paid another visit to our pet before dark and found it near the stick shelter, then went home to bed more hopeful.

Next morning, as soon as breakfast was over, we hurried to

visit our pet. The little shelter was as we had left it but we saw nothing of our little rock rabbit.

"It is probably out eating it's breakfast in the grass," Otis said hopefully as we started searching a little farther away. Then we found two little ears, nothing more. Papa had been right. We had made the mistake of taking it out of its natural habitat. We had learned another lesson the painful way.

Chapter XXII

Summer Episodes

NO PLANS FOR A HIGH SCHOOL in Othello had yet been made, but after the new two-story brick school building was completed two teachers were employed to teach the elementary grades. Laura Rogers, an experienced lower grades teacher, was employed to teach the first four grades; D. L. Haile moved to Othello to become the principal and to teach the four upper grades. The number of pupils attending had grown each year; in fact, the preceding term Mrs. J. W. Webster had for a time assisted the over-burdened teacher in the spring of 1910. It was becoming evident that in another year some of these eighth grade students would be ready for high school.

Xerpha graduated from the Ritzville High School that same year, and after working throughout the summer in the capacity of postal and store clerk for Tipton, went on to take college work at Pullman Agricultural College. Edward Gaines, a teacher in Ritzville with whom she was forming a friendship, may have had some influence in her selection of the agricultural college since he, too, was going on to Pullman. In furthering the interest, he made visits from time to time to the McCulloch homestead.

After working part of the summer, Nellie also returned to Ritzville for her junior year. Dona continued her work for the telephone company in Cheney until time for the fall term to begin, and I, too was going back to Cheney. Papa and Otis would be alone since Headley had obtained work away from home.

"Daughter, do you know what this is?" Papa asked as he handed me a train ticket and a coin at the depot in Othello the day I was leaving. He nearly always called me "Daughter."

"Yes, it is a five dollar gold piece," I answered, as I took the coin and ticket.

"Well, put it in your pocket and be careful that you don't lose it," was his admonition as he told me good-bye.

By mid-winter I was desperately in need of shoes and some warmer clothing. There seemed nothing to do but discontinue school at the end of the semester and return home to keep house for Papa and Otis.

It was quite evident they were in need of a housekeeper. Sagebrush makes a lot of debris, and to them, it had been simpler to brush the dust and trash behind the stove than it was to sweep it into the stove shovel to burn. The accumulation called for some shovel work to clear out the foot deep sweepings. The sheets and pillow slips had taken on an exaggerated tattle-tale gray, and I could have used some of Mamma's good home-made lye soap had there been any.

Some unwanted intruders had been brought in with someone's luggage a few years before, and by the time they were discovered had made a good start by multiplication. They had become firmly entrenched, not only on the beds, but in the cracks of the un-papered walls where they could grin defiance at all our efforts to exterminate them. We tried, but the only thing that would have been entirely successful would have been to burn the house down. We nearly did that accidently that spring when sparks from the kitchen range landed in the fuel box beside it, and flames were reaching up the wall to the ceiling when discovered. Quick action on Papa's part saved the house, leaving a charred wall to make us more alert.

"Otis, how can you sleep?" I asked him the next morning after I got home. Shortly after I had blown out the kerosene light and was dropping off to sleep, something was making me itch and squirm. After getting wide enough awake to realize there must be a reason, I quickly lighted the lamp in time to see a dozen or so of the uninvited night marauders racing to get out of sight. They were all sizes from pin head to a quarter inch, but already they were getting partly filled with the blood of their unwilling hostess.

"Oh, you get used to them, at least after killing off what you can," he cheerfully told me. "I keep the legs of the bed in cans partly filled with coal oil. They can't swim in that." He was trying to be encouraging, and helpful.

Either those bedbugs could swim in coal oil, or they outsmarted us by dropping from the ceiling onto the beds of their victims. Their nightly forays continued. One of the measures to outwit them was an application of poison at strategic places about the wooden beds and their wooden slats. The bed and springs where Papa slept downstairs were entirely of metal, and the front room was papered so it was easier to keep them to a minimum there, but the upper rooms afforded them ample space to multiply; and multiply they did.

At night after they had settled to their feast, I would hurriedly light the lamp and by a quick counter attack, head them off before they could get out of sight. Crushing them left traces of the encounter on the pillow slip and an offensive odor in the air. Next, the bedding was carefully searched for any that might have gone into hiding. Sometimes two or three such skirmishes took place before they either got reduced in numbers, or the would-be sleeper got sleepy enough to ignore further depredations.

While Headley and Otis were away from home for a few weeks that spring, I tried playing a game of hide-and-seek with them by moving to the other upstairs bedroom. The first two nights I slept fine, but by the third night they had caught up with me. After a few nights when most of them seemed to have moved to that end of the house, I moved back to my own room. It was rather interesting to see just how long it took them to figure out the switch.

The two boys went over to do some wheat seeding on the Warren quarter section that cornered on the May's homestead. Mary and Billie were in Kennewick where Billie was doing some plastering work. The boys batched and Otis was doing the cooking while Headley was seeding. He had even learned how to make biscuits, after a sort; in between household chores he stalked young ground squirrels, which were plentiful.

One evening near dusk, Otis stepped outside to draw a bucket of water from the cistern while Headley was finishing the chores at the barn. As he came back into the house he was confronted by something crouched inside the room off the entrance hall. It looked like a lynx or bob cat; he could see the tufted ears. Startled, he stepped back to call excitedly, "Oh Headley!" He expected it would spring onto him the next moment.

The crouched animal burst into whoops of laughter. Headley had slipped into the house unseen while Otis was at the cistern, and taking the skin of a lynx which had been killed sometime before, he lay just out of sight holding the skin in the semblance of a crouching animal. In the dim light, it looked very real to an eleven year old boy.

The two versions of his frightened reactions were very different. Headley's version was a weak quavery "Oh Headley!" Otis was quite sure it was a bold, vigorous, "OH HEADLEY!" Probably neither was quite accurate; Headley liked to tease.

Two summers before this, Otis and I had gone through an experience that tested our courage; or so we thought. It was the day before Memorial Day. Plans had been made for a trip to Cunningham to take a few roses to Mamma's grave from the yellow rose bushes she had planted at each side of the front door. We needed Billie's buggy in which to make the trip, but it was out on Frenchman Hill where Billie was helping Bill Goocher with some well-drilling. Billie had moved his family out there, and Mary was doing the cooking for the men.

Goocher drilled two or three wells out on the Hill about this time, one of which was on the place now owned by the May family. The one being drilled then was two or three miles beyond, a distance of about seventeen miles from our homestead. Our problem was to find a way to get the buggy to our place.

The day before we were needing it, Billie rode in on horseback and leading another horse to borrow a wagon from Papa.

"I didn't know you needed the buggy," he said, when we asked him why he didn't bring the buggy. "I could have brought it in if I had known."

"Papa, couldn't we go out with Billie and bring the buggy?" We were loath to give up the trip to Cunningham.

"I can't spare the time," Papa told us.

"Let Laura and Otis go out with me," suggested Billie, "They can bring it back." We were thrilled with the idea of driving back by ourselves.

"We'll be all right, Papa. Can we go?" There was no other way to get the buggy, so he gave his consent, and we were soon on the way with Billie in the wheat rack, and leading another team behind the wagon.

Though we had never been out on Frenchman Hill, we had been over much of the road as far as Hutchinson Lake, and Sam Hutchinson's place on lower Crab Creek. Our family had picnicked at both places while Mamma was still with us. We knew there would be wild lilies and pink phlox blooming throughout the sagebrush; besides, we would get to play with Willie. Of course we expected to get home long before dark.

The road lay along the foot of a long row of cliffs south of Deadman, Shiner and Hutchinson Lakes; a lonely road with no houses near the road between our home and the place the well was being drilled. It took nearly four hours to make the trip over the rough, rocky road.

We spent the afternoon in play, but as the day began to wane, we became more and more concerned about that long ride we were going to have to take alone. It would be dark long before those seventeen miles could be covered, and that long stretch of cliffs become more ominous as we thought of them. Lynx and bob cats were known to have their dens in just such places, and there might be cougars. Rattlesnakes could be lying in the road to cause the horses to take fright. Somehow, that road looked very different from that end than it had from home earlier in the day.

It was not until after supper that Billie had time to get the horses harnessed and hitched to the buggy. The sun was nearly down.

"Shouldn't we be starting for home?" we asked him as he came to supper. We had hinted as much to Mary a bit earlier.

"You eat your supper, and I'll get the team hooked to the buggy right afterward," he said as he washed up for supper. It seemed that supper was very slow in coming; the sun was sinking lower and lower, and home seemed a long ways away.

To our great relief, he not only got the buggy and team ready, but he put the saddle on his riding horse and prepared to go part of the way with us. It was nearly eleven o'clock and about eight miles from home when he turned the reins over to us.

"You'll be all right now," was his assurance as he swung into the saddle. "The horses will take you right home," then he headed back in the opposite direction. The tallest cliffs were behind us as we started the team toward home, but there were yet many smaller cliffs and outcroppings of rock to pass before we would get to our barn lot.

It was a clear moonlight night with lights and shadows changing shapes as the horses trotted along. The jingle of harness, the clop-clop of the horses hooves on the road and the rasp of the metal rims of the buggy wheels as they struck rock, were the only sounds in the quiet air except when the call of a coyote came from a distance. Two children, ages nine and thirteen, could think of a place they would rather be just then. That awful stretch of sagebrush and rocks lying between them and home, was a lonely place to be at night without adult company. Suddenly Otis gave voice to something that had been in my thoughts.

"Are you scared?" he questioned.

I wasn't sure of the answer to that question in my own mind, but if I said "Yes," it would probably scare him.

"No, are you?" I was trying to believe it was the truth. Back came his denial of such a weakness. He was used to being out hunting among the sagebrush and rocks with Johnny or Headley,

196

but this was the first time either of us had been in such surroundings alone at night.

We reasoned together that the horses were trotting calmly along with no show of fright. Their ears were not even pricked up as they would have been if danger was near. As long as the horses showed no alarm we could be reasonably sure nothing was near to cause trouble.

Finally we came to the dim road leading off northeast from the main road going to Othello, toward our homestead; only two miles across the flat yet to go. It was well past midnight when we drove into the barn lot. The house was dark. Papa had given up looking for us that night and the family had gone to bed; we would have to put the horses away. With no loss of time, we unhooked them from the buggy and removed the harness quickly to leave it laying on the ground. It took only a few minutes to take them to the barn, let them in and close the door without tying them in their stalls; then the kitchen door opened quietly and closed, with two relieved children inside.

We were soon in bed and asleep, but one of us was not to remain that way. Something had upset my inner equilibrium, which was relieved only by parting company with my supper.

Next morning we gathered the fragrant yellow roses and placed them in a can of water to take with us to Cunningham to place on Mamma's grave.

But now I was having problems of another kind. Papa frequently went over to see how the boys were getting along with the seeding of wheat on the Warren place, and was often away from right after breakfast until after dark. With only the hounds for company, (though they slept most of the day after a night spent in chasing coyotes), the homestead offered nothing to offset the loneliness. Papa had been unable to renew his subscription to the paper he had taken for many years, and the few books we possessed had been read through many times. I tried again to make bread so we could have a change from the daily biscuits, but without any marked success.

"Mrs. McCulloch, will you show me how to make light

bread?" After some futile attempts, I took my problem to her.

"Did you set up your sponge the night before?" she asked. "Save the water in which you boil the potatoes, and use that to make the sponge." She explained each step carefully. "Soak the yeast cake in a cup of lukewarm water until it is dissolved, add it and some sugar to the potato water, add the salt and enough flour to make the sponge. Set it in a warm place and cover it warmly overnight. The oven door is a good place after the range fire has died down."

"How do you know how long to knead the dough?" I thought that might have something to do with my failures in making bread that could be called light bread, for mine certainly was not.

"You knead it until it feels smooth and elastic in your hands with enough flour worked in so it isn't sticky, but not real stiff." She was a busy woman but never too busy to make me welcome with my problems in housekeeping. I often went up to the McCullochs. Eugenia Campbell, who was the teacher at Rising Star that year, was rooming and boarding there, and Flossie was attending again.

The number of pupils in the school had dropped still lower, with Flossie as her only eighth grade student. Sometimes when Papa had come home and gone to bed real early, I would light the lantern, quietly leave the house to walk the three quarters of a mile and visit with Flossie and Eugenia until bed time. Jess Knepper and another farm hand were working for Mr. Mac and there was more activity at their home. I would walk home again in the quiet night after enjoying the evening.

"Let's have a picnic over on Shiner Lake for Miss Campbell the day after school is out," Otis suggested a few days before the end of the term. He liked his teacher.

"We could make it a school picnic, and ask the rest of the boys and girls to go, couldn't we?" I thought it would be fun to include all of them.

"Do you suppose Papa would take us if we ask him? We could tell him it is for Miss Campbell?"

Papa was the school clerk that year and had become well acquainted with the young teacher.

"Papa, can we have a picnic for Miss Campbell and the rest of the school before she leaves?"

"We would have to go in the wheat rack." Papa thought it might not be quite suitable for the young lady to ride in.

"Do you think she would ride in the wheat rack?" we wondered. When Headley heard us making plans, he was in favor, so we talked Papa into going along with our plans. Eugenia was quite pleased and entered heartily into the plans though some of the pupils would be unable to go.

About mid-morning we picked up Eugenia, Flossie, Lillian Tipton, (a sister of Homer Tipton's) and Jess, who wanted to be included in the fun, and headed for the lake. In addition to the lunch boxes we packed, we took along a frying pan to fry any small fish we could catch.

Shiner Lake is nearly surrounded by cliffs, but there was an open place at the lower end where we made camp. Someone had left an old rowboat there providing a way for fun and fishing, and after an early lunch we left Papa to his fishing while we went exploring. Jess took Eugenia for a boat ride around the lake while the rest of us went for a hike along the edge on a small ledge. It afforded a trail two or three feet above the water line where we could walk following each other in Indian style. Shouting back and forth to the boaters, we discovered a clear beautiful echo coming back to us from the cliffs on the other side of the lake. The distance permitted brief sentences before the echo came back to us. Like in life, polite words brought back polite answers, but if we shouted "Shut up!" we got the same rude answer hurled back at us.

Intending to get back to camp to give the other girls a boat ride, we started to return along the rocky trail when suddenly, we were startled by a shriek and a loud splash. One of the girls had plunged into the lake when her foot turned on a loose rock. The water was only about three feet deep at the edge but it must have been a bit frightening to suddenly find herself on her back in the water. She was dripping from head to foot by the time she was pulled out.

That ended the picnic. We were nine miles from home and dry clothing. The boaters had seen the accident and were coming to shore as the horses were hitched to the wagon. Wrapped in the heavy quilt we had used to sit on at the picnic lunch, our casualty was taken home to be dried out.

Papa went to Ritzville shortly after this to prove up on the homestead, and get title to the land. In order to avoid the extra expense of a hotel room while up there, he took the train which left Othello about 2:45 in the morning. He was able to get his business concluded that day and caught another train home which got him there about 2:30 the next morning. It had been a long, wearying day, with no opportunity for sleep or rest until he got home.

Papa and I were alone about midday when I heard him make a queer noise from the nearby rocker where he had apparently been napping. Glancing up, I saw his head thrown back, his mouth open in stentorian breathing and his eyes set and glazed. In a panic, I jumped to his side and tried to arouse him. At first there was no response.

"Papa, what's the matter?" I stammered as I shook him. After a little he aroused some and said feebly, "I believe I'm dying."

"Oh no, Papa!" I was terrified. What should I do? The boys with the horses were away; there was no one nearer than the McCulloch's place and I could not leave him to go for help.

"Can you get me a cup of coffee?" he asked weakly as he aroused a little more. After drinking that he seemed a little stronger, and I was able to get him undressed and into bed. He seemed to have strained his heart, but after several days he was up and around again. Meanwhile, the boys came home again.

One day shortly after Papa was up again, I heard of a woman living in Othello who wanted a girl to help in the home. There were few jobs available for girls from which to choose and I was needing to earn some money. I went for an interview. It was expected that the hired girl would relieve the employer of all the heavier work including the washing, (by hand on the washboard,) ironing, (with irons heated on the stove,) scrubbing floors, (first with a broom and heavy suds, then rinsing twice with clear water and drying with a mop,) washing and drying the dishes, washing windows once a week, and part of the cooking for a family of four. For this I would receive two dollars and fifty cents a week with my room and board. It was a two-roomed house with the five of us sleeping in the main room on metal couches that were opened out at night. I slept with two children.

After several weeks, Billie came by one day to tell me that Mary had sent word I could come back with him to Kennewick if I would like. Right then I was somewhat in disfavor with my employer because of an accident in the kitchen a few days previously.

While washing the dishes at the little table beside the kitchen range, (there was no water or sink in the small house) the draining pan for the dishes was crowded too close to the edge and suddenly tipped off onto the floor with some of her fine china.

"Crash!" screamed those beautiful cups and saucers as they smashed, while I gasped in dismay at what had happened.

"Oh Laura! What have you done?" then answering her own question as she saw the broken cups. "You've broken all my beautiful Haviland dishes."

An inventory showed the damage had not been quite that extensive, but about six pieces were smashed and she was inconsolable over the loss. I thought there was a good possibility she might want to replace me if she couldn't replace the dishes and not realizing the high price of Haviland China I offered to work out their cost. My offer was refused. I decided to accept Mary's offer to come to Kennewick.

Early in July the Mays returned to their homestead, and I went to help Mrs. McCulloch and Flossie during the harvesting season. The dollar a day she paid me while I was there seemed very generous after my previous job.

201

Papa and the two boys had managed to cut the small crop of wheat before it was fully ripe so it could be used as hay, and stored it in the hay pen before we returned from Kennewick. But another loss came to him that summer when his largest farm horse, "Old Red," sickened and died. Headley then took the remaining horses and went to work in harvesting near Cunningham. The pay for the teams provided Papa with a little extra money which he badly needed for himself and Otis. I was still staying with Mary who was expecting another baby before the year ended.

"Do you have a sister Laura living with you?" the questioner was a strange woman we had never seen before.

"Yes, she is here," Mary told her and called me to learn what was wanted. I wondered what she could want with me.

"There is a Mrs. Wienke living out on the Sam Hutchinson place who is looking for a girl to help with the work," she explained. "She had an accident and needs someone to stay with her."

"Does she have a husband and children?" enquired Mary.

"Mr. Wienke is away working in the harvest field. It will be some weeks before he comes home. Meanwhile, she and the two little boys they are adopting are alone," she told us. "She got tangled up in the calf's rope the other day," she continued, "and hurt her ankle so badly she is unable to walk."

She explained that in addition to the housework and cooking there would be two cows to milk, which were due to freshen any day, their calves and some young pigs to feed. That part sounded more like a job for a man rather than a fifteen year old girl, and I was not sure I could handle the work.

"She will pay five dollars a week and I am sure you could do what she needs to have done," the lady assured me. "She desperately needs someone." That five dollars was quite an inducement and I decided to take the job.

It was eleven miles out to the Hutchinson place right on Crab Creek. There were no other houses within miles, and it set back over a half mile from the road leading from Frenchman Hill to

202

Othello. Mrs. Wienke proved to be a woman weighing nearly two hundred and fifty pounds, and when I later saw little Mr. Wienke I detected a strong resemblance to Mr. and Mrs. Hen Pecko, then running in the weekly comic cartoons. Dannie and Walter were the little five year old orphan twins the Wienkes had taken from a Spokane orphanage with the intent of adopting them.

One cow had freshened that afternoon and by the second day the other cow had delivered her calf, giving me two heavy milkers to separate from their lacteal fluid twice a day. It seemed to me it would have been much simpler to let their calves help me with that job, but I was directed to teach the calves to drink from a bucket instead of letting them suck their mother's teats for themselves.

Teaching those calves the artificial way of getting their nourishment instead of nature's way took time and effort besides a bit of messiness. They were eager to grab on to anything they could suck and taking the pail about a fourth full of the fresh milk, I would let them start sucking my fingers then try to lower my hand into the milk where they were supposed to start drawing the milk up between my fingers. Time after time their muzzle would be gotten into the milk only to have them lift their milky nose against me and bunt, or impatiently bunt the bucket because the milk was not going in the right direction. I learned not to put all their milk in one bucket at this stage by finding it was either spilled onto me, or the ground. After about three days of trying they finally caught on to what was expected of them and drank like the little lady and gentleman they were.

Another outdoor job was carrying water and feed to eighteen little pigs who were not yet big enough to root for their own food. However, they could squeal shrilly for it when they saw me coming. The older hogs were in a fenced field where they could get their food and drink without my help; but pigs are pigs. They do not like limits put on their foraging by fencing, and if there is a weak place in the fence or they can make one, they are sure to find it.

One day I chanced to see the boar just as he had gotten on the outside of the fence. It looked like it would be a simple job to drive him back in before he got farther away. I should have known better. He saw me coming and headed across the shallow creek which spread out about a hundred feet along there. Not to be outsmarted this early in the game, I went right on after him in an endeavor to head him back toward the pen. Back and forth we went through the shallow creek, and just when I thought I had him headed toward the way he should go, he would perversely do a quick turn in another direction. Finally, he headed off into a clump of willows where I could not hope to out-maneuver him; I returned to the house to get dry clothes.

Later when I saw him around the fence again I coaxed him along to the opening he had made with some feed in a pan. When he was safely inside I did some fence mending.

"There isn't enough work here to be worth five dollars a week," Mrs. Wienke told me at the end of the first week, "I am just going to pay you three dollars a week after this." With no way to get the eleven miles to town except to walk, and knowing I was an inexperienced girl, she was taking advantage of me. We had seen no one else the whole week I had been there and probably would see no one for weeks more.

They had a bunch of young horses that occasionally came up around the barn though most of the time we never saw them.

Someone apparently went through the barnlot one day and left the gate open to open country. We had not noticed it until we saw those young horses passing through.

"You will have to go and head them back, Laura," Mrs. Wienke called to me. "If they get away no telling when we'll ever see them again."

Without stopping to put anything on my head to protect it from the blazing sun, I started out to try and get around them before they got alarmed and started to run. Dodging around behind rocks and through sagebrush, I was almost successful when they saw me and, taking alarm, broke into a run. Running, panting, sweating, I kept on for a mile and a half through the

204

heat and dust until finally, at the foot of Frenchman Hill, they gave up and let me get around them. Very docilely they let me drive them back to the home place and fasten them in once more.

It left me with a splitting headache and a feeling of dizziness by the time I got to the house. Neither Mrs. Wienke nor the boys were in sight, but in a few minutes Walter appeared in the doorway with a message.

"Mamma says for you to come help fix the fence. The pigs got out again."

"Tell your mamma I can't come. I am sick from the long run in the sun." I couldn't see going out in the hot sun again after being so near a sunstroke.

In a few minutes I heard her coming through the kitchen door with the knee of the crippled leg resting on an old kitchen chair. I had often heard her use profanity on the little boys, but now she turned a stream of it in my direction as she told me how worthless and lazy I was, and ordered me to get out there and help mend the fence.

"Mrs. Wienke, I am going to town tomorrow if I have to walk," I told her quietly but looking her straight in the eye. "I have just had a three mile run after the horses, and I won't take profanity from anyone. You can get someone else to take my place."

She saw I meant it and tried to placate me. It must have surprised her that I would stand up to her for she had told several stories of fights she had had over the years with women who had differed with her, in which she came out best.

"You promised me five dollars a week when I came out here, then put it down to three," I told her. She offered to raise it back to the five again, but I wouldn't have stayed at any price.

The next morning I was up at four o'clock to get my suitcase packed and carried down near the road leading to town. It was Saturday and there might be someone going to town from a homestead out on the Hill. Then I went back, milked the cows, fed the calves and pigs, got breakfast and did up the dishes before taking up my stand down near the road.

Eventually, I saw a man in a buggy coming and called to him. It was Tom Berry, who knew my family, going into town. I picked up my suitcase to meet him when I heard a familiar rattle beside the road. I waited then until Tom drove over to where I was standing so I could point out the snake which he killed. We met Mr. Wienke on his way home before we got to town, relieving my mind on leaving her alone with only the little boys.

Chapter XXIII

Horse Herding

BILLIE SOLD THEIR LAND about this time and bought about twenty mares with their colts with the intention of raising horses. He had filed on a new homestead three miles west of the original claim where he would have access to open range land and a lake where his horses could get water. In the meantime they planned to remain at the first home until he could build a house on the new place. I learned of this when he picked me up in town after my ride in with Tom.

"I need someone to drive the horses over to one of the lakes for water," he explained as we drove home. "I have this plastering job to do, and I can't spare the time to haul water for them." I wondered if he was going to get Otis to do the herding.

"How would you like to do the herding for me?" he asked.

"Me?" I liked to ride, but I had never herded horses. "How often would they have to be taken over there? Everyday?"

"Yes. You would drive them over in the morning and let them graze along the way, then bring them back in the afternoon."

"What horse would I ride?" was my next question. I would be on horseback all day long between his place and the lake. That sounded like it might be interesting.

"You would ride old Blackie. If you will do this for me until the weather turns cold I'll give you a little black mare for your own." Later he pointed her out to me. A horse of my own! That was a real inducement, and I consented to take the job of horse herder.

Blackie was a tall, long-legged horse, so tall the stirrups had to be let out to full length to enable me to mount. His long legs carried us over the ground rapidly when it was needed, but he was very gentle. At the end of the first day in the saddle it was

207

torture either to sit or walk; to climb back into the saddle next morning was more torture, but after two or three days it eased off until a full day in the saddle gave no trouble.

Starting out about seven o'clock in the morning with a little sack lunch tied to the saddle horn, I rounded up the horses from the home pasture and headed them toward the open country. It was a distance of seven or eight miles across the flat to the lake where they could get good water. (It was the one just south of Crescent Lake). The horses spread out, grazing slowly, so that it took us until nearly noon to reach the lake. The black horse soon got onto the work of keeping them moving as we wove back and forth behind them. An occasional stop at an isolated homestead where some family was making a start was the only time I saw anyone throughout the day. Rarely, I met a rider looking for stray horses.

It was inevitable I should encounter rattlesnakes in that rough country, and hear rattlesnake experiences of other homestead people. On hearing the familiar rattle as my horse shied away from the danger, I first located the snake then took my horse back out of the danger zone and tied him to a sagebrush; then back to the battle. There were plenty of rocks handy for ammunition. Some were killed; some escaped by crawling under large slabs of rock where it was impossible to get at them.

One day while the horses were grazing near the lake, I stopped to visit Mrs. Brown, whose husband had taken a homestead claim just above the lake. They had two small children, a little two-year-old girl and a nursing baby. Mrs. Brown related a frightening experience she had earlier that summer, an experience that might have had tragic results if she had not kept her resourcefulness.

It was wash day. She had left the little folk in the house while she finished hanging out the clothes. She pinned the last garment on the line then picked up the gunny sack and dropped it back into the empty five gallon coal oil can in which she kept the soiled diapers, and went back into the house. The baby was fretting so she picked him up and prepared to nurse him. Sitting there in the small rocker with the baby at her breast, she felt the little finger on her left hand was commencing to tingle and itch. She rubbed it several times but when this did not relieve the tingling she examined it more closely. There were two small puncture marks on the side of her finger. Immediately she thought of the possibility of a rattlesnake bite, but she couldn't think of where one would have had a chance to bite her. She had not seen a snake. Then she thought of the gunny sack.

Laying the baby down, she went back out to where she had picked up the sack. There was the snake. First she killed it, for no rattlesnake must be allowed to escape, then she went back into the house to apply first aid. She was frightened as she realized her husband was away from home for the day, and she had the babies to think of. She first wound a string tightly around her finger between the punctures and her hand; then taking her husband's razor she made cuts across each puncture. By squeezing and sucking, she got rid of all the poison she could. There was no way of knowing how much of the poison had already gotten into the blood stream.

Mr. Brown was helping Charley Morgan in the harvesting on his homestead two miles away; but help for herself and the babies must be obtained before he would be home in the evening.

Putting the two little ones into the baby buggy, she wheeled them the two miles over the rough, rocky road under a blazing sun to the Morgan home. The men were hurriedly called in from the field and she was taken to the doctor in Othello. The supposed best remedy for snake bites at that time was whiskey in liberal amounts, and the doctor proceeded to fill her up on the remedy.

"I was sure sick afterward," she remembered, "But I am quite sure it was not from the snake bite."

One day as I was bringing the horses home in the late afternoon, one of the young mares got frightened by the carcass of Old Red which had been pulled down into the flat, and stampeded the whole herd off up the flat into the area of more cliffs and rocks. They ran for a mile or two before I could catch up with them some twelve or fifteen miles below where the O'Sullivan Dam now stands.

As I was skirting around to head them back, my horse suddenly gave a jump and I heard the warning rattle. After locating the snake at the base of a sagebrush, I rode back a little way and tied my horse to a sagebrush so he would not decide it was time for him to be getting home to his supper and leave me stranded. Watching where I stepped, for the possibility of a den of them being somewhere around was very real, (the terrain was just right for one) I went back to the one I had seen.

Various stories had been told about how far a rattlesnake could strike, from twice their length to six feet. Seeing the sun was not yet down, I decided to satisfy my curiousity and get the answer to the question. "Just how far could a snake strike at its best?"

Earlier in the day I had broken off a long slender willow branch that was growing beside a dried-up water hole, and had been using it to speed up the horses when they were inclined to loiter. It was just the thing to arouse that snake to its greatest striking power.

Trembling with excitement and the thrill of danger, I lashed the snake. First, with the leaves still on, the snake was stung to fury; the long leaf-covered switch could only sting, not damage him. The snake would strike at those elusive, stinging leaves repeatedly. At times it tried to escape, but a lash would send it back to the shelter of the sagebrush. At other times it darted toward me, whether to attack or escape in another direction, I do not know; but again the lash would send it back to the bush.

Then stripping the willow leaves to the bare stem about seven feet long, I stung the snake to greater fury. Its best efforts showed it had to keep at least a third of its length on the ground. It did not attempt to coil in rings, rather drew back like a flattened spring that took only a second to draw back and strike again. Time after time I lashed with the slender tip and it struck back furiously, all the time keeping up a continuous rattle. It made no attempt to bite itself as I had heard it said they would sometimes do when infuriated but with no way to escape.

Finally the lengthening shadows disappeared; the lonely call of a coyote sounded across the flat and was answered by another in an opposite direction. The sun had gone down. My herd was scattered up the flat and we were still miles from home. It was time to finish the snake with the ever-plentiful rocks lying all around, and gather the herd.

One morning when I went to round up the horses before starting out for the day, an unusual phenomenom was in clear view from the yard. There was a rise of ground between the May's place and town so that only the top of the high water tower showed from there; but this morning the whole town was elevated into clear view.

"Mary, come see how plainly Othello shows up this morning," I called to her. "I've never seen it like that before. I didn't know you could see Othello from here."

"That is a mirage," she said as she saw what I was looking at. "We've seen it before a few times." That was the first mirage I had ever seen and I couldn't understand how it could raise a whole town into view.

At first the horses were brought back to the home place at night, then Billie arranged to pasture them at Aunt Ellen's homestead, making the drive to the lake three miles shorter. The days were also getting shorter and the new pasture was situated in a wild lonely place bordering on a row of cliffs. The last mile as dusk was coming on in the evening was one that gave my imagination a lot of room for creepy feelings. The last half mile lay between two rows of cliffs, just the place for bob cats and lynx to have set up housekeeping. Coyotes began their gossiping across the wastelands at evening time adding to that lonesome feeling.

There was one particular place where a narrow break in the wall of cliffs permitted the horses to pass through to the pasture; this was the crucial spot where my imagination pictured some wild animal lying in wait to pounce. That none ever did in no

211

way lessened my fears of what might happen next time. I even learned to fasten the barbed wire gate open in the morning so I would be able to close it from atop the horse at night. Blackie and I may have had different reasons for the fast run to the top of the bench, past Aunt Ellen's cabin to where the fence-lined road joined the main road, but we lost no time getting there. Soon it would be dark by the time I got home.

"Mrs. McCulloch was taken very sick last night," Billie was talking to Mary one evening when he came home from town.

"Where did you hear that?" she asked as she poured some warm water from the tea kettle into the wash basin for him to wash before supper.

"I stopped in at Tipton's on the way home, and Xerpha told me," he answered as he soaped his hands to get rid of dust and plaster. "They are taking her to the coast to put her under a doctor's care over there."

"Did you hear what was the matter?" Mary's face showed her concern at hearing the nearest neighbor who had been so kind in her own illness should now be seriously ill.

"They are not sure yet," Billie answered as he pulled a bag of candy from his coat pocket and gave it to Willie.

"Here is some candy for Daddy's boy," he said to the small boy who was his pride. "Did you and old Longtail catch any jack rabbits today?" Then continuing his remarks to Mary, he said, "They seem to think it was a complete breakdown. They are all much concerned about her."

We wondered how Mr. Mac and Flossie would manage without her now. Xerpha was working in the post office and Flossie would be entering high school right away, and it seemed to us some other arrangements would have to be made to provide for the hired men who were working for McCulloch and Tipton on the farms under cultivation.

Some of the other homesteads were beginning to look deserted. Grandfather Adams had gone to live with other members of his family after the death of Grandma Adams. No one lived on the Showalter place after the Godseys moved to Lind; the James

Price family moved to the coast leaving their homestead house vacant. Other homestead men who were bachelors, proved up on their land then moved away. In some cases seeded wheat was blown out by the dust storms and it became necessary to borrow money from the banks to re-seed the land. Tipton gave credit to the families almost from one harvest to another, who would otherwise have been forced to leave the homesteads before getting title to the land. Banks were sometimes forced to foreclose when the crops were not sufficient to meet the obligations. Gradually the land was going into the hands of banks and land loan companies.

I was still occupied with herding horses, but starting out at day break on a chilly, frosty morning after breaking the ice in the horse trough so Blackie could drink, was losing its appeal. Othello was starting its first high school and it was time for me to return to the class room.

1909. First brick school building in Othello. The second row of windows above the balcony were used in the April Fool's Day exploit. Upper window, far R, where high school class of 1911 had their desks in the cloak room.

Chapter XXIV

High School Days

THE TWO-STORY BRICK BUILDING was almost bulging with the growing enrollment, and the two large class rooms, one on each floor, were assigned to the first six grades. In addition to these two main rooms, there were three very small rooms; one at the turn of the stairs between the first and second floors, used as the library, another at the head of the stairs on the second floor, a kind of anteroom which may have been intended for the principal's office, and another a short flight of steps up from this anteroom toward the belfry.

D. L. Haile was again employed as teacher, but with the addition of a ninth grade another teacher was needed. Eva Merrill, whose parents had been homestead people between Othello and Cunningham, was employed to teach the intermediate grades. Laura Rogers taught the three primary grades while Mr. Haile was the principal and taught the three upper grades.

Four students registered for the seventh and eighth grades; Ruth Barton and Nora Estep in the eighth and Strother and Archie Reynolds in the seventh grade. The Reynolds boys were not related. Strother was the son of J. W. Reynolds who owned a feed business in town, while Archie's parents were homestead people from south of town. To distinguish them we sometimes called them the "Town Reynolds" or "Country Reynolds."

Six girls, Flossie McCulloch, Edith Thorp, Lora Estep, Fannie Phillips, Florence Ogden and Lillian Hatfield registered for the ninth grade at the beginning of the 1911 school term. The first four girls were from the homesteads; Florence's father and brother published the newspaper and Lillian's father was running the Chavis livery barn.

"When are you going to start to school?" Flossie asked me

one evening as I stopped by their place to see her after putting the horses into the pasture. I would have to go from home when I started, and it was not going to be easy to go the three miles from there.

"I don't know yet. I had most of the first semester in Cheney." I remembered I had not been able to quite finish the first semester because of the la grippe and I would need to cover some of it again. "Could I ride with you and your father for a few days?"

"Why don't you come stay with us for two or three nights until you get started," she suggested. "Papa takes me in the little buggy."

A few days later I rode with Flossie and her father in the little one-horse rig to start high school in town. Otis went with me after that, riding horseback from home. It saved him the long walk to school alone since there were no other pupils going to school at Rising Star from the direction of our home. We rode Bert, and it took us about an hour to get to school on time.

One crisp, frosty morning we started to school about the usual time of eight o'clock. The frost lay almost like snow on the frozen ground. As we rode along the subject of Bert's occasional departure from good behaviour came up for discussion.

"Why do you suppose Bert has never tried to buck when we are riding him?" I asked him, remembering the time he had bucked Papa off.

"He bucked Headley off one time, too," Otis informed me. I hadn't heard about that.

Finally, one of us came up with the pert observation; "Bert knows it would do no good to try because he could never buck us off." The other rejoined very boastfully.

"Bert isn't man enough to buck us off." Both agreed it would be useless for him to try.

A half mile from home a wire gate stretched across the road and a short distance beyond there the road crossed the railroad track. As we approached the gate we noticed a long freight train was coming from Othello, its heavy puffs of smoke rising high into the still cold air as the big steam locomotive pulled the long string of heavily loaded cars up the grade. It was moving slowly and unless we got across the track before the train got there we might be late for school.

Otis jumped off and opened the gate for me to ride through, then fastened it quickly and got back on. Together we gave Bert a kick with our heels to get a fast start for the crossing. That was a mistake. Bert started, but not in the direction we wanted to take. He tucked his head down, gathered his muscles and went right up into the air with all four feet, coming down stiff-legged and his back arched into a good snapping position before we realized what was happening. The swiftly following second time he did it we parted company with the saddle and the horse to land together on the frozen ground.

Two more surprised and chagrined youngsters than we were as we picked ourselves up and looked at each other, would be hard to imagine. The same thought must have occurred to both. "Could Bert have understood what we had been saying?" We hadn't noticed his ears turned back to eavesdrop. If this was his way of teaching two young upstarts who was the better man, it was at least well timed.

"Are you hurt?" was Otis' first question to me.

"No, are you?"

"No, but now what shall we do?" was his next question. We were still two and a half miles from school. Bert had run off down into the field and was calmly grazing on the tender green wheat while he waited with unconcern to see our next move. He made no effort to evade us as Otis walked up to him.

"Are you scared to get on him again?" Otis queried me. I evaded a direct reply to that question by saying, "We have to get to school."

Carefully we soothed Bert with gentle pats and sweet words to show we had no hard feelings.

"Nice Bert!" "Good old horse!" Warily we climbed onto his back and gently started him toward the crossing. There was

217

model behaviour on his part, and ours. The train had come and gone and we were late to school.

Because of the distance from home for some of us we found places to stay in town where we could work for our room and board. Flossie came to stay with her sister Alice; Ruth found a place with Joe and Annie McManamon and Eva Merrill took me into her home. Otis reluctantly returned to the country school where Mabel Andresen was teaching the five children attending there.

Papa and Otis were alone now on the homestead for a while until Mary and Billie moved over to Papa's homestead where Mary could care for them and her family while Billie was building a house on their new homestead. A few days before Christmas, Gordon was born, giving Willie a little brother.

It was not only the distance which gave me reason to be glad to stay with Miss Merrill; it left one less mouth to feed at home.

The small room for the seventh and eighth grades did not permit space for the ninth grade, and the small room above it was too isolated as well as being hard to heat in winter. The problem of where to put the new high school was solved by putting it in the cloak room. This was a hallway about twenty feet long where the intermediate children hung their wraps. The space at one end not needed for wraps, was assigned to the ninth grade girls and desks were placed along one wall near the single window. It was an inconspicuous start.

Being hidden away in the cloak room had its advantages in some ways; it was not directly in line with the principal's desk, though he occasionally paid a little visit to see how the studying was progressing.

As the only representatives of the new Othello High School, we felt the need of some recognition that would take us out of the obscurity of the cloak room; some outward marks of our status such as class colors, pennants and an emblem.

"Girls, we've got to think up some way that we can get our class colors, class pins and pennants, or something to show we are in high school." Lora was no less in earnest even if she was having to talk in a whisper so her voice would not carry to Mr. Haile's ears in the outer room.

We were taking time out from studying ancient history to study our current problems. Obviously, these things were a vital need to our way of thinking, but they might not seem so vital to our parents beside such necessary items as shoes and other clothes. The personal finances with most of us who were homestead girls did not cover such items, and unless other means could be found to raise the money we were not likely to get the things we wanted.

"There ought to be some way to make some money if we could think of it," offered Fannie who was ready to go along with any plan that gave any hope of success.

"Could we make some candy and sell it?" asked Lillian. But where would we get sugar, chocolate, nuts and other ingredients. They would cost money, too.

"Could we put on a program and earn some money that way?" Florence had us all listening as her idea began to take shape even if we did think it would be a big venture for high school girls.

"What kind of program could we give that people would pay to see?" Flossie was of a practical mind and a bit skeptical that we could provide an evening's entertainment that the town people would pay to see.

"Oh, we wouldn't charge them to get in for the program," Florence went on, "That would just be a way to get them there."

"Then how would we make any money that way?" asked Edith. Some of us were just listening to the whispered talk going on around us, not yet having come up with more ideas.

"Sh-h-h," someone warned, "I think Mr. Haile is coming." Quietly, he tiptoed in to find every head bent studiously over her books.

Never having had any experience in class organization, and without a class sponsor to direct us, we made our own rules. Since just seven girls made up the class we took the name of the Seven Sisters Society. No class president was deemed necessary;

219

each Sister was on an equal footing with the others. Not only did we discuss ways and means of raising money in our cloak room sessions, but sometimes when Professor Haile came to our study hall to see how the studies were progressing, he found it turned into a beauty parlor as some girl worked at re-arranging another's hair style while one of the other girls read aloud from the ancient history lesson or from MacBeth. We were studying Shakespearean plays in our English literature. Mr. Haile might chide a little but he never turned thumbs down on our extra-curricular pursuits in the cloak room so long as we knew our lessons at class time. He may have considered "girls will be girls" and let it go at that.

We went to the small outer room for recitations, sometimes affording embarrassment to us and secret amusement to the boys in the other grades out there when we came to certain passages in MacBeth we considered too plainly spoken for public reading. To our relief, at one passage where MacBeth's enemy tells of his untimely birth, Mr. Haile quietly told the girl who was reading, "You may skip that next passage and continue on with the next."

Several plans for raising the money were talked over. We finally decided a program to be given at McMillan's hall offered the best possibilities. In order to carry through our scheme for raising money, it was first necessary to get Mr. Haile's consent since he was the principal of the high school. He was a bit dubious at first, but after hearing our plans and pleas he gave his consent with two conditions attached. We were not to involve him in any of our plans or preparation of the program we planned to give; nor were we to involve the school in financing it. If we went through with it we were to do it entirely on our own. We accepted his conditions being quite satisfied we were entirely capable of doing what we planned. We had met the first hurdle and cleared it.

Next, we approached Mr. McMillan in a body to arrange for the use of the hall. Fannie as the oldest was our opening spokesman.

"Mr. McMillan, we would like to rent the hall to give a program in about three weeks."

"Who is going to give a program?" he asked, astonished to be confronted by the group of girls with such a request.

"We are," several voices assured him.

"You girls are going to give a program?" This was a situation he had never seen before. "Why do you girls want to give a program? Is Mr. Haile in on this?"

"No, Mr. Haile isn't in on it, but he knows about it and has given us his consent if we don't bother him with any of the planning." We explained our need for money.

"How do you plan to pay for the hall? You know the price is ten dollars for the use of it."

"Mr. McMillan, we wanted you to be real nice and let us have it for half price," tall, red-haired Lillian coaxed him with her friendliest smile. We backed up her request with a chorus of "Please Mr. McMillan?"

"But girls, you didn't say why you want to give this program?" He was still puzzled at the unusual situation.

"Oh, we are the Othello High School," Florence told him. "We didn't want to ask our parents for the money to buy our colors, pennants and emblems, for some of the girls are from the homesteads and it would be hard for them to raise the money to buy these things."

One argument after another was given him as a reason for his going along with our request. When one girl paused for breath or ran out of arguments, another was ready with more. Sometimes we all talked at one time. Whether we out-talked him, or civic spirit and his sense of humor prevailed, he finally gave in and a date was set when we could have the hall. The second hurdle was cleared.

Florence could play the piano, so our program included music in the form of duets, trios, choruses and a piano solo, besides recitations and a short skit. For the social part of the evening we planned a candy booth, a coffee, sandwich and cake counter and a fish pond where patrons could fish out wrapped packages for a ten cent fee. We either made small gift items for the fish pond or solicited little items from the drug store and general stores. We expected to have help on the food items from our families and friends who were sympathetic to our high school problem. Before we got through with our planning for ways and means of bringing in more funds, we had devised a gypsy fortune-telling booth and a Salvation Army lass who was to circulate through the crowd soliciting funds for our needs. The last two schemes were designed to bring in clear cash.

We spread the word everywhere for we believed in advertising; the newspaper gave us good publicity. Since Othello was a railroad town with little in the way of public entertainment, we could expect a good crowd.

The evening arrived and found the hall crowded. The Sisters were excited and nervous, but elated when the time came to begin the program. It looked like everybody in town had come. Some of the nervousness may have been because we were without Mr. Haile's moral support at the last moment; he had received a summons from the County Superintendent of Schools that took him to Ritzville that day. We were indeed on our own. It was too late now to draw back; the show must go on.

Our audience was generous with its applause and sympathetic to the reasons for which the program was being given.

Flushed with the success of the first part of the evening's entertainment, Fannie, as the mistress of ceremonies, appeared on the platform to announce the part which was to bring in the money.

"Ladies and Gentlemen, Friends: This concludes the first part of the evening's entertainment, and we thank you for coming and for your applause. We hope you will stay and enjoy the social part which is to follow. We will be at the various stands around the room where refreshments will be on sale. At the stand on the right side of the room you will find sandwiches, cake and coffee. A booth of delicious candies is on the left. If you wish to try your success at fishing, Lillian will be there to bait your hook for one of the gift packages. Our gypsy will foretell the future of anyone who crosses her palm with a silver dime; and if a Salvation Army lass approaches you with her tambourine and a plea for assistance in our worthy project, you may recognize Laura in a new roll. We want you to have a pleasant evening together."

Meanwhile the various booths were opened and the girls took their places, ready to begin serving. The entire audience remained to patronize the food and other features. Lora, Lillian, Florence, Flossie and Fannie alternated among the different booths. Dark-eyed Edith, her hair in two long braids and wearing a colorful costume and long strands of bright beads, took her place in the little tepee. The Salvation Army lass in a dark blue dress, and with a hat carrying the familiar name in red across the front, circulated among the friendly crowd to accept donations.

Nearly everyone stayed for the entire evening, buying out our stock of food and gifts, and visiting with neighbors and friends. It was evident the young fellows required more than one reading by the charming little gypsy lass, and her dimes counted up to nearly six dollars before the evening was over. Donations to the Salvation Army lass were only a little less. When the funds were counted and expenses for the hall deducted there remained enough to purchase pennants, class colors and emblems. Othello High School had been successfully brought to public attention.

After having tasted a degree of success in giving our program, we began to look for other activities. It was suggested we might give a play. This time Mr. Haile went along with us. Not having any boys in the ninth grade and neither of the seventh grade boys wanting any part in the play we had selected, we pursuaded some of the homestead boys to take parts. They had been coming to our parties.

John Knepper from out on Crab Creek, was given the male lead with Lora playing the part of the leading lady. Herbert Michel from the Billington District took the part of the inn keeper, with me as his fuss-budget wife, and John Lee from the Rising Star District was the stage driver, the comedian. Johnny had grown to be a tall, lanky sort of lad with a drawl in his speech that fitted well in the comic role he played. Several others had parts in the play.

We had a lot of fun at rehearsals which were held twice a week under Mr. Haile's direction. Often other young folks came along to watch the fun and be with the other young people. One of the side awards to the girls was at the close of practice session when some boy got up the courage to ask, "May I take you home?" Othello had no street lights, so of course we were glad to have protection as we walked home through the darkened streets.

The play was well received, and for a time afterward we considered taking it to other schools, but this fell through as liable to distract from our studies.

A literary society had been organized at the Billington school five miles east of Othello where Mrs. A. O. Lee was the teacher. One day when A. O. Lee came in for his mail and groceries at Tipton's store, he told Lillian about the next literary program and box supper that was to be given.

"We would like to have you young folks come out and help us on the program," he told her.

"When is your next program?" she asked.

"It will be a week from next Friday evening. Could you get a group of the young people together, and come out?" Mr. Lee was interested in all the affairs of the community.

Lillian passed on the invitation, and we were all much excited over the prospect. John and Jess solved our problem of transportation by bringing in the big hay wagon which had been placed on sled runners because of the snow which had fallen.

There was room for the twelve or fourteen of us in the big wagon bed, the bottom of which was bedded with straw and quilts to keep us warm. Bells attached to the hames of the four-horse team added to the beauty of the winter night as they trotted along. Lillian, who was a little older, was usually our chaperone. If Xerpha was home from Pullman for the holidays she was included in the fun.

"Mr. Lee said he would like for us to give something on the program," Lillian reminded us. "John, you and Jess could sing a duet."

"Sing one of the cowboy songs you know," Nora suggested. We had heard them sing together at some of our parties and found they had real pleasing voices.

"Well, how about you and Lora singing something?" John knew they sang together at the little Presbyterian Church and was going to see they were included if he and Jess had to perform.

"Laura, why don't you give your 'tobacco spit' piece?" Lora asked. This was what she called the recitation I had given at Ritzville. Before the evening was over nearly all had been included in the program.

It was more fun to go as a group, and except when going to church we usually all went together in a wagon or bob sled if it was a social affair in the country.

The night we had a surprise party on Otto Dill out at his parents' homestead near the lake called either Owl Lake or Dill Lake, we went together in a flat bed, low-sided wagon. There were four children in the Dill family; the eldest, Otto, was near our age.

This time, Ollie Kellenberger, the widowed sister of the twins, was our chaperone. But Nora had a new boy friend, Walter Krause, who carried the nickname "Dutch." They decided to go in style so Dutch obtained a team and buggy from the livery barn in which to take Nora and Lora. The twins' brother, Ralph, went with them to drive the frisky team.

All arrived safely, but when we were ready to start home about midnight, there was trouble getting the livery team started. The horses balked at leaving the shelter of the barn and barnlot at that late hour. All of Ralph's efforts to get the team started producing no results, he got out of the buggy to lead them out of the barnyard intending to jump into the buggy when he got them going. Instead, they started on a fast run, giving him no chance to jump into his seat. Walter was not accustomed to either the team or the country, but it was now up to him to get the girls and himself back to town. The team would know the way back to the livery barn, so without anxiety Ralph got into the wagon with us for the ride back home.

Singing, laughing and talking over the things we had enjoyed at the party, we had gone about half way back to town when someone chanced to look back.

"Look, there's a buggy coming! Who do you suppose it could be at this time of night?" We all turned to look.

"They must be in a hurry. That team is sure running!" Rapidly it gained on us.

"Why, that's the team and buggy that Dutch and the girls were in," Ralph had recognized the horses as they came up to us and turned out to go around the wagon.

"But the buggy is empty!" cried Ollie. "They have had an accident! They may be hurt or killed!"

Our team was immediately turned around to go back and search for them while two of the boys followed the run-away team and buggy back to town. Rapidly, we drove back over the way we had come, stopping at frequent intervals to call and listen. After stopping several times, we caught an answering call from Lora off to the south of us.

"Dutch has got his leg broke," she was saying.

"Where is Nora? Is she all right?" shouted Ralph.

"We are both all right," Lora answered, "But Dutch is hurt. His leg is broken, and he can't walk."

"How did they ever get way off in that direction?" we queried among ourselves.

The wagon was left in the road while Ralph and some of the other boys reconnoitered to find a safe way to get the wagon near to the accident victims.

After leaving Dill's at such a rapid pace, the team followed the main road for some distance, then branched off onto a dim wagon track leading south instead of toward town. Walter succeeded in getting the team under control, but not being familiar with the road did not at first realize they had taken a

226

wrong road. When he found they were not going toward Othello he circled to get back onto the right road, not realizing the danger.

Still running, the horses and buggy went off a ledge of rocks about five or six feet high, turning the buggy over and throwing the occupants out. Walter's leg caught between the spokes of the wheel, breaking the leg. Neither of the girls had been more than bruised and frightened. The team plunged on in fright, righting the buggy, and dashed for home leaving the three stranded, helpless and alone at the foot of the ledge.

A sagebrush fire was started to keep them warm while the wagon was brought as near as possible among the rocks; then groaning in pain, Walter was taken back to town. It was nearing four o'clock in the morning when we at last got him to the home of his sister, Maude Anderson. Doctor Bardwell was called and we learned he had a compound fracture which had become badly swollen during the unskilled handling. After the doctor splinted it carefully, Dutch was sent on to the hospital in Saint Maries, Idaho, where it could be X-rayed before putting on the cast.

As Christmas time drew near the two school teachers, Eva and Laura planned a Christmas party for the more mature single people who liked to play bridge. Josie Gregg, who had a millinery and dressmaking shop in the Crawford building, Carl Tulles whose drug store was next to Josie's shop, Walter Zimmerman, the bank clerk, whose dark eyes and keen wit might enliven any party, A. B. Johnson, a boiler maker who worked at the round house and who later became one of Othello's early mayors, and a married couple by the name of Schoonmaker made up the party.

Eva received a box of mistletoe from out of the state to add to the gaiety of the evening.

"Where shall we hang this where it will be the most conspicuous?" asked Eva as Laura was admiring the odd plant with its white waxen berries. The Christmas tree had been decorated and the scent of fir filled the double room. The mistletoe was to be the final touch which would add to the fun of the festivities.

"We could have some over the entrance," Laura suggested,

"but I think we should have a spray right here below the chandelier." Laura was a roly-poly little woman who had a tightly laced figure suggesting a pouter pigeon, but whose friendly smile took in everyone. Acting on Laura's suggestion, a nice large spray was hung in the middle of the room.

Most of the evening was given to bridge before refreshments were served and the tree yielded up gifts for everyone. A lot of chaffing was going on about the mistletoe when Josie jumped to her feet and with her dark eyes snapping in fun, stood under the spray hanging from the chandelier with a "dare you" light in her eyes.

"All right, Carl, are you going to let her get away with that?" kidded Walt. "You have seniority rights here."

"Come on, Carl, here is your chance," challenged A. B. (Johnson was usually called A. B. by his friends.)

"Oh mercy, no!" groaned Carl in mock consternation. He was urged to accept Josie's dare to see if she would back down, but he couldn't be pursuaded to take up the gauntlet she had dropped, and was promptly labeled lacking in courage by the girls.

A civic organization was started before the winter was over when some of the civic-minded folk started the Othello Improvement Club. It might be better to say an effort was made to start one. Jim and Lucy McManamon took an active part in starting it with Jim as chairman at the beginning. The first meeting was held in the dining room of the Hibbard Hotel with a large segment of the population in attendance. It may have been partly inspired by some prospective developments that were advertised in the Portland Oregonian and the Spokesman Review in February, 1910. It had attracted attention with full page advertising.

A great prize contest was announced with an acre of fruit land at Othello Highlands, a beautiful building lot in Othello, and six other valuable prizes to be awarded the winners. Contestants were to write a letter telling why they thought Othello had a great future, and why it was a desirable place to locate.

The name of the company offering the contest was called THE OTHELLO IMPROVEMENT COMPANY,[1] with P. B. Newkirk the Managing Director.

With a great build-up on the future prospects, the American Slate Products Company was said to be erecting an immense plant, already under construction. When nothing further was done by way of construction after a few buckets of cement were poured into some holes in the ground, it seemed that any future progress for Othello could only be advanced by local people becoming organized. After a few meetings the Improvement Club turned into a whist club which helped to while away some winter evenings.

The winter passed and it was the morning of April Fool's Day. At school, the principal always went to the back entrance of the school building to see the children assembled into line and marched into their rooms in good order. He had just left the ninth grade girls in his room on the second floor, and had no sooner disappeared down the stairs when Fannie made a suggestion.

"Let's play an April Fool joke on Mr. Haile, and make him think we have ditched school for the day. We could hide up in the belfry. He wouldn't think of us hiding up there." The idea was quickly accepted by the rest of us.

The belfry was reached through the small room a short flight of steps above Mr. Haile's room. Slipping up the stairway and on through the door leading to the bell tower, we were soon seated on the ladder leading up to the bell; giggling at the surprise we were giving the principal.

Some ten minutes passed; then we heard steps coming up the short flight of steps to the room just outside the belfry door. We waited with baited breath to learn whether he would think of the tower. We did not have long to wait. The door leading to our hiding place opened and Mr. Haile looked up to where we were

---

[1]The story of the supposed development by the Othello Improvement Company is taken from the full-page advertisement in the *Portland Oregonian* of Feb. 27, 1910. A similar ad was run in the *Spokesman-Review* about the same time.

perched on the ladder. Our shout of "April Fool" was answered by another from him as he chuckled, then stepped back and locked the outer door before he retreated down the stairway.

On coming down to the upper room, we found the books we would need for our next class period had been laid on a shelf. Evidently we were to be kept prisoners until time for our first class period. He had neatly turned the tables on us; he doubtless expected us to put in the intervening time seated on the floor to study since there were no seats or desks in the room. But that kind of study did not appeal to us just then for the joke we had started had been turned against us unless we could find some way out of our dilemma.

The windows of the small room in which we were imprisoned looked out onto a flat roof over the front entrance of the building, but the ground was over two stories away. Then we saw the rope by which the flag was raised to the flag pole hanging temptingly near.

"We might slide down on the rope," one of the girls voiced what some of us were thinking.

"No, we might pull the flag pole down if we did that," cautioned Fannie. We discarded that idea.

That flat roof over the entrance was just outside the library window, and a way of entry through the library window if we could get down there, offered possibilities.

"Do you suppose the library window is unlocked," wondered Flossie. "If it isn't we would be out in plain view of the town from that roof."

"But how would we get down there?" "Suppose it is locked?" were some of the questions we asked each other. Urged on by a desire not to be outdone, we studied the possibilities. It was worth trying we decided.

"I am the tallest; I'll go first," offered Lora. "I can find out if the window is unlocked. If it isn't locked the rest of you can follow me."

She climbed out the window two and a half stories above the ground with two of the girls holding on to her hands while they

230

in turn were anchored by the others to prevent them from falling out. We let her down as far as we could reach from where she dropped about four feet to the roof.

"Girls, it's not locked," came her excited whisper. Now it was time for the rest of us to be let down one by one. In quick succession the rest of us followed and were soon standing with her on the balcony outside the library window.

Cautiously we raised the window, avoiding any noise that would give us away, then slipped through and tiptoed up the short flight of steps to Mr. Haile's door. We could hear the voices of the boys answering the teacher's questions as we waited almost breathless with excitement before knocking on the door.

"April Fool, Mr. Haile!" we shouted as he opened the door. The surprised look on his face was a most satisfactory reward for our efforts. We were now ready to settle down to study.

During her last two years of high school in Ritzville, Nellie stayed in the home of Sheriff and Mrs. George McCollom. No wages were paid to girls who were working for their room and board while attending school, but the McColloms were very kind to her. Sometimes, when the shoe problem became critical for her they bought her a new pair. But now, with graduation coming near when new clothes would be needed for the occasion, Nellie saw no way to get them. The four years with the barest minimum of clothing had been difficult, but this was a real crisis.

She finally unburdened herself to Mrs. McCollom. "What am I going to do?" she asked. "All the other girls will have nice dresses and I know Papa hasn't the money to buy me any." It was not customary at that time for the high school graduates in the small towns to wear cap and gown. She was sick at heart at the prospect and was almost ready to give up thoughts of graduating with her class.

"Nellie, we want to help you get your things so you can graduate with your class," Mrs. McCollom told her a few days later.

"We won't let our girl get up there in old clothes when all the other girls are wearing nice things," George added.

Material for a new dress was bought and made into a dainty white dress; shoes and stockings were supplied so that a young motherless girl could march happily in with her class to receive her diploma. Mrs. McCollom had filled the void to act as mother; and Nellie had become a high school graduate.

That same year saw the marriage of two homestead girls. Xerpha was again working as the postal clerk at the post office in Tipton's new store at the corner of third and main streets.

"Xerpha, I hear you are going to be married real soon. Is that true?" I enquired one day as I stopped by the post office.

"Yes, it is true," she replied with her modest smile.

"It is to Mr. Gaines, isn't it?" I was quite sure it must be, for while we were attending school at Rising Star we had sometimes seen him get off the train at Novara station, and walk up the hill to her home. Otis would tease her by punning, "Xerpha, I see you are going to Gaines something," or, "Have you Gained anything lately?" She always acknowledged his teasing with a quiet pleased smile.

Now she smiled her answer, "Yes it is Edward."

Their friendship had begun while Xerpha was attending high school in Ritzville where Edward was teaching school. As she went on to college in Pullman where he was continuing his studies in agronomy, the friendship developed more warmly. Now he came to claim his bride at the Tipton home in a quiet home wedding. Afterward, her mother, whose gradually returning strength permitted her to be at home once more, and other immediate members of the family walked to the depot with the bride and groom where they caught the late afternoon train to Pullman.

Edward and Xerpha were to become associated with Pullman College in developments which would benefit the farmers who raised wheat and other crops throughout the great Inland Empire. His name was to become well known by his work in developing better strains of wheat.

The other romance reached its climax the night a community dance was held at McMillan's hall. Jennie obtained permission

232

from her mother to spend the night in town with her sister Ruth. Ruth was working for Joe and Annie McManamon at the Hibbard Hotel where I was also working.

Jennie had been keeping company with Leslie Williams, the time keeper at the railroad round house. They came to the dance, but as Leslie seldom danced, they soon left. Nothing was thought of that until we got back to the hotel after the dance was over about three o'clock in the morning. Jennie had not returned. Ruth came to our adjoining room with a perplexed look on her face.

"What is the matter Ruth?" asked the other girl, Iowa Baxter, who was working with us at the hotel.

"Jennie isn't in my room, and I don't know what to think," she explained. "I wonder if Leslie took her home."

"Didn't she intend to stay with you tonight?" I asked.

"Yes, she did, but she might have changed her mind."

"It looks like she would have told you if she changed her mind," Iowa remarked. "Do you suppose those two decided to elope?"

"That is what I am afraid may have happened," Ruth told us with a worried look. "I am going down and tell Annie and Joe, and see what they think."

When breakfast time came and Leslie did not respond to the breakfast call, it looked like an elopement had taken place. It was the exciting topic of the day around the hotel. Later in the day when the Bartons came to town expecting to take their seventeen-year-old daughter home, it was to learn Jennie was missing and an elopement was suspected. Anxiously, they waited for some word of the missing couple, having no idea in which direction they might have gone, since both the east and west bound passenger trains met in Othello.

It was not until the early train from the west brought the missing couple back twenty-four hours later that we learned they had caught the two-thirty westbound train to Ellensburg where they were married.

233

Lower Crab Creek picnic, ca. 1910.

Chapter XXV

Picnics

PICNICS WERE ONE of the recreations for homestead families in the early days, though the places available for such outings were somewhat limited. An interesting place for some of the families and young folk who lived too far from Crab Creek to picnic there frequently, was the old abandoned silica mine which had discontinued operations some years before. It was in the Leone Valley area between Othello and Cunningham, some eight and a half miles east and two miles north of Othello.

The abandoned chambers and tunnels offered a cool and unique place for picnics in the hot summer. The columns supporting the ceiling came to hold quite a record of those visiting the mine as places were whittled smooth for the names and initials to be carved into the soft silica.

Records of the operation of the mine are scarce; but in 1898 two carloads a year were shipped from Hatton over the Northern Pacific Railroad. Two warehouses were built at the mine for storage until time for shipment. It was hauled by heavy wagon and four-horse team to the shipping point. Three holes were opened up into the side of the hill, with one of them extending some distance back and branching off into side tunnels. Pillars of the silica rock were left in place to support the ceiling. The silica had become exhausted and the mine closed down in 1901, but the loading platform and warehouses remained for some years longer.

Chunks of the rock were sometimes pounded fine and used as grit to feed the chickens by homestead people. Samples of both the rock and white powder had been brought to our place from the mine.

Dona had gone on picnics to the mine with Estella and her

brother Arthur, three of the Sneads, Grace, Ella and Delbert, Elmer and Roland Hedrick and others while we were living in Cunningham. But I had never seen the old mine until the summer of 1913 when Fannie and I were invited to go home with Ethel and Willard Simms after church one Sunday. We rode out with them in Willard's buggy.

In the afternoon, Herb Michel and Hugh Phillips came over and suggested we go and explore the tunnels of the old mine. That sounded like a good afternoon adventure. With three in Willard's buggy and three in Hugh's buggy we started for the drive to the mine.

We found some of the tunnels had collapsed from water seepage and winter flooding so it was unsafe to explore far into the tunnels. The dry white powdery silica and chunks of the semi-clear amber-colored rock were still laying around the floor of the mine, but the warehouses and platform had been removed. The columns which supported the ceiling of the main chamber just inside the entrance, still held the names and initials of those who had visited the mine, so we added ours to the many already registered there.

From year to year, community picnics were held on Crab Creek north of Deadman Lake to which people from all the surrounding area came. The first summer we were on the homestead we attended a 4th of July picnic and got acquainted with some of the families living north and west of us. These picnics were sometimes held on Labor Day instead of Independence Day, especially when the Pioneer's picnic was held at Neppel on Moses Lake with a three-day rodeo.

In the summer of 1913, a large celebration was planned at Nepel, now the present city of Moses Lake. It was just a small town with one hotel and a few small businesses on one street beside the lake. A spur line of the Milwaukee railroad extended out from Warden through Neppel to Ephrata, connecting that area with the main line of the railroad. The trains made the run daily except Sunday, with a passenger coach on the end of the train of freight cars to give passenger service.

"Are you going to the Pioneer's picnic up at Moses Lake?" asked Nora one day when I had gone up to visit her and Lora.

"I'd sure like to go, but I don't know whether I could get off from work." (I was waiting on tables for Mrs. Simonson in her small restaurant down on Main Street.) "Besides, I don't have any way to go. Are you going?"

"Yes, Brother Bill and Emma are taking us with them," Lora answered.

"He is taking a tent and we are going to camp for the whole three days," Nora added. I thought enviously how lucky they were. It would be fun camping for the full time of the celebration; but I knew that with four people in the two-seated hack, with a tent, bedding and food to last the three days there would be no room for another passenger.

"If you can find some way to get up there, you can sleep with us in the tent," they offered.

The more I heard about the coming picnic, the more I wanted to attend. When I talked with Mrs. Simonson she readily agreed to let me have two days off from work.

"Why don't you go up on the train?" someone suggested. "You could go up on Friday and come back the next day." The more I thought about that suggestion the better I liked it. To be what I thought suitably dressed, I bought a white ratine' dress to wear the whole time of the trip. It never occurred to me that it might be well to take along another dress, and with a dark summer coat which had been loaned to me as my only other item of wardrobe, I bought a round trip ticket and boarded the train early Friday morning.

When the train pulled in to the depot at Neppel, we found a large crowd waiting to meet friends at the train. The first familiar face I saw was that of a little red-faced German sewing machine agent I had seen in Othello from time to time, but who never aroused anything but aversion in me. He immediately came forward and attached himself to me as though I was just the one he had been waiting for, and offered to show me the way up to the hotel. Looking around desperately for some way of

237

escape without being rude, I saw the twin's brother Bill in the crowd.

"Oh! There you are Bill!" In glad relief at this chance of escape from the unwanted help of the short, unromantic-looking agent for the sewing machine company, I attached myself to Bill like a lost pup who had just found his best friend. "Where are the girls?" I asked. Then turning to Otto, I said, "I'm going with Bill to find my friends." But I wasn't to see the last of Otto.

Two exciting days with many kinds of contests followed; foot races for the boys and girls, horse races, bucking contests, calf roping and bull-dogging. Ralph, the brother of the twins, Art Phillips, Fannie's brother, and others we knew were among those taking part in the bucking contests.

"Ride 'im cowboy!" "Scratch him again!" Stick with him!" came the shouted advice from the interested spectators as the excitement of the events mounted.

The day was hot as July days in that arid country could get. By the time the contests for the day were concluded, we were looking for something cooler than a tent, and securing a boat which was powered by a small motor, we headed down the lake.

A low dam had been built across the lower end of Moses Lake where Crab Creek flowed out on its way to empty into the Columbia River just above the gap through Saddle Mountain near where Wanapum Dam now stands. An effort was being made to clear the lake of the mud carp so that game fish could be introduced. Just below the dam where only a small amount of water was escaping into the creek bed, we found dozens of the carp, many of them up to sixteen inches or more long, floundering helplessly among the rocks of the shallow stream bed.

Squeals of excitement came from the girls as they saw those large fish flopping in the shallow water. This looked like fishing opportunities at its best, and an opportunity that might never be ours again.

"Let's catch some and take them back to camp for supper," suggested Fannie who had joined us for the boat ride. Soon the four of us were scrambling for the big fish while Emma and Bill looked on in amusement from the boat.

"They will probably taste like mud," Bill warned us. "That is one reason they are trying to clean them out of the lake. They are mud carp."

In spite of his warning we each secured a flopping fish to add to the number being dropped into the gunny sack. We could not imagine those big fine-looking fish being anything but good to eat and were planning a fish supper from the ones we caught.

They smelled fine as they were fried a golden brown over the camp fire, but the first bite convinced us Bill knew what he was talking about. Sadly we discarded all of them.

By the early afternoon of the second day, most of the events on the program had taken place. Only the final dance would be held that evening for those who were remaining, so I walked down to the depot to learn when the train would be leaving for Othello.

"What time does the train leave?" I asked of the man at the desk.

"Oh that train left two hours ago," he informed me.

"The train's gone?" I asked in consternation.

"Yes, there won't be any more until Monday. Did you want to go to Othello?"

With a sinking feeling I turned to walk back to the tent knowing I did not have enough money left to pay for a hotel room and meals until train time Monday. What could I do? Besides, I had told Mrs. Simonson I would be gone only two days. If I did not show up at work the next morning she would wonder what had happened to me.

Back at the tent, it was being pulled down and things being loaded into the hack in readiness to leave for home right after the dance ended. They had a full load with no room to take another person. The same was true with the buggy in which Fannie had come with some of the Simms family. I was stranded, and it looked like I would have to sleep somewhere under the stars until Fannie offered to loan me two dollars to supplement what I had left.

My dress, which had been so white when I started to the picnic, was now so dirty from the dust and perspiration of the past two days the only thing to do was cover it up with the black coat. This added to my discomfort in the intense heat, but I went to the hotel and engaged a room.

At breakfast time, I was ashamed to appear in the dining room until after the other guests had eaten and left. Too, my limited funds would not permit more than two meals, and by eating late I should not have to go down at noon.

When I got back to my room, which by mid-forenoon was getting intensely hot, an idea came to me as I noticed the white bathtub in the bathroom. (Hotels were about the only place where there were bathtubs at the time.) I thought, "Why can't I wash out my dress in that bath tub? In this hot weather it will soon dry, and I can stay in my room and pretend I am sleeping until it dries."

Had the material been thin it would soon have dried, but that heavier ratine' was still damp as evening came on. I was beginning to feel the need of some food by this time, and hoping to find some store open I put on the damp dress and started out the hotel door. There was my would-be friend Otto, sitting in the shade of a locust tree not far from the door.

"Vere haf you been?" he asked, jumping up as he saw me. "I dit not see you in the dining room at dinner."

I am not sure that my explanation of over-sleeping sounded convincing, remembering how hot the day had been.

"Vere are you going now?" he asked.

I told him that since I had missed my supper, I thought I might find a store open where I could find some fruit. He fell into step with me, but every store and shop on the short business street was locked up.

"Let us get a boat and I vill take you for a boat ride on the lake. It vill be cooler on the vater," he offered.

"There are too many mosquitoes and gnats flying around at

240

this time of day." I countered his offer and turned back toward the hotel hoping to escape to my room where I could get out of my damp dress. I knew he would discover my dress was damp if he helped me into a boat.

"Vi don't you cum sit oudt here vere it iss getting cooler?" he invited in his strong German accent.

Doubtless he was trying to be nice to one who had waited on him many times, but an evening spent in the company of this little man with the foreign accent who appeared to be in his early forties, held no interest for me at seventeen. I proceeded on into the hotel to place an early morning call.

"Let me cum oop to your room and weesit a while," he next offered.

"No," I shook my head and said as civilly as I could, "I am going to bed early so I shall be sure and not miss the train back to Othello." In that oven-like room I would need to dispense with most of my clothing.

Once more in my room, I had a feeling I had not yet seen the last of Otto for the evening. The hotel was undergoing some enlarging, and my room was in the new part which had not yet had locks put on the doors. To be sure no one entered unbidden, I pulled the dresser across the door and then jammed the bed against the dresser so it could not be moved.

A half hour later I heard steps coming along the uncarpeted hall toward my room. They stopped at my door and there came a rap, then the door knob was turned.

"Who's there?" I called, knowing whose voice I'd hear in reply.

"It's me, Otto. Open the door. I've brought you some oranges, and bananas, and some ice cream and some nice tings." Even that bribery wasn't going to pursuade me to open that door just then, though I'd had nothing to eat since my scant breakfast.

"Well, I'm in bed," I told him. "You can set them down there by the door and I'll get them later." I didn't suppose he would, but I heard the rattle of paper, then his retreating steps down the hall. I waited a little while, then pulled the bed and dresser

241

away to open the door and peek down the hall. No one was in sight, but there on the floor at my door were the "nice tings" he had mentioned. Otto had been nice to me even though I had not been nice to him, but the slight feeling of regret it gave me did not prevent me from enjoying that delicious pint of ice cream in that hot room after I had again barred the door.

I never saw Otto on his next trip to Othello, but one day "Shorty" Fergen, the manager of the lumber yard came in to the restaurant for his noon meal.

"Your boy friend is in town." By the expression on his face I suspected who he meant, but asked very innocently, "Who do you mean?"

"Otto, of course," he answered bursting into shouts of laughter as he slapped his knees in enjoyment of the situation. I knew then Otto had told him all about the evening at Moses Lake. Shorty didn't let me forget Otto's name for some time, but I never saw Otto again.

As the Labor Day holiday drew nearer, the homestead folk living in the Deadman Lake area made plans for a big celebration at the usual picnic site on Crab Creek about a mile north of the upper end of Deadman Bluff. (We had always watched for the face outlined on the end of the bluff from a certain point as we passed.) Jim and Lucy McManamon, Ed and Tena Thurman and Minnie and Simon Morgan were the moving spirits in making the arrangements.

The site of the picnic was about seven miles from town so transportation for those living in Othello who wished to go, but were without means of getting there, found this provided by a "hay-burner" bus line. It was operated by Simon. The bus was a header box that had been fixed up with benches down each side of the wagon bed where his passengers could find seats. No padding or springs were provided to cushion the bumps: the fare was fifty cents each way. The "owl" bus would leave the picnic grounds on its last run at seven in the evening, and any who wanted to return to town must be ready to go home at that time. It took a little over an hour of bumpy riding to get from town to the scene of the festivities. Along with others, I paid my fare and climbed aboard over the high rear end of the wagon.

A large crowd had gathered at the grounds by the time our wagon load arrived, and stopped beside a rough pavilion which had been built for a place to visit and eat lunches, and for the dancing to come in the evening. Beside the pavilion, a kitchen and counter were set up where the wives of the sponsors dispensed ice cream, lemonade, sandiches, pie and coffee at modest prices. Firecrackers, torpedoes and other noise makers were also on sale.

A new feature was the merry-go-round. It was a homestead constructed affair, with a large upright pole in the center to which four side supports for two-passenger seats, extended out about three feet above the ground. A wide belt, (possibly one that was used at harvest time between the threshing engine and the separator) from the bottom of the pole to a gasoline engine set off on one side provided the power. Occasionally, the belt slipped off its track causing an interruption in the ride, but that was quickly adjusted and the merriment continued. Ed was operating the merry-go-round and collecting the five cent fares. The rides lasted about five minutes.

1913 Fourth of July picnic on Crab Creek.

Firecrackers were popping on all sides. Sometimes a giant cracker was set off to add to the noise and excitement. Mischievous boys delighted in dropping the lighted crackers onto the ground under the merry-go-round to hear the girls scream as they passed over the exploding fireworks. Neighbors, who saw one another only at rare intervals, stood around in groups talking over the crops and homestead news. A good bit of bantering and merriment was going on among the young folk, while the smaller children darted in and out among the crowd, or clung shyly to their mothers, a bit over-awed by the size of the crowd.

As the day drew to a close, families gathered their tired but protesting offspring, and hitching up the team to wagons, buggies or hacks, started for home. There would be the chickens to feed, the eggs to gather, the cows to milk and pigs to slop after they got home, and some had come from as far away as Smyrna, Beverly, Quincy, Ephrata, Moses Lake and Warden, and homesteads within that area.

The sound of the fiddler tuning up his fiddle, and the chords on the organ which had been brought from the Thurman home, coming from the pavilion drew old and young who were remaining for the dancing. Benches were arranged along the sides of the lamp and lantern-lighted room. The girls and women were now finding seats as they indulged in giggles and whispered conversation while they waited for the first dance to be announced; waiting in anticipation for some boy or man to approach with a bow and say, "May I have this dance?"

The eight inch boards of the floor with its cracks, was being made ready by being generously sprinkled with a powdered wax. The wax would be spread and worked into the floor by the feet of the dancers, and a fresh sprinkling of wax added from time to time during the evening.

"Get your partners for the first dance." The caller for the figures of the square dances had taken his place beside the organ on the little raised platform, and waited while enough couples to make four sets had taken their places. Then as the musicians

244

swung into the fast beat of "Turkey in the Straw," came the call for the first figure.

"Right hand to your partner and round you go, ala man left and do see do." Whether you had ever danced that particular dance before or not made no difference. You soon caught on.

With occasional pauses to give the musicians a rest, the dancing continued, sometimes interspersed with waltzes and two-steps, until the first hints of day appeared in the eastern sky. Aching feet and weary bodies that would never have admitted the charge, reluctantly yielded to the strains of "Home Sweet Home," or "Good-night Ladies," to return once more to the lonely homesteads. The picnic was over for another year.

For those who had come from town with no conveyance of their own, a large hay wagon was brought around and we climbed aboard. The sky grew brighter as we rode, giving the picture of a beautiful sunrise. The sun itself peeped up over the eastern rim just before we reached town and unloaded to go our various ways.

These settler's picnics were doubtless the fore-runners of, and inspiration for the Old-settlers' Othello-Corfu picnics now held annually at North Bend, Washington. Representatives of the old homestead families return from distant places each year to renew and rekindle old memories.

1913. Hardware store in the Crockett building, one of the first buildings in Othello, built by Hable. L. to R: John and Fannie McCulloch,
Everett Tipton, Flossie McCulloch, Mrs. H. J. Tipton, Ralph Tipton.

Chapter XXVI

More Homesteading

"MAMMA, WHY DID WE ever have to come out to a place like this to live?" wailed Hazel. Her younger sister Esther echoed the wails.

"There is nothing to see but all these rocks, and there isn't anybody to play with way out here."

"Now, now, girls," patiently Mrs. Haines tried to soothe them, "This is different from Kalamazoo, but you will get used to it, and we shall find things to do."

S. H. Haines came originally from Kalamazoo, Michigan to Walla Walla, then learning there was still homestead land available in the Pot Holes country, he filed on a quarter section in 1912. It lay just over the Adams County line in Grant County. The family consisted of his wife and two step-daughters.

They had been used to city life and the first sight of the new homestead with its stark isolation amid the sage brush and rock wastes was almost more than the girls could take.

"What can we do?" queried thirteen-year-old Hazel who was missing her friends.

"How would you like to pop some corn and make some popcorn balls?" suggested her mother. "Your father brought home a new Youth's Instructor with the mail this afternoon. You will have something new to read."

"Did he bring my paper?" asked Esther who was two years younger than Hazel, and always looked forward to the arrival of a childrens' paper called Our Little Friend.

"Yes, it came, too," her mother answered.

"Where is it?" squealed Esther in delighted anticipation.

"Let us get the dishes out of the way first," their mother cautioned, "Then we can have some popcorn balls while we read."

With the help of the two girls, the dishes were soon put away on the curtain-covered shelf, and the family settled down to some quiet reading.

Not always were the problems of isolation so easily solved. There was no school within walking distance, and it was too far for the girls to go either to Moses Lake or Othello.

The Mays had moved to their new homestead when the three-room house was nearly completed that same year. The sagebrush land stretched for miles to the north, broken here and there by outcroppings of solidified lava. In this more rugged location a keener watch for rattlesnakes was necessary. To the south and west of their place were more rugged cliffs. Bunch grass was again springing into growth for their grazing horses and cows. Mary and Billie were starting homestead life over again, only this time a town and the railroad were more conveniently near. No longer were the long hauls necessary from Hatton, Cunningham or Quincy, for groceries and other supplies for the homestead people in this area.

In this same year, O. F. Danielson took up homestead land on Crab Creek, five miles from the Ben Hutchinson homestead, but his family did not join him on the new claim until about 1917.

Other families along the creek had children who were becoming of school age. Jim and Lucy McManamon, with their three children had moved back to their land on Crab Creek; Charley Morgan's boy, Gilbert who was near Willie's age was now old enough to attend school. It was time to organize a school district to care for the children here. Heads of these families got together to form District No. 103. They erected a substantial two-room frame building, and on September 30, 1912, the school opened a twenty-four weeks term with Dona as its first teacher. It was also her first term of teaching school.

A short trial term was at first held in the Ed Thurman home before the school house was built and the regular school term begun. Dona roomed and boarded with the Thurmans during the trial term, but after that she rode from the May's place so Willie could ride with her to school.

Most of the children walked, even those coming from two and a half miles away. Blackie was again saddled for the teacher's transportation. Riding double with Willie behind the saddle, Dona set out at a sedate pace for the school; she was not one to endanger life or limb by fast riding. This worked well while the weather was mild, but along in mid-term the weather turned cold with deep snows and blizzard conditions. Not only was it impossible to wrap warmly enough to keep warm when riding horseback, but the horse had no shelter in which to stand during the day. Other plans had to be made.

The second room of the school building was fitted up for light house-keeping. Here Dona set up house-keeping taking the children who had the farthest to come, under her care while the blizzards and heavy snows lasted. Fires were kept burning in both stoves day and night, but school went on.

It was a real treat to the children on any homestead when Ben Hutchinson dropped in for a visit. Taking a child on each knee he told them Indian stories, sometimes talking to them in the Nez Perce language. Again, he would tell them stories of his cowboy days, or hair-raising stories about rattlesnakes. Not only did the children listen, wholly absorbed, but their parents, too, found Ben's stories fascinating. Occasionally, he stopped at the May homestead, and his tall form dismounting from his horse out by the horse trough brought Willie and Gordon on the run to see their friend. Ben had seen much history of the area in the making. Before he had his own herds and riders, he had ridden for Ben Snipes. His skill with the lariat was known and talked of wherever range riders gathered for a rodeo.

Our family life had seen much change, though Papa and Otis were still on the homestead alone for that winter again. Rising Star school had only three pupils attending now, with Belle Hoover the teacher for what was to be its last term before consolidation with the Othello school.

Papa's finances had reached an all-time low and some to whom he owed money were pressing him for payment, which he was in no way able to meet. During the previous summer while Dona was at home for a brief period, he explained his dilemma to her.

"Dona, I've been thinking it might be best to put the place in your name. It looks like I am going to lose everything else and I want to save the place for the younger children so they will have a home," he said. "There is a good chance that a lien will be filed against me, and that will take the horses and farm machinery," he explained.

Dona knew that with only the three horses he now had left, and only Otis at home to help him, he could no longer raise a crop of wheat.

"Would they be able to file an attachment on the homestead?" she asked.

"I am not sure," he answered, "but I don't want to chance it. Nellie is through high school; you will be teaching, and Headley is able to provide for himself. But Laura and Otis may need the home for a while yet." So the place was put in Dona's name.

Other changes in homestead life were coming to some whose children had grown past the grades in the country schools, or were getting married to make homes of their own. Some were getting too frail to carry on the wheat farming without the help of their sons. Joe and Fannie moved into town to start a small hardware store in the Crockett building at Second and Main Streets while their land continued to be farmed under Tipton's direction.

When Headley came home on a visit at the end of the summer's harvesting he approached Papa with some plans he was making.

"Papa, I met a girl while I was working over by Cunningham, and we are going to get married," he told Papa.

"Who is she?" Papa was just a little surprised, for he was thinking of Headley as just a boy since he was not yet twenty-one.

"Her name is Mollie Mattheis. She was helping cook for the harvest crew."

"If you get married where will you live? Would you plan on bringing her here?" Papa asked.

"No, we plan to live in Othello. I was thinking of going into business there."

"What kind of business?"

"I want to start a grocery store," Headley replied. Perhaps the limited food supply on our homestead the past few years had given him the urge to see shelves filled with all kinds of canned goods and other foods.

"Where will you get the money to start a grocery store?" Papa knew it would take more capital then Headley's summer wages had given him, and he would have no credit established with the wholesale houses.

"I thought we could get a loan from the bank, using the place here for security on the loan, and I could pay it off after the store is going good." Headley could see Papa's brow getting more furrowed at the suggestion of putting a mortgage on the homestead, and hastened to add, "Otis will need to go on to high school in Othello. He could stay with me and Mollie, and help in the store of evenings."

"But I have put the place in Dona's name so there would

The J. H. Tice grocery store, 1913. Courtesy Joseph H. Tice.

251

always be a home for Otis and Laura," Papa objected. "Now you want me to mortgage the place? We might lose it."

"It won't be like we sold the place," Headley assured him. "You won't be able to stay here by yourself much longer, and whenever you want to leave the homestead you can come and live with us."

"Have you said anything to Dona about this? She would have to sign any papers if you got a loan," Papa told him.

"Yes, I told her what I planned to do," Headley answered. "She said if you consented, she would rather put the deed in my name so I would be directly responsible to the bank, and leave her out of it."

Papa finally agreed somewhat reluctantly to Headley's plan, knowing he was no longer able to farm the land at his age.

The summer of 1913 saw Headley established in the grocery business in a new addition of the Crawford Building in downtown Othello. Roanie was brought into town to pull the grocery wagon, with Otis as delivery boy when not in school.

Chapter XXVII

Jack Rabbits, Coyotes and Badgers

WHEN WE FIRST MOVED to the homestead we frequently saw the long-eared, white-tailed jack rabbit as it bounded away through the sagebrush, but their number was kept somewhat under control by the coyotes. Then, as more coyotes were trapped by homestead boys for the bounty paid on each scalp, this upset in the balance of nature permitted a big increase in jack rabbits.

One summer Headley had set a trap in a dim coyote trail over across the deep coulee north of our place. Though the fur was no good in the summer, the bounty on them was his objective. He had been successful in trapping several.

While the harvest crew was resting in the shade of the house before returning to the field after their noon meal one day, Headley saw something like activity around one of the traps he had set. Getting a small telescope he had, it showed a dog-sized animal jumping around the site of the trap. It might be a coyote, or one of our dogs, or possibly a neighbor's dog that had gotten into the trap and been caught.

Quickly saddling one of the horses, he rode to see while the men waited with interest for his return. In about a half hour he was back with a coyote in tow on a long chain he had taken along, and which he had in some way managed to fasten to a strap he had put around the coyote's neck.

The dogs gathered around with hackles raised and growls deep in their throats, but none dared to rush in and attack the small animal that faced them with bared fangs and fur bristling on his back. Though out-numbered, it was evident that he would not go down to defeat without inflicting severe punishment on any dog that would have the courage to attack. None took his dare though urged on by the men.

But jack rabbits were increasing by leaps and bounds, in numbers as well as in their way of getting through and over the sagebrush. The potato crops were suffering under their whole-sale invasion, and in the winter when the bunch grass was covered by snow, the hay stacks became the mecca for all the rabbits in the country. Around these stacks upon which the homestead people depended to feed their farm animals, it looked like great flocks of sheep had been feeding there. Something had to be done. The number that could be killed by the rifles and shotguns of the boys and men took too much ammunition, and could never keep up with the birth rate of the rabbits. That was the birth-rate explosion of that decade.

Walt Danielson was out in his wagon one day when he saw one of the big jacks. This time he had a shotgun with him, and laying down the reins, he grabbed the gun and took aim intending to lay one more rabbit in the dust. The blast from just behind them frightened the team which took off for home and the barn. Having laid down the reins when he picked up the gun, the team had a good start and was gaining speed with every bound over the uneven ground. Walt managed to keep on his feet in the bouncing wagon while he snatched up the reins. Soon he brought them under control with no harm done, but Walt was more careful after that about dropping his reins.

The neighborhood men got together to discuss the situation. "We are going to have to do something about these jacks."

"How about a jack rabbit drive?" someone suggested, "I've heard you can clean out a lot of rabbits that way."

"How do you go about it?" questioned another who had never heard of driving jack rabbits.

"You build an angled fence with each side of the angle a quarter of a mile long, more or less. The fence has to be tight enough so the rabbits cannot get through. Then you get every-body lined up across the country with guns and clubs to drive the rabbits toward the wire trap," one of the men explained. It sounded like it might work, so a big rabbit drive was organized for the winter of 1917.

It was well advertised with arrangements for a special train from Seattle to bring all sport-minded hunters from the city for the big jack rabbit drive. A breakfast was to be served to those taking part in the drive.

The day of the big event came and so many had responded that the hunters were stretched out for five miles across the country. Spaced just a little way apart in a great semi-circle, they gradually drew in toward the fence, shooting any rabbits that tried to dodge between the hunters. Soon the jacks were leaping high here and there, looking for some way to escape the advancing men, but gradually merging toward the open end of the fence. It was evident that a vast number of rabbits would be enclosed within the two fence lines to be driven toward the apex. Thousands of rabbits were killed, and their numbers depleted, to the relief of those on the homesteads.

Other drives were held from time to time so that they never again increased to such numbers. As the white-tailed jack came under control and gradually decreased in numbers, there came a change in the kind of jacks. It began to be noticed that a black-tailed jack would be seen from time to time. These became

Jack rabbit drive breakfast served to those taking part. About 1913. Some came by special train from Seattle.

more prevalent until the white-tails were no longer seen. I never heard any explanation of how this came about, whether they migrated from some other area, or had been brought in.

Coyotes and badgers continued to make depredations in the flocks of chickens on the homesteads. Badgers were especially bad as they were not satisfied to take just one hen, but would kill for the pleasure of killing. A dozen or more dead chickens might be found on the chicken house floor when the farmer came to turn the chickens out in the morning. It was no problem for the badgers to dig under the side of the chicken house since there were no floors to balk them. A coyote usually snatched one from where the hens were feeding out in the open, and made off with it to the den.

Now and then a rabid coyote or badger was found and destroyed, but sometimes a dog was bitten by a rabid animal and in turn had to be destroyed.

After Dona had finished her term of teaching at the Deadman Lake School, she filed on some land north of Shiner Lake. Soon after, she and Fred Lee, who had been working for Billie, were married. They built a small house on her homestead and moved into it in the fall of 1914. A small chicken house was also built and a few chickens installed so that they might have fresh eggs.

One day toward evening when Dona was at the homestead alone, she heard a big commotion coming from the chicken house after the chickens had gone to roost. Hens were cackling and flying around inside the small building that she had closed for the night.

Taking a gun and the lantern, for the poultry house was only partially above ground, she went to investigate. As she opened the chicken house door it was immediately evident what was causing the disturbance. Two or three hens were already lying dead on the floor, and a badger was trying to catch another. Its eyes were like two small coals of fire as it paused in its blood-thirsty work when she opened the door.

She had no way of knowing whether it might be rabid, and it might bite the dog which had followed her, and pass on the rabies to it. Pushing the dog back, she raised the gun and shot the small destructive animal. Had it been undiscovered, it would have cleaned out the chicken house before morning.

Sometime afterward, Dona and Fred moved to the Simon Morgan place beside the lake and Deadman's Bluff. Simon had moved away, and the place offered possibilities for gardening with water from the lake.

During the summer harvesting season, Fred was away from home leaving Dona with two big dogs for company and protection. She kept them tied up to prevent their running around and leaving her alone at this lonely place, but she took them with her for walks around the lake.

One day she had returned from one of these walks and again tied up the dogs before going into the house. A few minutes later as she looked out the window toward the lake, she saw a coyote coming up the trail toward the house. It was the trail over which she and the dogs had just come. She watched it as it came, thinking it strange that a coyote would approach the house in the daytime, especially when there were dogs around. The dogs were beginning to make a fuss, when it suddenly occurred to her that this might be a rabid coyote. By this time it was too near the house for her to venture outside, for if it was rabid, it would immediately attack her. Then she thought of the dogs which were tied, and unable to get out of the way of the rabid animal.

The poor dogs were whining and growling in fear as the coyote approached them, with slaver drooling from its mouth. After a rebuff from the dogs it wandered erratically away. She was now convinced by the animal's strange behaviour that it was mad.

After assuring herself that it was gone, she went to look at the dogs to see if they had been bitten. She found foamy saliva where the coyote had mouthed over the dogs, but no place showed any bite. It seemed certain to her that the disease had progressed to the place where the animal's jaws were paralyzed; but in order to prevent the dogs from getting the dangerous saliva into their own mouths, she carefully washed away all traces from their bodies.

Later, she learned that some cowboys riding in the neighborhood had shot and killed a rabid coyote. She thought it must have been the same one she had seen.

Chapter XXVIII

Closing Homestead Days

THE WIND WHISTLED around the lonely homestead houses, and the dust gathered unmolested in the vacated houses where no woman's hand now kept it wiped away after each dust storm. A rusted wire clothes line leading from the small privy in the corner of the yard to the house where a loose end hung down, banged disconsolately against the house. But there were no ears to listen and know the wind was rising in another dust storm.

Though some of the land was under cultivation, other quarter sections lay idle, lacking water to bring its potentials to life. There were those who saw the great potentials, and were working to bring about the day when the union of land and water would bring their hopes to fruition.

Rory McDonald had been found dead in his little cabin. The loneliness that he had tried to banish with drink had done its work. Until his estate could be settled and the heirs found, Papa remained in his little cabin to look after the few animals Rory had owned.

Otis had just finished another year in the Othello High School, and stopped by to see how Papa was getting along.

"Papa, I saw Willie Lang down town today. He is working for Drumheller. He said Drumheller needs another man on his ranch. I think I'll see if he will take me on."

"What kind of work? His cattle are all under fence now," Papa remarked.

"He wants riders. People go through and cut the barbed wire and his cattle get out," Otis told him. "There are miles of fence that have to be checked and kept mended. There would be other work with the cattle, too."

"Go ahead," Papa encouraged him. "There will be lots of

work around a cattle ranch, and there isn't much work to be found now."

So for a time Otis worked on the George Drumheller ranch. Riding fences was only part of the work in connection with the large ranch, and other boys from the homesteads whom he knew found work there. Sometimes George's daughter Jessie, and her friends came up to spend part of their summer vacation on the ranch, and joined the riders in riding fence.

Along with many other places, the bank had taken over our homestead to satisfy the unpaid mortgage. Reluctantly, Sheriff McCollom had held a sheriff's sale of the machinery on our place to satisfy a lien which had been placed upon it. Homesteads gradually went into the hands of banks and loan companies until within a few years much of the land was no longer owned by the original homesteaders.

Frank and Bert, the two remaining horses, had been sold a while before the lien was obtained. The last we heard of Frank, he was sold to a man who took him to Alaska. At Anchorage he was again sold, this time to a Chinese truck-gardener in the Matanuska Valley. He was used to peddle vegetables to the housewives in Anchorage, and was reported to be pleasing his new master in the fine job he was doing. Bert was purchased by a man who had learned of his bent for bucking at odd moments, to be ridden in rodeos. Doubtless, Bert got all the bucking he wanted when he found the bucking strap buckled in place.

Orley Sanders, who had married Alice McCullom the year before, now left his homestead northeast of town, and moved into Othello. His bride of less than a year was found to have contracted tuberculosis. The care of this disease was not so well understood then, and gradually she failed until she was laid to rest in the little Adams Cemetery.

Nellie had not returned to the homestead after graduating from high school, but had gone on to Cheney. The opportunities for work and more education were greater there. In Cheney she met and married Dennis Riordan, a music student at the Normal. They went to make their home in Spokane.

For some time I had been working as a waitress, having started at the Hibbard Hotel while I was in high school. As openings for this work in Othello were limited, I secured a job in the railroad lunchroom in Malden.

One day the chief railroad detective covering that work on the C. M. & St. P. Railroad from Montana to the Coast stopped in for a little talk. I had become acquainted with him as he came into the lunchroom from time to time on his trips back and forth.

"Why don't you get out of this kind of work," he asked after some conversation. "This is no kind of work for you."

"What kind of work could I do? I wasn't able to finish high school." I had gone on to Ritzville, but without financial aid I had found it necessary to quit and go to work.

"Why don't you go to Spokane and take a business course? You could take a secretarial course," he went on. "If you do there will be a job waiting for you in my office when you finish."

At the time this seemed beyond my finances, and about Christmas time I went back to Othello and went to work at the "beanery" there. But I kept remembering what the railroad detective had said, "If you will go take the secretarial course, there will be a job for you in my office." So in June I quit the lunchroom and boarded the train for Spokane.

Homestead children were taking their places in world affairs. Perhaps they had learned through the hardships their parents had undergone on the homesteads to meet their problems and work them out.

About this time our country became involved in the first world war. Otis might soon be called, so he quit the cattle ranch to continue his education at Cheney where he took ROTC training.

Not all homestead children can be traced, but some have made real contributions in various lines. Some have remained to help develop the land, now under irrigation and fulfilling

261

its early promise once voiced by the early people; "If we just had water, this soil would grow anything."

Xerpha McCulloch Gaines has long been connected with the Agricultural College, now Washington State University. Along with her husband, she has contributed much to agriculture in Eastern Washington as an agronomist. In 1963 she was named State Mother of the year.

Sons of Herbert Michel have gone in for extensive farming and cattle raising around Othello. The beautiful Black Angus and Hereford cattle owned by Clayton Michel are under fence on irrigated land where once range cattle starved in the winter. Some of the land he now owns sold for as little as thirty-five cents an acre during the depression of the early thirties.

Another prosperous ranch where thousands of the Angus and Hereford cattle grow sleek and fat, is that of Don Damon, the son of Fred Damon whose parents homesteaded around the turn of the century. Don's ranch has its headquarters at what was once the Jabe Couch homestead. Could Jabe, whose son Reddin now lives in Wenatchee, return to the site of his original homestead, he would never recognize the place. But he would recognize the name of Damon as that of an old-time friend.

A meeting place for many who grew up on the homesteads is at the Old Settlers' Picnics held yearly at North Bend, Washington. William Laurenz, who became an official with the Boeing Company of Seattle, now flies up from San Francisco to talk over old times with Lloyd Nelson who first developed and patented the pack board which was adopted by the Boy Scouts and the U. S. Army. His brother Fred meets with the pioneers there, too. W. L. (Bill) Gochnauer, who still lives in Othello, goes over to meet and argue with Charley Toskey about early day events, such as which year saw the start of Othello.

Lora Estep Waters, for many years department head and buyer for one of Seattle's large department stores, and now National Vice-President of the Women's Auxilliary of the Veterans of Foreign Wars, comes with her Sister Blanche to meet Nora and Walter (Dutch) Krause from Malden in Eastern Washington.

Dutch has retired from the railroad after driving the big diesel engines for years on the Milwaukee from Malden to Othello. At Othello, Gordon May picks up this same train and pilots it on to Cle Elum.

Two other homestead boys, Gilbert Morgan and Will May keep the tracks in repair as section foremen from north of Othello to the Columbia River. All are interested in the great development that is now taking place in the Great Columbia Basin.

In one small section of Othello where the locust trees set out by other hands, have grown tall and sheltering, are a few homes in which live a few of those who were first to homestead and cultivate the land, and envision the possibilities of the soil when irrigation would come. Feeble are their steps. Their hair has grown white with the passing years as they watched their land fulfill their prophetic vision.

In the little cemetery, once a part of Grandpa Adams' homestead, may be found a row of markers. Neighbors, who once lived near one another on the homesteads, now rest side by side in neighborly fashion. There, as on many of the roads throughout the area, you will find the names of those who once were neighbors in the homestead days of long ago.

Rising Star School Record of Teachers

Copied from files in the office of the County Superintendent of Schools

By courtesy of Mrs. Mary Pearce

Teachers	Directors	Date of Contract	Term
Pliny Hayden	Byron Hayden Chas. Showalter J. F. Lee, Clerk	Jan. 25, 1904	12 weeks
Pliny Hayden	Byron Hayden F. M. Adams Chas. Showalter	May 2, 1904	8 weeks
Mildred Love	Byron Hayden F. M. Adams Chas. Showalter	Nov. 22, 1904	20 weeks
Emma Langworthy	J. F. Lee J. H. McCulloch Chas. Showalter, Clerk	Nov. 3, 1905	20 weeks
Gertrude Lee	J. F. Lee J. H. McCulloch	Sept. 4, 1906	24 weeks

*(Gertrude resigned in December 1906)

Teachers	Directors	Date of Contract	Term
Nellie Phillips	Chas. Showalter John H. McCulloch J. F. Lee	Jan. 29, 1907	8 weeks

*(Mrs. Phillips finished out the term, apparently)

Teachers	Directors	Date of Contract	Term
Nellie G. Phillips	F. L. Barton J. F. Lee	Sept. 30, 1907	24 weeks
Emza R. Hiday	F. L. Barton Ralph Barton	Aug. 31, 1908	28 weeks
Emza Hiday-Godsey	Ralph Barton F. M. Rankin Mrs. J. H. McCulloch	Feb. 15, 1909	28 weeks
Eugenia Campbell	Mrs. J. H. McCulloch J. W. Tice Byron Hayden	Oct. 19, 1910	24 weeks
Mabel Andresen	Byron Hayden J. W. Tice	Sept. 11, 1911	32 weeks
Belle Hoover	Byron Hayden J. W. Tice J. F. Lee	Oct. 3, 1912	28 weeks

*Comments by the author. Where only two directors are named, there was doubtless a holdover of the third previously listed.

Othello School Record of Teachers

Copied from school files in the Adams County Superintendent of Schools

By courtesy of Mrs. Mary Pearce

Teachers	Directors	Date of Contract	Term
Laura Irvin	M. W. Thurber		
	M. Chavis	Trial term	12 weeks
	F. Bagwell		
	A. E. Lee, Clerk	Mar. 28, 1903	20 weeks
J. W. Hicks	Wynass Chavis	Oct. 12, 1903	14 weeks
	F. Bagwell		
	A. E. Lee, Clerk		
Wm. G. Cook	R. M. Chavis	Oct. 6, 1904	20 weeks
	A. E. Lee, Clerk		
Mary Tice	William Ruppert	Aug. 23, 1905	24 weeks
	J. W. Hicks, Clerk		
Theresa Bocteau	No further record on this		
Abbie Goodwin	M. Chavis	Oct. 14, 1907	28 weeks
	H. Gregg		
	F. Bagwell		
Grace L. Grantham	F. Bagwell	July 10, 1908	36 weeks
	M. Chavis		
	H. Gregg		
D. L. Haile	C. S. Warn	May 21, 1910	36 weeks
Laura Rogers	M. E. Morgan		
	J. W. Webster		
D. L. Haile	J. W. Webster	Sept. 2, 1911	36 weeks
Laura Rogers	James McManamon	Sept. 11, 1911	36 weeks
Evaretta Merrill	M. N. Schoonmaker	Sept. 27, 1911	32 weeks
Geo. Crandall	J. W. Webster	June 8, 1912	
Laura Rogers	James McManamon	April 17, 1912	36 weeks
Evaretta Merrill	M. N. Schoonmaker	April 17, 1912	

Index

CPSIA information can be obtained
at www.ICGtesting.com
Printed in the USA
FSHW011929040519

9 780874 221749